2004

W9-DFM-693

TELEVISION

TELEVISION

The Limits of Deregulation

Lori A. Brainard

LYNNE
RIENNER
PUBLISHERS

BOULDER
LONDON

Published in the United States of America in 2004 by
Lynne Rienner Publishers, Inc.
1800 30th Street, Boulder, Colorado 80301
www.rienner.com

and in the United Kingdom by
Lynne Rienner Publishers, Inc.
3 Henrietta Street, Covent Garden, London WC2E 8LU

Library of Congress Cataloging-in-Publication Data
Brainard, Lori A., 1968–
    Television : the limits of deregulation / Lori A. Brainard.
      p. cm.—(Explorations in public policy)
    Includes bibliographical references and index.
    ISBN 1-58826-244-8 (alk. paper)
    1. Television broadcasting—Deregulation—United States. 2. Television
broadcasting—United States. I. Title. II. Series.
    HE8700.8.B7   2003
    384.55'1—dc21
                                        2003047161

British Cataloguing in Publication Data
A Cataloguing in Publication record for this book
is available from the British Library.

Printed and bound in the United States of America

The paper used in this publication meets the requirements
∞ of the American National Standard for Permanence of
Paper for Printed Library Materials Z39.48-1992.

5 4 3 2 1

Contents

Preface

IT GOES WITHOUT SAYING THAT AMERICANS GET THE VAST BULK OF
their news, entertainment, and sense of society from television.
Television transmits to us, and mediates, our shared experiences. But
despite television's role in our lives, few of us know much about the
larger debates surrounding television as a policy issue.

In writing this book, I wanted to investigate how policymakers
shape and control the powerful social force that is television. I also
wanted to shed light on debates within the fields of public policy and
regulation studies. The seeds for this volume were first planted when
I read Martha Derthick and Paul Quirk's book *The Politics of
Deregulation*. Derthick and Quirk investigated airline, trucking, and
telephony deregulation, seeking to explain why, after decades of regulatory protectionism, regulators and policymakers suddenly
reversed direction and engaged in deregulation. Derthick and Quirk
capped their analysis with the generally optimistic conclusion that
those examples of deregulation demonstrated that the U.S. political
system had tremendous capacity for policy change that represented a
diffuse public interest rather than a narrower, particularistic industry
interest. The book challenged the prevailing view that the U.S. political system was incapable of reaching policy closure, was susceptible
to gridlock, and was prone to pandering to business interests.

When I approached Derthick and Quirk's book, I had a cursory
prior knowledge of television policy. My sense was that television
deregulation was neither as smooth, as swift, nor as consensual as
airline, trucking, and telephony deregulation. I wanted to see if this
impression was correct and, if so, why television deregulation was so

different. A larger question that nagged at me was whether, to the extent that airline, trucking, and telephony deregulation demonstrated that the U.S. political system "worked," the divisive, slow, and ambiguous nature of television deregulation meant that the system, or at least the television policy system, was "broken."

While investigating these questions, I benefited from the support and guidance of many others along the way. Because this book is, at least in part, about the power of ideas and a diversity of viewpoints, it is only fitting to first thank my colleagues in the School of Public Policy and Public Administration at The George Washington University, who constantly seek to create an intellectual community based in a wide range of ideas, approaches, and perspectives. I genuinely appreciate their encouragement and collegiality. I have also benefited from the research assistance provided by Sarah Epps, Melissa Merrell, and Christina Sgroi.

R. Shep Melnick and Sidney M. Milkis contributed to my early thinking on these issues, as did Christopher J. Bosso, who continued to read drafts and provide feedback, support, and a sounding board for my ideas. The Dirksen Congressional Center and the Caterpillar Foundation, as well as the Goldsmith Awards program of the Joan Shorenstein Center on the Press, Politics, and Public Policy at the John F. Kennedy School of Government, Harvard University, provided financial support for some of the research that has culminated in this book.

Several anonymous reviewers furthered my thinking on this topic and kept the work interesting, and I thank them for their careful attention. Leanne Anderson of Lynne Rienner Publishers combined patience, enthusiasm, and a sense of humor. Jason Cook copyedited the manuscript and Karen Williams professionally ushered it through production.

For their help in guarding against "writer's isolation," I thank my sisters, Diane Judd and Susan Lawson. The memory of my mother, Dorothy Brainard, and of the hope, encouragement, and caring she showered on me over the years, was a constant source of inspiration as I wrote this book.

Finally, I thank my husband, Bob Liebowitz. He has shared this journey with me, even as it meant forgoing vacations, doing all the cooking while I wrote, and then listening to me talk incessantly about television policy during our dinners. This is for him.

TELEVISION

1

Regulation and Deregulation in Theory and Practice

THIS BOOK INVESTIGATES THREE EFFORTS TO DEREGULATE THE TELEVI-
sion industry since the mid-1970s. Despite considerable effort, the
result was incremental and incomplete deregulation and episodes of
*re*regulation as the political left and right, a wide array of interest
groups, the major political parties, and key policymakers waged a
pitched battle for several decades across all of the institutions
responsible for television policy. This book explains why.

Considering television policy is worthwhile not just because it is
an industry that captures so much of our attention and is perceived to
influence everything from elections to toothpaste purchases, but
because it tells us so much about U.S. politics and policy generally. It
also provides striking examples of how regulatory policy and the categories we use to understand it (categories such as "economic regulation" and "social regulation") are influenced by perceptions, political reasoning, and rhetoric, not just a narrow conception of economic
"rationality." Indeed, in the television case we find that a combustible mixture of economic issues and social issues led to failure to
produce any coherent policy consensus.

The first effort to deregulate television occurred in the mid-
1970s, when Representative Lionel Van Deerlin (D–Calif.) attempted
but failed to pass legislation deregulating the industry. The second
effort occurred during the 1980s, when the Reagan administration,
with limited success, sought to deregulate television administratively
by appointing proderegulation commissioners to the Federal
Communications Commission (FCC), the regulatory body responsible for television. The third effort culminated in passage of the 1996

Telecommunications Act, which, contrary to the rhetoric surrounding the legislation at the time, produced further incremental television policy change.

The incremental nature of television deregulation sits in stark contrast to efforts to deregulate other industries. Between 1975 and 1980 the United States experienced a spate of deregulation efforts. Many of these efforts, especially in the important infrastructure sectors of transportation and telecommunications, were successful in the sense that policymakers achieved relatively quick and decisive results.[1] More telling, deregulation not only induced firms in the affected sectors to change the way they conducted business, but it also forced scholars in political science and public policy to alter their assumptions about change in the U.S. political system. Scholars who spent a great deal of time explaining why radical policy change did not and could not occur, now had to explain why whole sectors of the U.S. economy, in particular the airline, trucking, and telephone industries, had gone through such fundamental change in such a short period of time.

Not surprisingly, while these scholars generally agree on the facts of deregulation, they disagree on the larger causes. Indeed, scholars find evidence for all kinds of theories in the deregulation successes of the airline, trucking, and telephony cases. Some argue that deregulation ultimately was caused by economic contradictions inherent in regulation. Others argue that deregulation occurred because firms that would benefit from it sought it. Still others argue that deregulation was the result of an issue and institutional context that favored the creation of a broad consensus around the idea of deregulation and that enabled policymakers to override the policy preferences of the previously protected industries.

What is to be gained from studying a case—the television example—in which deregulation was more ambiguous? To the extent that the television example constitutes a case that is remarkably different from the relatively clear examples of airline, trucking, and telecommunications deregulation, investigating it can sharpen our understanding of the central debates about regulation and deregulation. Previous scholars of deregulation sought to account for regulatory change in light of the then-prevailing wisdom about policy stability in the United States. This book, by contrast, wonders about the comparative stability of television policy amid broader policy flux and in light of the subsequent prevailing wisdom about policy change.

To that end, this book examines three different theories of regulation and regulatory change. *Market forces* theories typically suggest that regulation and regulatory change reflect changes in the underlying economic or technological conditions (or both) of an industry. Theories of *industry determinism* suggest that regulation and regulatory policy change are direct responses to industry demands and that these policies clearly reflect the interests of the affected industry. A more broadly based *contingency* framework suggests that regulation and regulatory change result from, and are contingent on, a less deterministic array of factors, such as new ideas or institutional changes and, more important, the interaction between ideas and institutions. These theories direct our attention to important factors—economics and technology, industry influence, ideas, issues, and institutions—to consider in understanding the television story. Simultaneously, understanding television deregulation in reference to these factors also will shed light on which theory of regulatory change holds more explanatory power.

Regulation and Deregulation: Concepts and Theories

When we open a newspaper or turn on television news, we often find politicians, policymakers, and pundits bandying about such terms and phrases as "deregulation," "regulatory reform," or "regulatory relief." Politicians may benefit from such imprecise language, but any study seeking to sharpen our understanding of the saga of television regulatory policy must clarify these terms.

Marc Eisner, Jeff Worsham, and Evan Ringquist define regulation as "an array of public policies explicitly designed to govern economic activity and its consequences at the level of the industry, the firm, or individual unit of activity."[2] This definition is useful for several reasons. First, it directs our attention to decisions and actions made *by government* that impinge on economic activity—rather than, for example, those decisions made voluntarily by firms to control their own activities. Second, it directs our attention not only to specific regulations (such as pronouncements mandating that television broadcasters air a set number of hours of children's programming every week), but also to *patterns* of government regulations. The definition also encompasses the idea of intentional action by government, even though there might be (and often are) unintended consequences of regulatory policies. Finally, by noting that regulations are directed at the industry, firm, or individual, this definition concerns policies that operate at the microeconomic, rather than macroeconomic, level; these are actions that induce individual firms to change their behavior.

The term "regulatory reform" means many different things to many different people—which is why politicians of many ideological stripes like it so much.[3] It literally denotes changes to regulation and, depending upon the person using it and the context in which it is used, may mean a rationalization, streamlining, or reordering of regulation, even a strengthening of regulation. Thus it is important to bear in mind that in practice the choice is not necessarily between regulation and deregulation. Rather, regulatory policy change often involves alteration of various policy tools—such as licensing and certification; price, rate, and quantity controls; product quality, technical, and performance standards; subsidies (direct and indirect); and assignation of property rights—used in particular regulatory arenas.[4] Alternatively, regulatory reform might mean a decrease or removal of regulation. This latter meaning is more strictly in line with the definition of deregulation given by Martha Derthick and Paul Quirk as "the removal, to whatever degree" of earlier regulations.[5]

The wave of deregulation that occurred in the 1970s and 1980s did not directly address the entire economy but rather the "infrastructure industries" that form its backbone.[6] The transportation and telecommunications industries, for example, facilitate commercial and social interaction by promoting and expediting the movement of goods, services, and people. Any changes in this sector naturally would have major ripple effects throughout the economy and society. Moreover, "deregulation" is somewhat a misnomer in that some regulations were kept in place. Deregulation was targeted at a specific type of regulation, known as economic regulation, as opposed to social regulation. This distinction is important for the ensuing analysis, so further discussion of it is warranted here.[7]

Stemming from the Progressive and New Deal eras, economic regulation focuses on the problems of monopoly—when no competition exists—on the one hand, and excessive competition, on the other, and their respective effects on prices and service. It also focuses on the problem of scarcity, which results from an undersupply of an important resource, such as the frequencies that television broadcasters use to send their programming to viewers. Thus, economic regulation controls prices, entry into and exit from an industry, and the allocation of business rights.

Because the microeconomics of each industry historically have differed, economic regulation typically is industry-specific. Having said this, one certainly can argue that "waves" of regulation and deregulation also mirror changes in prevailing scholarly and political thinking about dominant problems. One can say that the New Deal wave of regulation was a response to one temporal set of problems, while the deregulation wave was a response to an entirely different set of problems, to more sophisticated sets of arguments about the merits of less regulation, and sometimes to the eventual pathologies created by earlier regulation. So, regulation is sector-specific, but within broader ideological or analytical contexts.

Mirroring the sector-specificity of economic regulation, government agencies responsible for implementing economic regulation also usually have sector-specific jurisdictions. Economic regulatory agencies usually operate under broad and vague statutory mandates to regulate in the "public interest." Such agencies, therefore, typically have vast discretionary authority to interpret the public interest as they see fit. That discretion, coupled with their vague mandates, makes economic regulatory agencies prone to "capture," which Barry Mitnick describes as a form of "reverse regulation" whereby regulated firms and industries over time come to dominate the agencies that are supposed to control them.[8] Indeed, by the 1960s, such cozy mid-level relationships between the agencies and the regulated industries (as well as with key members of Congress) came to be called "iron triangles" because of their endurance over decades, though the image of iron triangles began to break down in the 1970s.[9] The quasi-corporatist nature of iron triangles had origins in the deference to bureaucratic expertise inculcated by the Progressive and New Deal eras.

Social regulation, on the other hand, addresses the social effects of economic and business activity, or as Mitnick notes, "activities with a direct impact on people," such as pollution, occupational safety, consumer protection, and equal employment opportunity.[10] Unlike economic regulation, social regulation cuts across industry lines, and therefore the agencies responsible for implementing it operate across the economy. Social regulation came to dominate the policy agenda in the early 1970s, when capture theory was at its peak and during significant abuses of discretion, such as the Watergate scandal. Thus the legislative statutes involved in social regulation, again reflecting changes in thinking about the desirability of deference, typically award less discretion to social regulatory agencies than to their economic kin. Given that these agencies exist essentially to force firms to absorb the costs of social responsibility, coupled with the rise of consumer advocacy and the public interest movement, far more overt political conflict surrounds social regulation.[11]

Not surprisingly, by the late 1970s, students of public policy began to argue that the iron triangle construct no longer held—or at least that it was relevant only to certain business sectors—and that regulation, especially social regulation, now occurs in the context of what Hugh Heclo calls "issue networks"—unstable and fluid policy communities consisting not just of private-sector actors, agency regulators, and congressional experts but also of public interest groups, citizen advocacy organizations, and even academics.[12] Whatever geometric conception one uses, the political and policy reality is messier and less predictable.

These concepts and terms are important vocabulary because, in the debates surrounding television policy, the distinction between economic regulation and social regulation is not as clear as it is in textbooks. Nevertheless, as important as these terms are for *describing* regulation, they are of little help in *explaining* regulation and, more important, regulatory change. We therefore look to three models that offer competing explanations for where regulation comes from and under what conditions it goes away.

Market Forces Theory

The market forces theory of regulation often is referred to as "public interest" theory because it emphasizes that regulatory policies are intended to serve the broader public interest by compensating for instances of market failure.[13] Because it focuses on the economic origins of regulation or deregulation, it views economic and technological forces as independent variables to which policymakers respond. Moreover, there is an important normative element to this theory, to the extent that it holds a presumption in favor of the marketplace and to the extent that it presumes that government must step in and engage in regulation only when the market fails or to improve the marketplace. The economic theory is closely related to models of the policy process that emphasize the role of analysis, what Deborah Stone refers to as the "rationality project."[14] In this model, goals are identified, alternatives are considered systematically, and policy decisions are made on the basis of politically neutral expert analysis as to which alternative is most likely to achieve the stated goal.[15]

According to this theory, airline regulation was initiated in the 1930s to rescue an infant industry from the effects of corrosive competition. Trucking regulation was adopted at about the same time to prevent similarly destructive competition within the industry and, equally important, between the trucking industry and the railroad industry during an economic depression. Telephone regulation was necessary to protect consumers from the monopoly power and monopolistic prices of what essentially was a national utility. These policies were deemed to be in the public interest because they would preserve important industries and protect consumers from harmful economic effects.

The market forces theory suggests that deregulation occurred as a response to changes in the economic and technological conditions underlying these industries. For example, in the 1970s the combination of high inflation and high unemployment made economic regulation appear inefficient and expensive. Similarly, airline and trucking regulation came to be seen as unnecessary because these industries matured and stabilized and their economic conditions improved. Technological change made a natural monopoly in telephony decidedly *un*natural. Given such changes in the fundamental nature of these industries, in perceptions about the desirability of market intervention, and in the economy generally, regulations that impeded the "normal" functioning of markets finally could be lifted without harming the broader public good; in fact, lifting them could promote it.

Industry Determinism Theory

The industry determinism theory differs from the market forces theory of regulation in that the former is based on the "rational choice" approach to the study of politics, which views industry actors, political actors, and policy actors as engaged, first and foremost, in pursuing their own self-interests.[16] As a result, the industry determinism theory makes no assumptions about whether or not regulatory policy serves, or ought to serve, the public interest. Indeed, such a theory concludes that regulation often serves private interests, and any notion of protecting the public interest is purely secondary. Similarly, the industry determinism theory concludes that, far from using rational policy analysis to correct for market failures, regulation often is used, at the behest of the regulated firms, to bypass markets altogether.[17]

This theory, then, implies that the power of private-sector actors is the important independent variable in policy.[18] As the argument goes, firms and industries sought regulation to protect their financial interests. Policymakers, who are seen as rational actors seeking reelection, and agency personnel, who are seen as seeking to maximize their budgets and jurisdictions, responded favorably to industry requests for regulation.[19] Regulation subsequently became a form of protectionist corporate welfare.[20] So, for example, this theory viewed airline, trucking, and telephone regulation as an attempt to protect active airlines, trucking firms, and the AT&T telephone monopoly from natural (and beneficial) competition.

By extension, this theory also suggests that deregulation was a response to industry interests. That is, it suggests that the regulated industries and firms (or new firms seeking entry) wanted deregulation, demanded it, and got it.[21] Where once regulation was deemed essential to their needs, changes in economic conditions and industry structure led them to demand regulatory changes that would continue to maximize their advantage. This, of course, is in line with the notion of capture discussed earlier.

Contingency Framework

The contingency framework[22]—so labeled to denote that policy outputs are mere possibilities conditional on factors that are themselves fluid and uncertain—views regulation and regulatory policy change as less deterministic, and more conflictual, than do market forces and industry determinism theories. This approach thus regards motivations other than economic self-interest and values other than economic rationality as relevant. The contingency approach holds a wide array of factors, such as ideas, beliefs, perceptions, and institutional arrangements, to be present in policy and regulatory change. As these factors are very fluid and difficult to pin down, unlike the more easily abstracted (and even measurable) independent variables associated with the other two theories, analyzing them is a far messier and more complex enterprise. Nevertheless, as this book will demonstrate—especially with regard to television policy—we are sacrificing elegance for greater descriptive and explanatory power.

Unlike the market forces theory, the contingency framework assumes that microeconomic conditions and rational analysis are not necessarily the central factors in policy change. In other words, simply because the economics of the airline, trucking, or telephone industry changed does not mean that policy change automatically followed. Nor does it mean that policymakers or citizens take their leads from scripts produced by economic or technological change. This approach does not suggest that economics do not matter but that economic factors compete with others within a larger issue and institutional context.

Unlike the industry determinism theory, the contingency framework suggests that policy decisions are not necessarily reducible to rational, self-interested motivations. It also assumes that politicians and policymakers may actually be interested in passing good public policy even if and when it does not mirror the policy wishes of private-sector actors—or at the very least, that politicians and policymakers may have their own policy concerns that are not consonant with private-sector wishes. Moreover, while the industry determinism theory seems to assume that money equals power and therefore that private-sector actors are a powerful force in our political system, the contingency approach assumes that there are other forms of influence in our system (for example, votes, an ability to mobilize public opinion, and an ability to persuade) and that these forms of power are dispersed throughout our system, including among citizen advocacy and nonprofit organizations.

The contingency approach creates important conceptual space for the role of ideas, values, and competing images of the public good. Deborah Stone, for example, emphasizes the role of ideas, political reasoning, and rhetoric. She looks at how we argue about issues, or as she puts it, how we try "to get others to see a situation as one thing rather than another."[23] For example, she argues that a great deal of our political life involves defining the "public interest," which (like regulatory reform) means different things to different people. Stone notes: "There is virtually never full agreement on the public interest, yet we need to make it a defining characteristic of the polis because so much of politics is people fighting over what the public interest is and trying to realize their own definitions of it."[24]

This approach also stresses the role of governing institutions. For example, E. E. Schattschneider, noting that "organization is the mobilization of bias," argues that institutions structure political conflict.[25] Hence, he argues, institutions (through their governing rules, norms, or culture) necessarily rule out the participation of some actors, organizations, and interests while ruling in that of others. Taken to its extreme, one variant of a focus on institutions skates close to institutional determinism and focuses on how institutions structure the preferences of the people who operate within them. Institutional arrangements are important, as this variant holds, because different arrangements will lead to different policy decisions.[26] Still other scholars argue that, besides institutional structures, we must pay attention to the intellectual backgrounds, professional and personal ambitions, and ideological preferences of policymakers.[27] In any case, institutions matter, a point not made in either of the other two theoretical frameworks.

In recent years scholars have made great strides in integrating analyses of ideas and institutions. The work of Frank Baumgartner and Bryan Jones warrants special attention here.[28] Looking specifically at the phenomenon of policy change, Baumgartner and Jones argue that policy is not necessarily a "rational" response to either economic change or industry demands. They note, "In the long sweep of American politics, one is less tempted to claim that cozy arrangements between politicians, interest groups, and the media will prevent change and more likely to ask when and how new policy arrangements will emerge."[29] To answer this question, Baumgartner and Jones advance the notion of "punctuated equilibrium," by which they mean that a policy construct may remain relatively stable for long periods of time only to go through a remarkable spasm of change in a relatively short period of time. They argue that punctuated equilibrium, of which economic deregulation was an example,[30] reflects changes in dominant problem definitions, which in turn increase the salience of issues to more actors, mobilize resources, and force issues into new institutional venues that are more receptive to policy change.[31]

The boundaries between these three theories of regulation and regulatory policy change often are blurry. Thus, for example, economic and technological changes often produce new interests, which then affect the larger issue context. Or the market forces theories might be an extreme case of a particular set of ideas—economic rationales for regulation—in play. Nevertheless, the three theories emphasize very different factors as important independent variables, and those differences are highlighted here in order to mark the boundaries of debate. The market forces theory stresses economic and technological conditions above all. The industry determinism theory reduces causality to the policy preferences of private-sector actors. The contingency framework, attentive to variation and uncertainty and to a deeper form and conception of political competition, emphasizes ideas and institutions. As theoretical constructs, these theories and approaches are rather abstract; they become more concrete when used as lenses through which to view how the process of deregulation of the airline, trucking, and telephone industries worked in practice.

Regulation and Deregulation in Practice

In the 1930s, Congress created the Civil Aeronautics Board (CAB), the Interstate Commerce Commission (ICC), and the FCC and delegated to these agencies discretionary authority over prices for, entry into, and exit from the airline, trucking, and telephone industries respectively, in order to create stable sectors and ensure service. The airline and trucking industries essentially were regulated as cartels. Using their control over entry, the agencies determined which firms would be allowed to offer services and granted permission to serve a particular market. In these cases, the burden of proof—that additional or new service would meet the public interest, convenience, and necessity—was on firms seeking to enter the particular industry. It was a high burden of proof indeed. The agencies restricted entry, hoping to provide for a reasonable but not destructive amount of competition.[32] The FCC regulated AT&T as a monopoly, thus restricting entry altogether. Not only did this provide for stability in the telephone system, but it also provided the FCC with a rationale for mandating that AT&T wire the country to promote universal telephone service.

The CAB, the ICC, and the FCC also controlled prices that the regulated firms charged their customers. In the airline case, regulators set minimum prices to avoid destructive fare reductions, and set maximum prices to ensure and promote ridership. Truckers set their own rates collectively. Though the ICC retained final price authority, it rarely rejected industry agreements. In fact, it was usually the ICC that raised rates.[33] Rate-making for telephony took place by informal negotiations between the FCC and AT&T, though AT&T was the dominant partner.[34] With the New Deal regime being quasi-corporatist, such arrangements were the norm and they looked a lot like capture, though with the benefit of industry stability.

By the 1970s, in the context of structural changes in the U.S. economy and intellectual changes in economics, deregulation came onto the public agenda and airline, trucking, and telephony deregulation looked more or less alike. According to all definitive accounts, specific deregulatory policy changes began in the agencies, which slightly opened up entry to new firms and began to allow competitive pricing. Affirming these deregulatory initiatives, Congress passed the Airline Deregulation Act in 1978 to phase out the authority of the Civil Aeronautics Board and to abolish the agency entirely at the end of 1982. In 1980, Congress passed the Motor Carrier Act to end collective rate-making and to buttress ICC efforts to reduce restrictions and open up entry. Congress did not pass legislation deregulating the telephone industry, but approved deregulation by defeating a bill sponsored by AT&T that would have codified the telephone monopoly, just as the federal courts were assessing it. Court-ordered divestiture of AT&T occurred in 1984.

In each case, opposition to deregulation came primarily from dominant industry actors—the regulated firms—who feared uncertainty and structural chaos. They argued that deregulation would result in higher prices and loss of service, especially to smaller communities in which service-provision would likely be less profitable. For its part, AT&T warned that disruption to the industry caused by deregulation would undermine the stable and affordable provision of universal telephone service. Eventually, however, the protected industries capitulated and ceased overt lobbying efforts to defeat deregulation.

In each case a broad coalition of interests pushed deregulation forward. Liberals applauded deregulation because it would break the alleged collusion between government and business and because it promised lower prices and better service to consumers. Conservatives worked to advance deregulation because they saw it as a method of combating inflation and affirming the nation's reliance on free market principles. Firms shut out of these markets supported change, as did firms in other industries that stood to benefit from lower prices and more choice.

It is worthwhile to distinguish the process of economic deregulation of the 1970s from that of social deregulation. Social deregulation began in the 1980s, stemming from a critique by free market conservatives of the costs of such regulation. Conservatives also evidenced a desire to fight inflation, which they viewed as exacerbated by the costs of social regulation, and a preference for relying on free market forces. By contrast, liberals opposed social deregulation, which they viewed as an attempt to remove the obligation of corporations to behave in socially responsible ways. The politics of social deregulation thus have been far more acrimonious. As a result, social deregulation has been far less complete.

Taken together, these examples demonstrate some key common characteristics. First, economic deregulation occurred primarily between 1975 and 1980, though importantly the seeds of change had been sown many years earlier. Second, deregulation was applicable to a particular type of industry. Robert Britt Horwitz notes that the industries that underwent deregulation were infrastructure industries, which constitute "essential modes or channels that permit trade and discourse among members of society."[35] They bind society together. Third, deregulation applied to industries and firms that were governed by a particular institutional form; that is, industries and firms subject to economic regulation administered by independent agencies that operated under vague mandates, possessed significant discretion, and were accused of capture. Fourth, in spite of such allegations of capture, regulatory agencies actually took the first policy steps in deregulation. Finally, deregulation later was codified or approved by Congress.

Scholars find evidence for each of the three theories of regulatory policy change in the airline, trucking, and telephone examples. Economic and technological change was clearly important, as structural changes in the economy began to expose regulatory protection as inefficient, and as a contributing factor to inflation. John Meyer and his colleagues hint at a theory of industry determinism and suggest that by the 1970s the airlines in particular were seeking less pervasive regulation.[36] Other scholars alternatively emphasize the role of Congress[37] or that of the agencies and their chairmen.[38] Martha Derthick and Paul Quirk stress the role of ideas and argue that the way in which the idea of deregulation was framed allowed the broad coalition of political liberals and conservatives to come together. They also note that the fragmented political system allowed for numerous points of entry for those advocating change.[39]

The Television Example

In the mid-1970s, television policy exhibited many of the same characteristics discussed above. First, the television industry also is an infrastructure industry that brings people together both in commerce and in discourse. Television transmits and mediates our shared experiences and provides a central function—advertising—in our economy. Second, as in other instances, new technology, in the form of cable television, was changing the underlying structure of the industry. Third, the agency responsible for regulating television, the Federal Communications Commission, economically regulated the industry and, like the Civil Aeronautics Board and the Interstate Commerce Commission, faced charges of being captured by the regulated television broadcasters. Fourth, despite allegations of capture, the FCC had begun some deregulation, as it slightly relaxed restrictions on cable television, a nascent competitor to broadcast television. Fifth, as with the other sectors, economists had been advocating television deregulation for years. Finally, in Congress, the House Subcommittee on Communications was set to consider omnibus legislation to deregulate the industry. On paper, television looked like another candidate for deregulation.

Indeed, in his study of television deregulation, Horwitz argues that television deregulation did follow a path similar to that of airline, trucking, and telephony deregulation.[40] As Horwitz argues, cable was freed of regulatory constraints. The television environment thus expanded and the newly emergent abundance and competition undermined the underlying rationale supporting all of television regulation—that the frequencies on the electromagnetic spectrum used by broadcasters to distribute programming were scarce and thus required allocation by government. Gone with scarcity, according to Horwitz, was the underlying justification for the full gamut of regulation. Deregulation proceeded accordingly. Horwitz thus emphasizes the similarities between the deregulation of television and that of other industries.

Nevertheless, the facts of television deregulation legitimately lend themselves to different interpretations and the argument in this book is that television deregulation took a trajectory that was remarkably different. Omnibus legislation deregulating the industry failed during the 1970s. This is especially notable because the House and Senate Commerce Committees, which were responsible for much of the deregulatory legislation dealing with airline and trucking policy, were unable to pass similar legislation dealing with television. Subsequent television deregulation would occur later than it did in other industries and take longer. Television deregulation also would be incremental, incomplete, and subject to dramatic policy fluctuations and institutional warfare. Television regulatory policy, then, constitutes a notably different story.

What can we gain from studying such an ambiguous example of deregulation as television? First, television is interesting in its own right and we all care about the issue to some extent. Yet most of us turn on the television and watch what comes out of it, whether for recreation or edification, and give very little thought to the policies behind it. Beyond the intrinsic interest of television policy, the issue has remained on the public agenda since the mid-1970s, providing us with an extensive public record.

The television example also is a good case with which to scrutinize theories of regulatory policy change. That technological change in television was so dramatic makes this a good example to use in assessing the explanatory power of the market forces theory of regulatory change. Because the television industry is widely perceived as being politically powerful, this is a good example with which to consider the value of the industry determinism theory. Similarly, that television engages political interests in a way that airlines, trucking, and telephones do not, makes this a particularly compelling case with which to consider the role of political institutions and ideas.

Finally, because television deregulation was so different from that of the airline, trucking, and telephone industries, investigating it will help us to gain a deeper insight into which framework for understanding regulatory policy change best approximates reality generally. The cases of airline, trucking, and telephony deregulation present evidence supporting each of the three theories of regulatory policy change. But because those cases are so similar to each other, it is difficult to isolate important factors, and so the debate rages on. It thus is useful to juxtapose these similar cases with the distinctly different television case. For if we can discern what was different about the television case, it will shed light on which factors were more important in other cases of deregulation.

The Plan of Study

This book documents the ways in which television deregulation was different and analyzes and explains the differences in light of the theories of regulatory change discussed above. The investigation compares the evolution over time of six specific television policy issues: cable television competition with television broadcasters, television station licensing policy, television station ownership policy, the Fairness Doctrine, equal employment opportunity and affirmative action ownership policies, and children's television policies. These issues are a fairly representative sampling of television regulations, they were all the targets of efforts to deregulate, and they allow us to investigate both the economic and the social aspects of television policy. These policy issues are compared not only to each other, but also to the deregulation of the airline, trucking, and telephone industries.

Chapter 2 focuses on the historical origins and development of television policy and how it came onto the public agenda in the 1970s. In the process, it sketches the historical and institutional contours of television regulation. Chapter 3 takes up the economic and technological factors in the debate over television deregulation. The market forces theory suggests that television deregulation was so ambiguous because technology did not sufficiently mature to make deregulation viable, or that technological change went unnoticed by policymakers. Nevertheless, technological change in television was both rapid and substantial (at least as much as that in other infrastructure industries), and key policymakers advocated policy change based on technological development, yet no conclusive deregulation emerged.

Chapter 4 investigates the role played by the television industry. The theory of industry determinism would suggest that television deregulation was so incremental and incomplete because "the industry" did not want deregulation. However, the various sectors of the television industry in fact advocated deregulation. Why they did not get deregulation, to the extent to which they wanted it, offers important insights into how industry influence is filtered through the larger issue and institutional context.

Chapter 5 takes up the factors encompassed by the contingency framework—the issue and institutional context—for understanding regulatory policy change. The contingency framework suggests that television deregulation was so inconclusive because the issue and institutional context was not conducive to rapid change and policy closure. In short, liberal and conservative public interest groups opposed television deregulation and, with their allies in Congress (who had their own policy concerns), were successful in preventing significant deregulation by asserting new, predominantly social ideas justifying continued regulation. Opponents of deregulation thus expanded the scope of the debate beyond what took place in other, clearer examples of deregulation.

Chapter 6 summarizes the book's findings and explains how this analysis helps us to understand television policy and regulatory change. I argue that the incremental nature of television deregulation resulted from an unfavorable issue and institutional context, in which economic, social, political, and cultural factors worked at cross purposes to each other and ultimately stymied significant deregulation, and further explain the linkages between ideas and institutions on the one hand, and technological change and industry influence on the other. I conclude with a discussion of the larger lessons and implications of the book's findings for regulation and regulatory change, arguing that a contingency framework holds the most explanatory power for economic deregulation generally (or in the television case, the comparative lack of it). I argue that the distinction that scholars and policymakers alike make between economic and social regulation ought to be reconsidered, and that the normative assumptions we make about policy change in the United States ought to be rethought.

Notes

1. By "success," I do not intend to convey a normative position toward deregulation nor any evaluation of outcomes. Rather, echoing Charles Lindblom, who asserted that the test of a good policy is whether there is agreement about it, I use "success" to refer to the relative alacrity with which policymakers were able to agree on policy change. Lindblom, *The Intelligence of Democracy.*

2. Eisner, Worsham, and Ringquist, *Contemporary Regulatory Policy,* p. 5.

3. See, for example, Breyer, *Regulation and Its Reform.*

4. Eisner, Worsham, and Ringquist, *Contemporary Regulatory Policy,* pp. 13–18.

5. Derthick and Quirk, *The Politics of Deregulation*, p. 34.

6. On the nature of infrastructure industries, see Horwitz, *The Irony of Regulatory Reform*, p. 11.

7. The classic literature distinguishing economic regulation from social regulation includes Bardach and Kagan, *Going by the Book;* Breyer, *Regulation and Its Reform;* Lilly and Miller, "The New 'Social Regulation'"; Mitnick, *The Political Economy of Regulation;* Vogel, "The 'New' Social Regulation"; Weaver, "Regulation, Social Policy, and Class Conflict"; Weidenbaum, "The New Wave of Government Regulation of Business"; and Wilson, *The Politics of Regulation.*

8. Mitnick, *The Political Economy of Regulation*, p. 14.

9. See, for example, Cater, *Power in Washington;* Freeman, *The Political Process;* McConnell, *Private Power and American Democracy;* and Redford, *Democracy in the Administrative State.*

10. Mitnick, *The Political Economy of Regulation*, pp. 15–16.

11. Vogel, "The 'New' Social Regulation," pp. 162–171.

12. Heclo, "Issue Networks and the Executive Establishment." See also Berry, "Subgovernments, Issue Networks, and Political Conflict"; Brainard, "Presidential Leadership, Interest Groups, and Domestic Policymaking Summitry"; and Bosso, *Pesticides and Politics.*

13. See, for example, Breyer, *Regulation and Its Reform;* Greer, *Industrial Organization;* and Scherer, *Industrial Market Structure.* On market failures, see Stokey and Zeckhauser, *A Primer for Policy Analysis.*

14. Stone, *Policy Paradox*, p. 7.

15. On rational analysis, see Simon, *Administrative Behavior.* For approaches to policy and program analysis, see Quade, *Analysis for Public Decisions;* and Stokey and Zeckhauser, *Primer for Policy Analysis.*

16. See, for example, Downs, *An Economic Theory of Democracy.*

17. For a liberal view of this perspective, see Kolko, *The Triumph of Conservatism;* and Kolko, *Railroads and Regulation.* For a conservative view, see Stigler, "The Theory of Economic Regulation."

18. Different authors attribute this private-sector influence to different factors. Theodore Lowi and Grant McConnell, for example, attribute the influence of industry to the ideological context of the U.S. system, which views democracy and private autonomy as correlates. See Lowi, *The End of Liberalism;* and McConnell, *Private Power and American Democracy.* Mancur Olson, for example, attributes the dominance of business interests to the political stability found in the United States. See Olson, *The Rise and Decline of Nations.*

19. On the receptivity of members of Congress to demands by business interests, see Mayhew, *Electoral Connection.* On agency personnel, see Niskanen, *Bureaucracy and Representative Government.*

20. Becker, "A Theory of Competition Among Pressure Groups"; Buchanan, *The Demand and Supply of Public Goods;* Buchanan and Tullock, *The Calculus of Consent;* Peltzman, "Toward a More General Theory of Regulation"; and Posner, "Theories of Economic Regulation."

21. MacAvoy, *The Regulated Industries and the Economy;* and Carron and MacAvoy, *The Decline of Service in the Regulated Industries.*

22. I use "contingency" rather than "neopluralism." See McFarland, "Interest Groups and the Policymaking Process." I use "contingency" to stress the approach's relationship to the other theories reviewed here, thus emphasizing the relative conditionality of regulatory and policy change rather than the relative determinism of economic and industry determinism theories.

23. Stone, *Policy Paradox,* p. 9.

24. Ibid., p. 21.

25. Schattschneider, *The Semisovereign People,* p. 71. On the role of institutions generally, see March and Olsen, *Rediscovering Institutions;* Shepsle, "Studying Institutions"; Evans, Rueschemeyer, and Skocpol, *Bringing the State Back In;* and Hoberg, *Pluralism by Design.*

26. Shepsle and Weingast, "Institutional Foundations of Committee Power"; and Riker, *Liberalism Against Populism.*

27. McCraw, *Prophets of Regulation;* Wilson, *The Politics of Regulation;* and Mucciaroni, *Reversals of Fortune.*

28. Baumgartner and Jones, *Agendas and Instability in American Politics.*

29. Ibid., p. 235. See also Harris and Milkis, *The Politics of Regulatory Change.* The analysis by Harris and Milkis converges nicely with that by Baumgartner and Jones. Both analyses argue that we must step back from a singular focus on ideas or institutions or policies so that we can better understand how these factors *interact* in order to produce regulatory change. Nevertheless, the approaches of these authors differ in several important ways. While Harris and Milkis look at ideas, broadly understood, about regulation (what they call "regulatory regimes"), Baumgartner and Jones look at specific problem definitions of specific issues over time. Further, Harris and Milkis seek to identify broad historical patterns in business-government relations, while Baumgartner and Jones look at micro-level changes in specific areas of public policy (but which themselves are reflections of macro-level dynamics). Finally, therefore, Harris and Milkis identify broad qualitative shifts in regulation generally, while Baumgartner and Jones seek to understand how change specifically occurs. These two approaches thus are complementary.

30. Baumgartner and Jones do not investigate economic deregulation directly but do suggest that deregulation is an example of punctuated equilibrium. See Baumgartner and Jones, *Agendas and Instability in American Politics,* pp. 210–213.

31. For more on problem definition, see Stone, *Policy Paradox;* Dery, *Problem Definition in Policy Analysis;* and Rochefort and Cobb, *The Politics of Problem Definition.*

32. For analyses of airline regulation and deregulation, see Behrman, "Civil Aeronautics Board"; Meyer et al., *Airline Deregulation;* and Bailey, Graham, and Kaplan, *Deregulating the Airlines.* For analyses of trucking regulation and deregulation, see Childs, *Trucking and the Public Interest;* and Alexis, "The Political Economy of Federal Regulation of Surface Transportation." For analyses of telephone deregulation, see Horwitz, *The Irony of Regulatory Reform;* Vietor, *Contrived Competition;* Wiley, "The

End of Monopoly"; and Geller, "Regulation and Public Policy After Divestiture."

33. Childs, *Trucking and the Public Interest,* p. 158.

34. Horwitz, *The Irony of Regulatory Reform,* p. 134.

35. Ibid., p. 11.

36. Meyer et al., *Airline Deregulation,* p. 36.

37. Wiley, "The End of Monopoly"; and Geller, "Regulation and Public Policy Divestiture."

38. Behrman, "Civil Aeronautics Board," pp. 76–86.

39. Derthick and Quirk, *The Politics of Deregulation.*

40. Horwitz, *The Irony of Regulatory Reform.*

2

The Developing "Television Problem"

WHEN CONSIDERING REGULATORY HISTORY, SCHOLARS REFER TO "regulatory regimes." By this they mean that we can understand longitudinal waves of regulation and regulatory change only by focusing on changes in three elements: ideas, institutions, and policies.[1] Ideas are the underlying justifications for government intervention in business activities. Institutions, defined broadly, include not only the formal and informal structures and processes through which policymaking takes place, but also interest groups (both private and public) and other organized policy actors. Policies are the actual constraints that government places on business. Waves of regulation—that is, dominant paradigms of regulation as distinct from policy-specific modalities—are said to be qualitatively different owing to variations in the composition of these three elements.

The New Deal regime of regulation that emerged in the 1930s as a response to the Great Depression was characterized by ideas that supported government intervention in business activities in order to stabilize industries, allocate scarce resources, and promote industrial and economic growth and development. An important institution of the New Deal regime was the independent regulatory commission—itself a legacy of the Progressive Era—a device intended to rationalize and "depoliticize" regulation. These commissions, given wide discretion by vague legislative mandates, often produced capture of commissions by the businesses they were supposed to regulate. The New Deal regime also experimented with corporatist arrangements, such as the Tennessee Valley Authority. Thus New Deal policies, such as economic regulation, often favored industry interests, though, at least at the beginning, not necessarily at the expense of the broader public interest. Indeed, policymakers often viewed industry interests and the public interest as synonymous.

Take, for example, airline, trucking, and telephone regulation. In the airline and trucking cases, Congress was in part responding to widespread concern about destructive competition; that barriers to entry in each industry were so low that more firms would enter the field than traffic could support. Policymakers believed that in an overly competitive environment prices would fall so low that financial instability would ensue and result in the loss of service to the public. In the telephony case, Congress was responding to the economic idea that AT&T's telephone monopoly was a natural monopoly. Through this expansion of federal regulatory authority, Congress also was responding to Americans' fear of the free market amid the Great Depression. Finally, regulating these industries exemplified Americans' faith, at the time, in the ability of government intervention to produce the intended economic benefits of affordable prices and stable service amid their distrust of the ability of markets to correct themselves. Early television regulation was similar to airline, trucking. and telephony regulation in several important ways.

The Early Years:
Chaos, Scarcity, and the Regulatory Response

Imagine walking into a room, expecting to sit quietly and listen to some music. Instead, the room is filled with people all loudly expressing themselves in a variety of ways and on a variety of topics, all at once. Some talk about their day while others discuss current events. One person gives the recipe for the fabulous dinner he made last night. A trio in the corner plays musical instruments. A pair over by the window discusses a movie. Some just gossip. One person reads the news aloud, or maybe it's poetry; it's tough to tell with so many people making noise at once. When you try to tune into one person's or group's particular conversation, or song, or piece of poetry, the others seemingly get louder, crowding out your every attempt to focus. It is an exercise in frustration.

This is what it was like to switch on a radio (the technological and regulatory predecessor to television) at the beginning of the twentieth century. Radio (and television) broadcasting takes place over the electromagnetic spectrum, or airwaves, and in the early days of broadcasting more broadcasters wanted to air programming than the available spectrum could support. The result was excessive competition, or chaos. Broadcasters, all airing programming simultaneously, stepped on each other's signals. A listener tuning in confronted static. The central problem, which would become the underlying justification for all broadcast regulation, was spectrum scarcity. In this context, policymakers deemed the airwaves a scarce public resource and called for regulation.[2]

On February 23, 1927, Congress passed the Federal Radio Act, created the Federal Radio Commission (FRC), and instructed the commission to rationalize the industry and thereby preserve the availability of radio service to the public. While the statute vested responsibility for radio broadcasting in the FRC, the Interstate Commerce Commission (ICC) was responsible for telephone regulation. As part of his New Deal, however, President Franklin Roosevelt proposed to consolidate responsibility for all communications regulation into one agency, noting:

> I have long felt the need that, for the sake of clarity and effectiveness, the relationship of the Federal Government to certain services known as "utilities" should be divided into three fields: transportation, power, and communications. The problems of transportation are vested in the Interstate Commerce Commission and the problem of power . . . in the Federal Power Commission. In the field of Communications, however, there is today no single government agency charged with broad authority.[3]

Clearly, Roosevelt was identifying the infrastructure industries relevant to the economy at the time and was attempting to rationalize those industries through government regulation.

Responding to President Roosevelt's concern, in 1934 Congress passed and the president signed the Federal Communications Act. The law created the Federal Communications Commission (FCC) to oversee the entire communications industry, which at this point consisted only of radio, telephony, and telegraphy. Outside of creating a new commission and consolidating communications regulation, the 1934 act replicated, nearly verbatim, the 1927 Radio Act. When Congress passed and President Roosevelt signed the 1927 and 1934 acts, television did not yet exist, in any commercial form at least. Nevertheless, when television was invented, in the middle to late

1930s, it was folded into the 1934 Communications Act. As is so often the case with new technology, policymakers seek analogies to current technology and regulate the new technology in a similar manner. The new technology of television was most analogous to radio—a television essentially is a radio with pictures. Television also utilizes the airwaves and, as in the case of radio, there were more television broadcasters wishing to air programming than the spectrum could support. So policymakers, in this case the FCC commissioners, determined that television would be regulated in the same manner as radio.

The FCC, a classic independent regulatory commission, is composed of five commissioners, no more than three of whom may be from the same political party. The commissioners serve five-year terms. The chair, selected by the U.S. president, presides over commission meetings and coordinates the commission's work. The commission also combines legislative, executive, and judicial functions. A rule, order, or opinion of the FCC has the full force of law, which the commission also implements and enforces. The FCC also adjudicates disputes. As such, and given the vague mandate to regulate in the "public interest," the FCC, like other independent regulatory commissions, has vast discretion.

Given its "independent" form, the FCC has a complicated relationship with its political principals. The president nominates commissioners and selects the chair, and thus can shape the commission's agenda profoundly by appointing members sympathetic to the views of his or her administration. The president also is advised on communications issues by the National Telecommunications and Information Agency, housed in the Commerce Department. Further, the Justice Department weighs in on antitrust matters in the communications field.

On the other hand, the FCC also is beholden to Congress. Commissioners must be confirmed by the Senate. Further, Congress controls the FCC's budget and can exercise significant influence over the agency's agenda and actions. Finally, certain congressional committees are responsible for oversight of the commission. In particular, the House and Senate Commerce Committees (and their subcommittees on telecommunications) have jurisdiction over the commission and communications policy generally. Committee members, and especially subcommittee members and their staffs, are often experts on the issues. In addition, the House and Senate Judiciary

Committees also have jurisdiction over antitrust issues and therefore over antitrust and consolidation matters in the communications industry.

Given these relationships to the president and to Congress, it is a wonder that these commissions can be considered "independent" at all. Most often, and especially during times of divided government (when one political party controls the White House and the other Congress), the independent regulatory commissions find themselves in the awkward position of having to be responsive to political principals of conflicting ideological and policy stripes. Finally (and as will be made evident in Chapter 5), the complex relationship between the FCC, Congress, and the president stems from the fact that each body has its own jurisdictional interests and its own relationship to the public at large.

The Authority to License

The FCC's main regulatory tool is its authority to issue scarce licenses to television broadcasters to operate on specific frequencies (channels), or as the inventor of television, Philo T. Farnsworth, later put it, "to slice up the pie in the sky."[4] According to the 1934 Communications Act, the FCC is to do this in order to ensure the "public interest, convenience and necessity." This form of entry regulation epitomized the New Deal regime.

Television broadcasters receive their licenses for free, which constitutes a significant subsidy. With that subsidy and the use of a scarce public resource, however, regulators expected that television broadcasters would act as fiduciaries for the public, or "public trustees," and that broadcasters would retain their licenses only as long and insofar as they served the "public interest." The FCC would define the "public interest" and operationalize it through the licensing process.

Because there were so many television broadcasters competing for scarce licenses, the FCC employed a comparative process by which the commissioners evaluated the merits of various license applicants against each other. Given a broadcaster's public trustee status, the FCC focused on programming in particular. Indeed, as Stephen Breyer notes in his text on regulation, "To award a television license in the public interest . . . requires consideration of 'good programming.' Programming is, after all, the final product that television provides for the public."[5] The vagueness of the public interest concept allowed the FCC to define it, and in the early years of broadcasting the commission interpreted it to mean, for example, that a broadcaster must serve its local community with news and public affairs programming.

Regulating Industry Structure: Ownership Rules

In addition to requiring all radio and television broadcasters to obtain licenses, in the early 1940s the FCC promulgated rules limiting, to three, the number of broadcast stations any one person or corporation could own. By the mid-1970s the limits had been revised upward so that any one entity could own up to seven AM radio stations, seven FM radio stations, and seven television stations.[6] These ownership limits were a tool of economic regulation, designed to ensure that broadcasting remained competitive and that stations would not fall into the hands of a few. The primary early concern here was economic. This was an antimonopoly measure, but also reflected a notion of the public interest in the free flow of ideas.

Given the assumption that broadcasting should remain competitive, why did policymakers allow group ownership at all? First, they believed that economies of scale would provide resources for more expensive and, presumably therefore, "better" programming.[7] Second, strong group owners could serve as potential competitors to the three dominant networks of the time (for this was, of course, prior to the widespread use of cable television).[8] Finally as Robert Britt Horwitz notes, "Based on the fact that, in the early days of television, all the nascent television networks had scrambled to acquire many stations, the FCC came to the unproved conclusion that multiple ownership facilitated the formation of networks."[9] So the FCC wanted to strike a balance between allowing group ownership and limiting it, between presumably improving the "quality" of programming and ensuring competition. In this sense, the FCC was acting much like the Civil Aeronautics Board (CAB) in regulating airlines and the ICC in regulating trucking. Each agency was trying to find the proper mix of, and balance between, too much competition and too little.

Though regulators placed limits on television station ownership in order to preserve competition and guard against monopoly, they also believed that a desirable by-product of these regulations would

be "diversity." That is, they believed that diversity in station ownership presumably would lead to diversity in programming and, by
extension, to a diversity of viewpoints that could be heard over the
airwaves. Social goals thus were intertwined with the economic goal
of competition.

These ownership regulations spawned a complex and fragmented, yet interconnected, industry structure. The broadcast television
sector is composed of several kinds of firms: individually owned stations, whether owned by a person or corporation; group broadcasters,
which own more than one station and range from small to large; and
networks (for example, ABC, CBS, and NBC), which own a number
of stations usually at or near the regulatory limits but which are distinct from individually owned stations and group broadcasters in two
ways. First, the FCC does not regulate networks; rather the agency's
jurisdiction extends only to stations. Therefore, for example, while a
station owned by ABC is subject to FCC regulations, the ABC network itself is not. Second, networks also have affiliations with stations they do not own. Thus, for example, an individually owned station, or a station that is part of a group, may affiliate with a national
network for the rights to distribute that network's programming.
Stations that are neither owned nor affiliated with a network are
called "independents."

In general, stations, groups, and networks may produce their
own programming or they may purchase programming. Broadcast
television firms earn their revenues, which they use to purchase programming, from advertisers. Each firm tries to air programming that
is popular enough to attract a large audience. Advertisers purchase
airtime from a television firm in order to advertise their products,
and they pay the television firm according to the number of people
those ads reach (as measured through ratings). Alternatively, advertisers may not want to reach a large audience; instead they might
want to reach the "right" audience. For example, the manufacturer of
very expensive watches may not want to reach a large or wide audience, but instead will be more satisfied reaching a smaller, select
audience comprising a large proportion of viewers who can afford
luxury timepieces. Thus television firms produce and purchase and
air programming that they think will attract the audiences desired by
advertisers.

By promulgating ownership regulations, the FCC was trying to
find a balance between facilitating the formation of group broadcast-

ers and networks that could produce and buy programming with mass appeal, and discouraging monopoly in both the advertising market and in the marketplace of ideas.

The Fairness Doctrine

In light of the public trustee status of broadcasters, the FCC promulgated a "social style" regulation—though one with roots in the scarcity problem. The Fairness Doctrine instructed television broadcasters to air programming covering controversial issues of public importance and to do so fairly. The FCC promulgated the Fairness Doctrine because it was concerned that, given spectrum scarcity and therefore the limited number of channels available, programming might not reflect a diverse array of perspectives and viewpoints. And given that broadcasters were using (and profiting from) the public's airwaves, they had an obligation to serve that public. The agency also worried that broadcasters might use their licenses to further their own political ends (for example, by favoring particular candidates or parties for office). Finally, the FCC reasoned that there was a compelling public interest in broadcasting and therefore the public must retain some control over the medium. Thus, as Steven Simmons notes, "The idea of a shared First Amendment right in broadcasting between broadcaster and listener was being suggested."[10] Regulators reasoned that while broadcasters have a First Amendment right to free speech, viewers and listeners have a right to hear a variety of viewpoints on the important issues of the day. In promulgating the Fairness Doctrine the FCC tried to strike a balance between these competing rights.

The first official pronouncement of the doctrine came in 1929 when the Federal Radio Commission refused to renew a broadcaster's license on the grounds that the company editorialized unfairly. In its decision, the FRC stated that in an environment of scarcity,

> The standard of public interest, convenience, or necessity means nothing if it does not mean this. . . . In so far as a program consists of discussion of public questions, public interest requires ample play for the free and fair competition of opposing views, and the commission believes that the principle applies . . . to all discussions of issues of importance to the public.[11]

The FCC reiterated this principle more explicitly and forcefully in 1941 when it stated: "Freedom of speech on the radio must be

broad enough to provide full and equal opportunity for the presenta-
tion to the public of all sides of public issues. . . . The public interest—
not the private—is paramount."[12]

Cable Regulation and Broadcaster Protection

In the 1950s, technological development created a competitor to television broadcasters. Using coaxial wires, cable television operators
could transmit broadcast signals to viewers hitherto unable to receive
such signals, or unable to receive them clearly, due to geography. At
first, since these cable systems were little more than passive "pass
through" mechanisms, broadcasters viewed cable as a great boon.
Now able to extend the reach of their signals, broadcasters also could
reach larger audiences. Able to reach larger audiences, they could
charge more for advertising and thereby increase their profits.

Initially, subscription rates charged by cable operators were regulated by local authorities (owing to the status of cable systems as
local monopolies), while the federal government shunned jurisdiction. As cable technology developed, however, cable system operators were able not only to extend the reach of broadcast signals but
also to import them and export them as well. Thus a broadcaster in
Boston, for example, now found itself not only competing against
other Boston-area broadcasters but against broadcasters from, say,
Tennessee, whose signals were being imported into the Boston area
via cable. Broadcasters viewed this increased competition as a threat
to their large audiences, advertising revenues, and therefore profits.

In a 1958 decision the D.C. Circuit Court of Appeals provided
the FCC with a rationale to restrain cable television operators. The
court held that "economic injury to an existing station . . . becomes
important when on the facts it spells diminution or destruction of
service. At that point the element of injury ceases to be a matter of
purely private concern."[13] The court reasoned that television broadcasters ought to be protected from competition because they served a
public purpose. Failure of the industry due to unrestrained competition would harm the availability of that service to the public.

Looking very much like a captured agency, the FCC assumed
jurisdiction over cable and enacted a series of highly restrictive regulations to protect television broadcasters. For example, the FCC
enacted a slew of signal carriage rules. Among these were "nonduplication" rules, which restricted cable system operators from importing
the programming of distant signals when local broadcast stations

were already showing those programs, thus protecting broadcasters from audience fragmentation. This rule prevented the viewer from turning on the television set and having to make a choice between watching a particular program on one channel versus another. For example, in the absence of nonduplication rules, a viewer might be faced with choosing between a local station airing the *Mary Tyler Moore Show* and a cable system importing a distant signal airing the same program at the same time. The viewer might, by chance or by choice, watch the distant channel, thereby disadvantaging the local station (i.e., fragmenting the audience and therefore lowering the ratings and profits of the station). Equally important, the FCC restricted cable systems from importing distant signals into any of the top 100 television markets unless it could demonstrate that doing so would not harm local broadcasters.[14] This was comparable to actions by the CAB and the ICC that placed the burden of proof on those firms seeking entry into these respective industries.

The FCC justified this protection of broadcasters by noting that broadcasters provide important services—such as news and public affairs programming—to their communities. Thus, the argument went, the rules were not so much designed to protect television broadcasters per se as they were meant to protect the services provided by broadcasters to the public.

From 1934 until the middle to late 1960s, then, this system of television regulation functioned like a classic iron triangle, complete with connotations of FCC capture by television broadcasters. Congress passed the vague 1934 Communications Act, mandating that the FCC use its discretion to award broadcast licenses in the public interest, and then left the commission to its own devices. The FCC, using its discretion, awarded licenses to broadcasters who thrived under the system and were generally happy with it. The FCC protected licensed broadcasters from competition from unlicensed broadcasters (broadcasting without a license was illegal) and from cable operators. Television regulation reflected the dominant regulatory regime.

The Public Lobby Wave

Beginning in the 1960s, a new regulatory regime emerged, which later came to be called the public lobby regime.[15] Changes in policies thus resulted from new institutional characteristics and new ideas. An important institutional change occurred in Congress. In 1974 a swarm of new, younger, and more liberal members of Congress won election and took office wanting to be more entrepreneurial and more activist—especially with regard to consumer and quality of life issues. Happily for them, they were able to produce several important changes in the congressional institutional structure that gave individual members additional staff and resources that they could use to be more active.[16]

Simultaneously, public interest groups were granted standing to participate in regulatory proceedings and to sue agencies in court.[17] It was this ruling, in part, that gave rise to what Jeffrey Berry calls the "advocacy explosion."[18] Groups claiming to represent the broad and diffuse public on matters ranging from consumer to environmental and safety issues acquired new resources and legal legitimacy with which to mobilize and become active across nearly all areas of public policy.

Concurrent with these institutional changes, new ideas began to circulate throughout the policy system, as policymakers and activists increasingly wanted the private sector to absorb more of the costs associated with conducting business. This entailed two different policy manifestations. One such policy manifestation was the rise of social regulation: rules forcing business to take responsibility for problems such as pollution, workplace safety, and quality of life issues generally. Another manifestation of these changes, however, was an emerging consensus about the desirability of economic deregulation. In the latter case, policymakers began to pick up on the critique of regulation advanced by economists, that economic regulation was inefficient, and political scientists, that economic regulation, to the extent that it entailed capture of regulatory agencies by business, subverted democratic processes. By the late 1960s and early 1970s, the relevant regulatory agencies began to open up entry to competitors.

The forces in U.S. society and government that gave rise to the public lobby regime also affected television regulation. With new resources, individual members of Congress began to get more involved in the details of regulatory policy and oversight.[19] Congress had not intervened in FCC policies since passing the 1934 Communications Act,[20] but in the 1970s members of Congress became key, powerful, and active (and rather constant) participants in television policy. This new interest in communications policy especially was driven by younger and more liberal Democrats.

Along with more active members of Congress, public advocacy organizations entered into debates over television regulation. An important 1966 appeals court decision, *Office of Communications of the United Church of Christ v. Federal Communications Commission,* gave the broader public, and organized interests that claimed to represent diffuse interests, the right to participate in FCC proceedings and the right to seek judicial review of agency decisions.[21] In the airline, trucking, and telephony cases, public advocacy groups came from the broader public interest and consumer movement. In the television case, however, new public interest groups formed to focus specifically on television issues. During this time period the television public interest "movement" was a loose confederation of liberal groups. Many grew out of the civil rights movement, such as the Citizens Communications Center (a public interest law firm), the National Black Media Coalition, and the Office of Communications of the United Church of Christ, and were particularly concerned with issues affecting racial minorities (such as minority employment at television stations, programming geared to minority interests, and programming related to the important public issue of civil rights). The Office of Communications of the United Church of Christ actually was the first such group to concern itself with media issues and was the plaintiff in that 1966 landmark case, which gave standing to public interest groups on communications policy issues. The National Citizens Communications Lobby, headed by former FCC commissioner Nicholas Johnson, came out of a more general "public interest" perspective (and therefore sought to ensure public participation in television regulatory matters), while the Committee for Open Media was rooted in academia. Action for Children's Television, founded in 1968 and headed by Peggy Charren, concerned itself primarily with children's television issues, though it participated in broader communications issues as well.

Academics also became increasingly active in television policy issues. Sociologists, for example, studied the portrayal of women and racial and ethnic minorities in the media. Psychologists studied the effects of television, and portrayals of sex and violence, on the population as a whole and on specific subgroups. Academics participated directly in television policy by issuing reports and studies, testifying before Congress, submitting responses to agency regulatory proposals, and the like. They also indirectly influenced policy by producing books and appearing on television news programs and in newspapers as commentators on the effects of television on society. They thus contributed to the increasing salience of television policy.

Stemming in part from this transformation in the institutional characteristics of the television regulation system, and from the expanded configuration of interests brought about by the injection of new stakeholders (and therefore new ideas) into the television policy subsystem, in the 1960s the FCC began to formulate additional public trustee regulations. These regulations, reflecting the social regulation paradigm of the public lobby regime, were layered on top of the New Deal paradigm of economic regulation.

Equal Employment Opportunity Rules

In 1969 the FCC became the first and only economic regulatory agency to promulgate industry-specific equal employment opportunity (EEO) rules. This is significant because the Equal Employment Opportunity Commission (EEOC), established in 1965, was mandated to ensure nondiscrimination across U.S. business and industry generally. And while other agencies responsible for economic regulation (such as the CAB and the ICC) left equal employment matters relating to their regulated industries up to the EEOC, the FCC promulgated its own.

In prohibiting discrimination on the basis of race, religion, color, and national origin, the FCC required each broadcaster to adopt a program of affirmative employment practices.[22] The FCC's EEO rules required broadcasters to inform sources of qualified minority applicants of the employment programs and enlist their help in recruitment, continuously campaign to avoid discrimination, and continuously review station employment structures to ensure full participation of all organizational units in the EEO program. In 1970 the FCC began requiring its licensees to file annual employment reports consisting of statistics on minority employment as well as written EEO programs enumerating their efforts to recruit minorities.

In 1978, noting that minorities constituted approximately 20 percent of the U.S. population but less than 1 percent of television (and radio) broadcast station owners, the FCC took steps to ensure minority ownership of television stations. For example, the commission announced that a person or corporation who sold their station to minorities would qualify for a capital gains tax deferral. Similarly, in cases where more than one person or corporation competed for a television license, the FCC announced that preference would be given to a minority.[23]

Children's Television Rules

Children's television regulations also were promulgated during the 1970s. Action for Children's Television, a group of Boston-area mothers concerned with the quality of children's television programming, lobbied the FCC to create a rule aimed at reducing the number of commercials during children's programs and at requiring broadcasters to air children's educational programming. To preempt FCC action, television broadcasters agreed among themselves (through the National Association of Broadcasters, the primary organization representing the interests of radio and television broadcasters and networks) to limit the amount of advertising during children's programming. The FCC adopted the industry's self-regulatory policy as its own in 1974. Similarly the FCC "urged" broadcasters to air programming suitable for children, as part of their overall commitment to serve their communities, but did not require them to do so.[24]

The FCC commissioners attached all of these social, "public trustee" regulations to the basic New Deal paradigm of economic regulation. In fact, these policies were extensions of it. They all hinged on the twin pillars of the New Deal paradigm—scarcity, coupled with the need to award licenses to broadcasters to serve the public interest. The scarce spectrum could support only a few broadcasters in each market. With so few television stations, each broadcaster found itself attempting to appeal to the mass audience and often ignored audiences considered to be nonmainstream, such as minorities and children. Regulators also thought such rules appropriate for businesses considered public trustees.

The injection of new groups into television regulation thus led to new kinds of policies requiring broadcasters to assume more responsibility under their public trustee status. Certainly broadcasters found social, or public trustee, regulations—such as EEO regulations, the Fairness Doctrine, and children's television regulations—onerous. They complained that the former violated their freedom to hire whom they chose and that the latter violated their right to free speech—but such regulations were not strictly enforced. The FCC was extremely hesitant to revoke a license of a broadcaster that failed to adhere to these regulations for fear that it would open itself up to allegations of infringing on the First Amendment right to free speech. And while broadcasters were not happy with implementation of children's television regulations (again owing to First Amendment concerns), that the broadcast industry itself wrote those regulations made them more palatable.

Rethinking Cable Regulation

By the 1970s the FCC, like the CAB and the ICC, began to ease the regulatory burden. Specifically, the FCC began to rethink its constraints on cable television. In 1972 the commission relaxed the regulatory burden altogether for cable system operators in small markets.[25] The 1972 rules also eased many of the regulatory requirements for cable systems operating in larger markets, but in a very controlled way and in exchange for public trustee requirements. For example, cable systems operating in larger markets would henceforth be able to import distant signals, but their numbers were limited. Syndicated exclusivity rules required cable systems to black out any program that was being shown on the same day by local over-the-air broadcasters. Larger cable systems would be required to offer a minimum of twenty channels, to originate local programming, and to furnish public, educational, and government access channels. Finally, the FCC's EEO regulations were extended to cable in this period.[26]

Just as the Civil Aeronautics Board and the Interstate Commerce Commission took steps to deregulate their respective industries, by 1974, with the creation of a Cable Television Reregulation Task Force (itself a misnomer since its goal was to relax the rules restricting cable), the FCC began to reconsider its 1972 rules. As a result of the task force's efforts, the FCC further eased many of its 1972 rules. For example, in 1974 the agency amended its rules to permit importation of late-night programming without restriction. The agency deleted its requirement that cable systems engage in local origination of programming. Finally, the agency relaxed the syndicated exclusivity rules for smaller cable systems.[27] Nevertheless, despite this slight relaxation in the restrictions on cable, the sector remained highly regulated so as to protect broadcasters from competition.

Summarizing Regulatory Development

An astute observer would notice many similarities between the development of regulation for television and the development of regulation for the airline, trucking, and telephone industries. In particular, all are infrastructure industries and each was a focus of government efforts, as part of the New Deal regime of economic regulation, to rationalize U.S. business and industry with an eye to finding a proper balance between too much competition and too little (or in the case of telephony, compensating for a lack of competition altogether). In each case, the regulatory agency tended to protect from external competition the regulated firms for which it was responsible.

To be sure, there was one notable difference. In the television example, we observe the overt and purposeful intertwining of economic and social regulation. In other cases, social regulations were promulgated independently of the underlying economics of the industry. Thus, for example, air safety regulations were based on the externalities rationale and the assumption that increased competition would not ameliorate (and might even exacerbate) safety concerns. Such air safety rules were promulgated by the Federal Aviation Administration, not the Civil Aeronautics Board, which was responsible for economic regulation of the industry.

By contrast, in the television case, public trustee regulations were layered on top of the New Deal regime of economic regulations, its underlying scarcity rationale, and the lack of vigorous competition in the industry. According to the regulatory logic, then, ameliorating the scarcity problem, and increasing the level of competition in the industry, would undermine the need not only for economic regulations in television but for public trustee regulations as well.

In light of the similarities, and despite these differences, just as economists criticized airline, trucking, and telephone regulation for being inefficient, they also criticized television regulation. Indeed, in the 1950s economists began to argue that extensive regulation of broadcasting was unwarranted. Their primary target was the FCC's licensing authority. Economist Leo Herzel was the first to advocate that price mechanisms and the market be allowed to allocate frequencies, rather than being an administrative process that involved the government in editorial decisions.[28] Relieved of the need to allocate frequencies, the economics literature concluded, government would have no basis on which to intervene in program content.[29]

Similarly, considering the state of television and the technological changes that the industry was undergoing (as manifested in the development of cable television), economists began to conclude that such changes called into question the whole paradigm of television regulation. For example, Roger Noll, Merton Peck, and John McGowan, after an economic analysis of the industry, argued that the expansion of the television environment (through cable as well as through other technologies such as satellite) would ameliorate the problem of spectrum scarcity, since cable doesn't use the airwave spectrum and can air many different channels. In an era marked by an abundance of television, the FCC would no longer need to issue "scarce" licenses. Without the need to license, the FCC would no longer need to be concerned with program content and the business practices of its licensees. The market could reign.[30]

Despite these early similarities, as the television issue took on added salience it became much more complex, as we can observe by investigating the conflict that began to surround television policy in the mid-1970s.

Defining the Television Problem: The Metaphor Is the Message

Because perceptions about the nature of a policy problem define its politics, one good way to understand the nature of political conflict is to assess competing definitions of policy problems. For example, economists drove airline, trucking, and telephony deregulation by defining the problem as one of economic inefficiency. Problem definition also can occur through a seemingly much less analytical, even intuitive process of constructing narratives, of telling stories about the causes, consequences, and possible solutions to public problems. Thus, as Deborah Stone writes, problem definition is the

> strategic representation of situations. Problem definition is a matter of representation because every description of a situation is a portrayal from only one of many points of view. Problem definition is strategic because groups, individuals, and government agencies deliberately and consciously fashion portrayals so as to promote their favored course of action.[31]

Problem definition thus shapes political conflict by emphasizing different dimensions of an issue. This, in turn, often implies competing policy prescriptions.

If the "problem" of television—"scarcity"—seemed simple up through the 1960s, beginning in the mid-1970s competing images of reality began to emerge, first through books by academics and activists, then through government reports, and finally in a series of comprehensive FCC oversight hearings held in 1976 by the Communications Subcommittee of the House Interstate and Foreign Commerce Committee. The debate that ensued offers a vivid demonstration of the process and politics of problem definition and of Deborah Stone's instruction that problem definition, as a form of storytelling, often includes reasoning by "metaphor and analogy. It is trying to get others to see a situation as one thing rather than another."[32]

A "Vast Wasteland"

In the mid-1970s, a central, overarching problem definition subsumed two distinct subsidiary strands of argument. The central metaphor around which interests and activists coalesced was that television constituted a "vast wasteland," a phrase coined in 1961 by then–FCC chairman Newton Minow in a speech to the National Association of Broadcasters. Minow, who was appointed to the FCC by President John F. Kennedy, challenged broadcasters to sit before their television sets for one entire day:

> You will observe a vast wasteland. You will see a procession of game shows, violence, audience participation shows, formula comedies about totally unbelievable families, blood and thunder, mayhem, violence, sadism, murder, western badmen, western good men, private eyes, gangsters, more violence, and cartoons. And endlessly, commercials—many screaming, cajoling, and offending.[33]

In short, Minow was offering a vivid and distinct definition of the television problem: TV stinks. And what is more, by airing such programming, television broadcasters were abusing the public trust. Minow went on to chide television broadcasters for not taking their fiduciary responsibilities more seriously, noting, "Gentlemen, your trust accounting with your beneficiaries is long overdue. Never have so few owed so much to so many."[34]

"Vast wasteland" subsequently went on to become the dominant metaphor for the way people thought about (and continue to think about) television—not only in debates by policymakers and interest organizations, but also in the minds of the larger viewing public. Indeed, the speech and the metaphor so resonated throughout society that the latter subsequently became a part of our popular culture and has been featured in book titles, in Bartlett's *Familiar Quotations,* as an answer to a Trivial Pursuit question, and even on the Law School Admissions Test.[35]

In his speech, Chairman Minow argued that television should be enriching and informative (as well as entertaining and recreational), and that it should make citizens aware of their world. These were consensus objectives for television, a consensus understanding of the "public interest" in television. Nearly everyone agreed, and still does, that these are appropriate goals for television (after all, who would argue that television *should* be a vast wasteland?). Though Minow's speech identified a significant television problem, it offered no specific policy prescriptions. Rather, subsumed under this central, overarching understanding of the television problem were two very different problem definitions, each of which had its own array of interest organizations, its own metaphor and narrative, and its own distinct and separate policy implications.

A "Virtual Stranglehold"

One strand of the larger debate over television pitted cable companies, public interest groups, and economists against television broadcasters and the FCC. In this view, broadcast television interests had captured the FCC, which in turn protected broadcasters from competition from cable. Cable companies, public interest groups, and economists argued that the three television networks at the time (ABC, CBS, and NBC) unfairly dominated the attention of U.S. viewers. They wanted the FCC to build on its relaxation of cable regulations initiated in the early 1970s and continue to open up entry to cable. Barring that, they wanted Congress to force the FCC to do so. Doing so, they argued, would break the control that the three networks had over television programming, and thus the ensuing competition would improve television programming itself.

According to this view, that television constituted a "vast wasteland" stemmed from the fact that three large corporations dominated television. Ted Turner now is known as the colorful media mogul who pledged $1 billion to the United Nations and whose vision bore CNN. Nevertheless, in the early and mid-1970s, Turner was the chairman of the board of the fledgling Turner Communications (which consisted primarily of WTBS, an Atlanta-based broadcast television station—which is now part of the AOL Time Warner empire). Turner, although a broadcaster, advocated cable deregulation, wanted to take on the three major networks, and best voiced the concerns of those who believed that the television industry was far too concentrated:

> You have to remember there are three supernetworks . . . that are controlling the way this nation thinks and raking off exorbitant profits, and most of these local stations . . . are just carrying those network programs that are originated out of New York. They have an absolute, a virtual stranglehold, on what Americans see and think.[36]

Advocates for cable television (including cable firms and public interest groups) also argued that the dominance of the networks contributed to the "vast wasteland" problem because the lack of competition allowed the networks to be unresponsive to the great diversity of the viewing audience. Thus the networks treated viewers as passive recipients of programs without input into television programming. Jesse Jackson, then head of Operation PUSH (but better known today as a sometime presidential candidate and head of the Rainbow Coalition), elaborated on this criticism and argued that the broadcast television system particularly excluded minorities and that cable promised to be different. Jackson noted, "The greatest impact of cable TV is that, as an alternative, it is a viable protest—if it is true to its calling—against network TV monopoly."[37] Because advertisers try to attract large audiences, broadcast television programming often was not geared toward racial minorities, rural viewers, poor viewers, and those not perceived as likely to buy the products that were being advertised.

In the 1970s public interest groups and economists thought that the then-new cable television service would address this problem. Because cable companies earn a portion of their revenues from fees paid directly by viewers, cable programming theoretically would be able better to meet viewer demand. And because of the expanded number of channels, cable programs would not have to seek a mass audience. As Russell Karp, president of Teleprompter Corp. (a cable company), argued:

> Cable television has the potential to remedy the main defect of commercial television—the lack of diversity caused by the scarcity of the broadcast spectrum and the dependence of broadcasters solely on mass-appeal advertisers. Cable television, not subject to these limitations, can make an enormous difference in the quality and diversity of television programming.[38]

Hence, in addition to the standard program types then offered by broadcasters, cable potentially could offer niche programming such as high drama, symphony, and Broadway theater.

Because cable companies in the 1970s usually were local operations, licensed by municipalities and serving, in some cases, geographical entities no larger than the average-sized neighborhood, cable advocates thought that citizen-viewers would be able to collaborate with cable systems to determine programming. At the very least, viewers could vote with their wallets. In the case of pay cable services (movie and other premium channels), noted Curtis T. Whitehead, director of the Cable Project for the Citizens Communication Center, a public interest law firm, "the family links paying directly to the choice of programming."[39]

Television broadcasters, on the other hand, wanted to restrain cable. Of course, they had their historical antipathy toward competition. But they also believed that they were subject to unfair competition from cable companies. In carrying broadcaster signals, cable system operators simultaneously carried broadcasters' programming. Broadcasters, of course, either produced their programming themselves or paid the copyright owners (usually movie and program production houses and Hollywood studios) for the rights to air the programs. According to a 1976 law, cable companies paid government-set fees into a fund, which the government then distributed to television broadcasters. But broadcasters continued to complain, noting that the fees were not set by the market and therefore were unfairly low. From the perspective of television broadcasters, cable system operators were stealing their product.

This strand of the debate over the television problem thus had much in common with the debates that came to be centered on airline, trucking, and telephony regulation. In each of these cases, policymakers and activists alleged that the regulatory agency had been captured by the businesses it was supposed to regulate and therefore was engaging in economically inefficient regulatory protectionism, thereby hampering the natural workings of the marketplace and depriving consumers of new and improved services that would be more responsive to their demands. In the television case, advocates of cable television wanted restrictive regulations removed from the cable sector. They wanted deregulation of cable television.

A "Toothless Tiger"

A second strand in the debate over the television problem did not look at all like that surrounding airline, trucking, and telephone regulation. Rather, public interest groups, continuing to argue that the FCC had been captured by broadcasters, suggested that the commission was not using its regulatory powers to the fullest extent possible and rarely enforced its own policies. The FCC was, as Jesse Jackson then put it, a "toothless tiger."[40]

The imagery, and the implied narrative, is compelling: television broadcasters and viewers alike are wandering the vast wasteland of television. The public relies on the tiger (the FCC) to police the broadcasters and ensure that they are serving the public (and the public interest). The tiger approaches broadcasters, flicks its tail, makes a menacing growling noise, and opens wide. Alas, it has no teeth. Television broadcasters, not the tiger, rule the vast wasteland. In other words, the vast wasteland stemmed from inadequate regulation. Thus, beyond the cable television issue, public interest groups defined the problem as too little regulation and lax regulatory enforcement. They wanted more of each. We can see this line of reasoning more specifically by looking at the controversies surrounding particular regulatory policies.

Broadcaster licensing.   One such controversy dealt with the FCC's central regulatory tool, broadcaster licensing. On the one hand, public interest groups argued that the FCC was falling down on its job of using the licensing process to ensure that only broadcasters serving the public interest received licenses. Public interest groups wanted the FCC to revoke, or decline to renew, the licenses of broadcasters who were not serving the public interest. As Barry Cole and Mal Oettinger complained:

A renewal application has never been denied solely because of a failure to meet community needs and problems, an excess of commercials, a lack of public service announcements, or an inadequate amount of news, public affairs, or other nonentertainment material. Nor has a combination of these misdeeds ever resulted in denial of a renewal application. No renewal has ever been denied solely for failing to live up to programming promises.[41]

On the other hand, broadcasters argued that a three-year license term created an onerous burden. The 1934 Communications Act limited the broadcast television license term to three years in order to prevent broadcasters from assuming a vested property right in their frequencies. Similarly, the act's license terms were designed so that broadcasters could not reap a financial windfall by selling their valuable frequencies, which are, after all, public property. Broadcasters argued that three-year license terms were too short and too disruptive. Specifically, they argued that longer, even indefinite terms would enable them to engage in better strategic program planning, acquire long-term financing, and produce better-quality programming. Television broadcasters voiced the fear that they would make large investments in programming and in facilities only to have their licenses revoked or not renewed.

Ownership rules.   A similar dynamic occurred around the FCC's broadcast station ownership limits. A report by the U.S. comptroller-general noted:

> Although the Commission cannot determine the effect on diversity of its multiple ownership rules, it can measure the impact on ownership concentration by analyzing available ownership data. However, it doesn't. Except in the course of formulating ownership rules, the Commission performs no overall ownership analyses. Nor does it maintain aggregate ownership statistics.[42]

This of course opened up the FCC to the charge that it performed very little follow-up monitoring on its own policies—indeed, that it had no idea whether its policies even attained their stated goals.

Public interest groups argued that ownership regulations were meaningless because they were not stringent enough and because the FCC was unwilling to force divestiture. The FCC was unwilling to force divestiture because of its concerns for industry stability and therefore broadcasters' ability to provide service to the public.[43]

Hence, whenever the FCC promulgated ownership regulations, it pegged those limits essentially according to what broadcasters wanted. It never promulgated limits lower than what broadcasters already owned because it did not want to raise the divestiture questions. Horwitz notes that this "softened the industry's opposition to the rule."[44] Critics, however, argued that because the FCC was unwilling to set stricter limits, enforce them, and force divestiture, ownership limits had little effect.[45]

The Fairness Doctrine. Controversy also surrounded the Fairness Doctrine in the mid-1970s. Simmons pointed out that questions remained about whether the doctrine was effective. One of the most serious problems with enforcement of the Fairness Doctrine was what Simmons calls the "problem of issue."[46] In brief, in enforcing the Fairness Doctrine the FCC was left to define such concepts as "issue," "controversial," and "public importance." Simmons argued:

> In attempting to define a controversial issue of public importance, the Commission has looked to vigorous debate between substantial elements in the community, thus excluding the ideas of the small minority. . . . If a lone pariah's ideas or those of a small group are scoffed at by the rest of the community, there is no debate and therefore no fairness requirement.[47]

Hence, many argued that the Fairness Doctrine did not accomplish all that policymakers intended. Unpopular, minority viewpoints did not receive consideration over the airwaves; rather, the Fairness Doctrine acted to legitimize various points of view falling within the mainstream. Similarly, the enforcement of the doctrine by the FCC and the interpretation of the doctrine by broadcasters implied that only two sides to issues must be discussed. Simmons argued, "Given the complexity of many controversial issues . . . the FCC reinforcement of a licensee's bipolar orientation appears antithetical to the doctrine's stated objective."[48]

Broadcasters, on the other hand, called for repeal of the Fairness Doctrine and full recognition of the industry's First Amendment rights. Speaking before the California Broadcasters Association, Wilson Wearn, then chairman of the National Association of Broadcasters, proclaimed: "Since 1922 when broadcasting began, the Government has tried to intervene in programs, tried to substitute its judgment for that of the licensee. The very fact that we use the airways is more reason for the First Amendment to apply to us, not less, because it makes broadcasting so much easier to manipulate."[49] In other words, broadcasters argued that the very fact that they were subject to a modicum of government control—by virtue of the fact that they required a license from the government—meant that they were potentially vulnerable to government intrusions on their freedom of speech. Therefore, as the argument went, there should be a heightened concern for broadcasters' First Amendment freedoms, rather than a lessened concern.

Some television broadcasters also argued that the expansion of television, brought about by the development of the UHF band of the electromagnetic spectrum as well as the nascent cable television industry, made (or would make) scarcity a thing of the past. For example, though Fred W. Friendly, a former president of CBS News and an astute observer of Fairness Doctrine debates, did not believe that scarcity already had ended, he did note the promise of new technologies then on the horizon and suggested that their growth would mitigate the need for the doctrine.[50] Hence there was a general sense among television broadcasters at the time that scarcity no longer was an issue, or at least would not be an issue for much longer, and therefore that the justification for government intervention in program content was eroding.

Equal employment and diversity. In the middle and late 1970s the FCC's equal employment opportunity policies and practices also were embroiled in controversy surrounding three main issues: (1) the job categories and classifications used in the FCC's EEO forms; (2) the type and number of stations required to submit written EEO programs; and (3) the level and sincerity of the FCC's enforcement of its EEO regulations.

In preparing the form to be used by broadcasters in meeting their EEO obligations, the FCC borrowed job categories and classifications from the Equal Employment Opportunity Commission. Such categories included "skilled craftsman" and "unskilled laborer," classifications that are not applicable to television broadcasting. After an analysis of eight stations (television and radio), the Civil Rights Commission found that stations did not agree on the categories into which various job titles should be placed. In spite of this, however, the FCC declined to change the job categories on its form, prompting some citizen groups to argue that the FCC placed a low priority on EEO regulations.[51]

Activists also argued that the FCC was not effectively enforcing its EEO rules and regulations, as judged by the statistics on minority employment in the broadcasting industry, both television and radio. Upon inspection, Nolan Bowie of the Citizens Communications Center found that improvement in minority hiring between the time when the FCC adopted its EEO rules and 1977, was not significant. He showed that in 1971, minorities held 9.1 percent of all jobs in broadcasting and only 4.6 percent of all jobs listed under the "officials and managers" category. By 1977, these figures had increased only to 13.3 and 7.4 percent respectively.[52] Similarly, in 1976 Jesse Jackson argued:

> The truth is that presently blacks and nonwhites have minimal input in the communications industry, period. A study published by the FCC disclosed that only 7.8 percent of the broadcast industry employees are black; 5/10th of 1 percent are oriental; 4/10 of 1 percent are American Indian, and only 3 percent are Spanish speaking. Again, the higher you filter into the ranks the fewer blacks and nonwhite persons are represented.[53]

Additionally, according to Cole and Oettinger, "United Church's own calculation of the year's annual employment reports suggest that stations misclassify job categories, especially higher-level categories: 78 percent of the full-time jobs in television are listed as managerial, professional, technical, or sales."[54]

The controversy over the participation of racial minorities in the television industry also extended to ownership of broadcast and cable television facilities. Public interest groups generally, and specifically those that were mobilized through the civil rights movement, argued that for a true diversity of ideas to be seen and heard on television, minorities must not only work in the television industry but must have the opportunity to own television facilities. Related to this issue was the concern that the First Amendment right to free speech extended only to those who were wealthy enough to own television facilities. Hence, Charles Tate, executive director of the Communications Resource Center of the Booker T. Washington Foundation, argued: "Today the First Amendment is a promise to minorities. It will not become a full-fledged political and legal reality until there is a radical change in the ownership and control of the electronic media in America."[55]

The public interest perspective was thus the argument that television constituted a "vast wasteland" because the FCC was a "toothless tiger," unwilling to create stricter regulations for television broadcasters and unwilling to enforce the regulations that it did promulgate. The policy prescription embedded in this argument, therefore, was for more regulation, not less. This strand of the larger debate over television thus was not at all similar to the debate over cable television, and therefore was vastly different from the consensus that was building over airline, trucking, and telephone deregulation.

Tensions and Paradoxes in Television Policy

The early development of television regulation embodied several policy tensions that were absent in airline, trucking, and telephone regulation—and these had significant potential implications. In the television case, the New Deal regime of economic regulation was extended to include significant social regulation as well. These social regulations were logically and legally dependent on the underlying "scarcity" rationale. This created certain attendant paradoxes and contradictions that were exposed in the mid-1970s, when the newly emergent actors in television politics sought to define, and prescribe remedies for, the television problem.

Interests involved in the debate disagreed on the specific causes for why television had become a "vast wasteland" and therefore on the potential policy remedies. On the one hand, cable companies, public interest groups, and economists argued that television constituted a vast wasteland because the networks captured the FCC and had a "virtual stranglehold" over programming. They thus wanted cable signal deregulation, on the assumption that added competition between cable companies and television broadcasters could produce more diverse programming that would be more responsive to a wider array of viewer demands and interests. On the other hand, public interest groups had vested interests in regulations—especially social regulations—that they wanted to protect. They argued that television was a vast wasteland because the FCC was a "toothless tiger" that was not working hard enough to enforce its own regulations. Public interest groups thus wanted more regulation, especially of broadcasters. These two different understandings of the television problem thus suggested remarkably different, contradictory, even schizophrenic policy prescriptions: both regulation and deregulation. This was paradoxical to the extent that deregulation of cable signal rules would undermine the scarcity rationale and, with it, the basis for any regulation at all. It was also paradoxical because public interest groups argued both sides simultaneously. While in other infrastructure cases "regulatory reform" was coming to mean "deregulation," in the television case no such consensus developed.

Frank Baumgartner and Bryan Jones note that the process of arguing over and defining public problems has several important effects. They note that a public debate over problems increases issue salience and mobilizes both supporters and opponents of policy change. Further, they note that the politics of problem definition can drive issues into new institutional venues because, as they argue, "when controversy increases, the venue of decision-making authority is more likely to change."[56] For decades after passage of the 1934 Communications Act, Congress had not involved itself in television policy. With the increase in the salience of, and political mobilization around, the television issue in the mid-1970s, this was about to change.

Notes

1. Harris and Milkis, *The Politics of Regulatory Change.* The regulatory regime concept has been used independently by different authors. In addition to Harris and Milkis, see also Hoberg, *Pluralism by Design;* and Eisner, *Regulatory Politics in Transition.* Their understandings of the concept are similar but do include some notable differences. For example, Hoberg's version of the concept is intended to apply only to the regime of social regulation that emerged in the 1960s and 1970s, though he does not argue that a regime is locked in time. Harris and Milkis as well as Eisner use the regime concept to place our understanding of regulatory policy in a broader historical and philosophical perspective. The distinctions between Harris and Milkis's and Eisner's regime concepts are based on the elements they view as composing a regime. Eisner, for example, sees a regime as composed of ideas, institutions, and interests. Harris and Milkis focus on ideas, institutions, and policies. Nevertheless, Harris and Milkis define institutions broadly to include interests of various kinds.

2. For a discussion of the various regulatory options that policymakers entertained, see de Sola Pool, *Technologies of Freedom,* esp. chap. 6.

3. Quoted in U.S. House of Representatives, Committee on Interstate and Foreign Commerce, *Regulation of Broadcasting,* p. 27.

4. Quoted in Schwartz, *The Last Lone Inventor,* p. 168.

5. Breyer, *Regulation and Its Reform,* p. 79.

6. U.S. Comptroller-General, *Selected FCC Regulatory Policies*, pp. 96–110.

7. Noll, Peck, and McGowan, *The Economic Aspects of Television Regulation*, p. 104.

8. U.S. Comptroller-General, *Selected FCC Regulatory Policies*, p. 109.

9. Horwitz, *The Irony of Regulatory Reform*, p. 173.

10. Simmons, *The Fairness Doctrine and the Media*, p. 21.

11. U.S. Federal Radio Commission, *Great Lakes Broadcasting Co.*, reprinted in Kahn, *Documents of American Broadcasting*. See also Simmons, *The Fairness Doctrine and the Media*, pp. 31–33.

12. U.S. Federal Communications Commission, *In the Matter of the Mayflower Broadcasting Corporation and the Yankee Network*.

13. *Carroll Broadcasting Co. v. Federal Communications Commission*.

14. U.S. Federal Communications Commission, *Second Report and Order*. See also Greenberg, "Wire Television."

15. While Harris and Milkis call this the "public lobby" regime, Hoberg refers to it as the "pluralist" regime. Harris and Milkis as well as Hoberg are essentially referring to changes in policies resulting from the emergence of public interest groups. Harris and Milkis, *The Politics of Regulatory Change;* and Hoberg, *Pluralism by Design*.

16. On institutional changes, see Dodd, "Rise of the Technocratic Congress"; and Bosso, *Pesticides and Politics*, chap. 7.

17. For a discussion of the emergence of public interest groups and the judicial doctrine of standing, see Hoberg, *Pluralism by Design;* and Berry, *The Interest Group Society*.

18. Berry, *The Interest Group Society*.

19. Dodd, "Rise of the Technocratic Congress"; and Bosso, *Pesticides and Politics*, chap. 7.

20. Except for passing legislation dealing with a technical matter in 1962.

21. *Office of Communications of the United Church of Christ v. Federal Communications Commission*, 359 F. 2d 994.

22. U.S. Federal Communications Commission, *Nondiscrimination in Employment Practices*. See also Bowie, "The Communications Act of 1978," pp. 146–147; and Cole and Oettinger, *Reluctant Regulators*, pp. 160–167.

23. U.S. Comptroller-General, *Selected FCC Regulatory Policies*, pp. 111–113.

24. U.S. Federal Communications Commission, *Children's Television*.

25. U.S. Federal Communications Commission, *Cable Television*.

26. For further discussion of the 1972 cable rules, see LeDuc, *Cable Television and the FCC;* and Besen and Crandall, "The Deregulation of Cable Television."

27. U.S. House of Representatives, Subcommittee on Communications of the Committee on Interstate and Foreign Commerce, *Hearings on Regulating Cable Television*, pp. 1241–1242.

28. Herzel, "The Public Interest and the Market." Herzel was followed by others who advocated vesting broadcasters with private rights in their frequencies through the marketplace. Coase, "Federal Communications Commission"; Demsetz, "Toward an Economic Theory of Property Rights"; Kalven, "Broadcasting, Public Policy, and the First Amendment"; DeVany et al., "A Property System for Market Allocation"; and Levin, *The Invisible Resource.*

29. Demsetz, "Toward an Economic Theory of Property Rights"; Kalven, "Broadcasting, Public Policy, and the First Amendment"; DeVany et al., "A Property System for Market Allocation"; and Levin, *The Invisible Resource.*

30. Noll, Peck, and McGowan, *The Economic Aspects of Television Regulation.*

31. Stone, *Policy Paradox,* p. 133.

32. Ibid., p. 9.

33. Minow, "Address to the National Association of Broadcasters," reprinted in Minow and LaMay, *Abandoned in the Wasteland,* p. 188.

34. Ibid., p. 189.

35. Minow and LaMay, *Abandoned in the Wasteland,* pp. 3–4.

36. Ted Tuner, chairman of WTBS, quoted in House Subcommittee, *Hearings on Regulating Cable Television,* p. 464; see also similar testimony by Representative John M. Murphy (D–N.Y.), p. 225, and Clay T. Whitehead (former director of the Office of Technology Policy, Executive Office of the President), p. 17.

37. House Subcommittee, *Hearings on Regulating Cable Television,* p. 464.

38. Ibid., p. 356.

39. Ibid., p. 759.

40. Ibid., p. 732.

41. Cole and Oettinger, *Reluctant Regulators,* p. 134.

42. U.S. Comptroller-General, *Selected FCC Regulatory Policies,* p. 96.

43. Ibid., pp. 98, 101.

44. Horwitz, *The Irony of Regulatory Reform,* p. 173.

45. U.S. Comptroller-General, *Selected FCC Regulatory Policies,* p. 96.

46. Simmons, *The Fairness Doctrine and the Media,* p. 146.

47. Ibid., p. 159.

48. Ibid., p. 191.

49. Quoted in "Broadcaster Finds Rights Endangered," p. 67.

50. Friendly, *The Good Guys, the Bad Guys, and the First Amendment,* esp. chap. 13.

51. For further discussion, see Cole and Oettinger, *Reluctant Regulators,* pp. 160–167.

52. Bowie, "The Communications Act of 1978," p. 159. These data are confirmed in Cole and Oettinger, *Reluctant Regulators,* pp. 169–170.

53. House Subcommittee, *Hearings on Regulating Cable Television,* p. 730.

54. Cole and Oettinger, *Reluctant Regulators,* p. 170.

55. House Subcommittee, *Hearings on Regulating Cable Television,* pp. 1119–1120.

56. Baumgartner and Jones, *Agendas and Instability in American Politics,* p. 34.

3

Changing Policy to Accommodate Technology?

BY 1980, DEREGULATORY POLICY CHANGE FOR THE AIRLINE, TRUCK-ing, and telephone industries was complete. Congress had passed legislation deregulating the airline and trucking industries and defeated legislation that proposed to codify the AT&T monopoly in telephony.[1] By contrast, though policy change for television arrived on the public agenda at precisely the same time as that for the airline, trucking, and telephone industries, congressional approval of television deregulation did not happen in the 1970s. Rather, television deregulation took much longer, and was far more ambiguous. Despite three significant efforts by key policy-makers to deregulate the industry, Congress still was addressing television deregulation well into the 1990s. With the eventual passage of the 1996 Telecommunications Act the net television policy change was incremental and incomplete deregulation. Further, this period witnessed several important instances of television reregu-lation. The broad paradigm of television regulation remained in place.

This chapter examines the divergent path of television policy change from 1978 to 1996. The period encompasses three major efforts at deregulation. In 1978, Representative Lionel Van Deerlin (D–Calif.), then chair of the House Telecommunications Sub-committee, sought to repeal the 1934 Communications Act and replace it with an entirely new, deregulatory statute. In the 1980s the Federal Communications Commission (FCC) and its Republican chairman, Mark Fowler (and his successor, Dennis Patrick), attempted to deregulate television administratively through the rule-making process. Finally, in 1996 Congress passed and President Bill Clinton signed a new Telecommunications Act into law.

In discussing the substance and process of television deregulation, this chapter also examines the market forces theory of regulatory policy change. This theory suggests that regulatory policy change is a clear response to changes in economic and technological conditions.[2] Such a theory would suggest that changes in economic or technological conditions were key variables in airline, trucking, and telephony deregulation. During the 1970s the dual effects of low growth and high inflation decreased demand for transportation. Coming on the heels of significant technological advancements in transportation (such as the development of widebody jets), gross overcapacity resulted. Further, the airline and trucking industries had matured and stabilized. Technological change was an important factor undermining FCC regulation of the AT&T monopoly. For example, new companies found cost-effective ways of providing phone service (to compete with the service offered by AT&T), obviating a telephone monopoly. In this environment, therefore, regulations that hindered the "natural" workings of the marketplace could be removed without harming public welfare. Indeed, the perception of those advocating change was that deregulation would actually prove beneficial to the economy and consumers alike.

In this vein, a market forces theory of television policy change might suggest that television policy followed such a divergent path because the underlying economics and technology of the industry had not sufficiently matured. Alternatively, it suggests that technological and economic change in the television industry went unnoticed by policymakers, who therefore failed to advance a deregulatory agenda. Yet as this chapter demonstrates, economic and technological change in television, especially technological change, was at least as substantial as it was in the airline, trucking, and telephone industries. Moreover, key policymakers advocated television deregulation on the basis of "technological change." Nevertheless, television policy change was decidedly incremental. In short, despite significant technological change, television deregulation was highly ambiguous and episodic.

Episode 1: The Failed 1979
Rewrite of the 1934 Communications Act

The "toothless tiger" and "virtual stranglehold" metaphors that were central to placing television on the policy agenda in the mid-1970s contained within them open pleas for congressional involvement. Both metaphors, and the problem definitions and policy prescriptions to which they gave form and voice, implicated an FCC that failed at regulating the television industry for which it was responsible. The institutional changes of the 1970s, which decentralized Congress and empowered individual members, almost invited members of Congress to answer the pleas for congressional involvement in television policy. Members of Congress responded to the invitation with a flurry of legislative introductions and competition with the FCC and the U.S. president over control of policy turf.

Beginning in the mid-1970s members of Congress jumped into the television debate with both feet. Near the end of a series of FCC oversight hearings, on August 6, 1976, Representative Lionel Van Deerlin, chair of the House Communications Subcommittee, announced that Congress should undertake a "basement to penthouse revamping" of the 1934 Communications Act.[3] Van Deerlin's initiative was the start of two decades of congressional involvement in television policy.

On March 29, 1979, after three years of study and several months of hearings surrounding an experimental bill, Van Deerlin introduced the Communications Act of 1979 (H.R. 3333), a rewrite of the 1934 Communications Act.[4] Van Deerlin and his staff spent an enormous amount of time studying television issues and were acutely aware of the technological changes in the industry, the various economic and social tensions embedded in television policy, and the attendant political controversies subsumed under the "virtual stranglehold" and "toothless tiger" metaphors.

The Bill

Van Deerlin attempted to respond to the policy prescription implied by the logic of technological development and advocated by economists. His main objectives were to deregulate cable and remove government from program content. Van Deerlin believed that the cre-

ation of new television outlets, via the deregulation and subsequent
expected expansion of cable television, would facilitate competition,
reduce scarcity, and thereby mitigate the need for government intervention in programming.[5] He thus sought to restore full free speech
rights under the First Amendment to television broadcasters. Van
Deerlin argued, "If Thomas Jefferson were writing the Bill of Rights
today, he would make clear that the First Amendment applies to
broadcast . . . journalism."[6]

Van Deerlin recognized that television regulation involves a
complex mix of policies and goals. Television policy involves economic regulation but also social regulation that touches on First
Amendment concerns, as well as issues surrounding various concep-
tions of morality. As a former broadcaster, Representative Van
Deerlin was deeply concerned about government intrusion into programming, yet he feared that complete deregulation would place certain social objectives at risk. Therefore, wherever possible he wanted
to substitute intervention in the marketplace (economic regulation)
for intervention in speech (a form of social regulation). Instead of
mandating that broadcasters produce diverse programming, Van
Deerlin preferred to use policy to structure the industry so that varied
programming would occur naturally. Van Deerlin's underlying philosophy was clearly evident in the bill, as shown in Table 3.1. What
is clear is that H.R. 3333 was somewhat anomalous to legislation
deregulating other infrastructure industries. It entailed some economic deregulation, in particular with regard to cable signal carriage and
broadcast television licensing. Nevertheless, it also proposed to
strengthen some economic regulation (particularly ownership limits)
as it also promoted social deregulation.

H.R. 3333 retained public interest language in its regulatory
standard, but as Van Deerlin noted at the time, this was a purely sym-
bolic gesture, designed to attract support from television broadcasters, who equated "public interest" with broadcaster protectionism,
and from public interest groups, who viewed themselves as protecting public rights in television.[7] Rather, Van Deerlin intended to legislate a presumption of deregulation and provide for regulation only
where the market was deficient. The competition that Van Deerlin
envisioned would result from deregulating cable television. The bill
provided for federal preemption of local cable regulation, meaning
that the federal government would assume total jurisdiction over
cable (including cable rates, which hitherto were regulated at the

Table 3.1   The Communications Act of 1979—H.R. 3333

Issue	Extant Policy	H.R. 3333
Regulatory standard	Public interest, convenience, and necessity	Where marketplace forces are deficient in serving the public interest[a]
	Economic Issues	
Cable	State/local regulation	Prohibit state and local regulation;[c] transfers jurisdiction to federal government[b]
	Federal signal carriage rules	Federal signal deregulation[c]
	Copyright compulsory license	Repeal copyright compulsory license;[c] substitute retransmission consent[b]
Broadcast television licensing	3-year term	Indefinite after 10 years[c]
	Allocation via comparative hearing	Allocation by lottery[a]
	Free licenses	Spectrum fee
Ownership limits	7 stations	7 stations—written into law[b]
	Social Issues	
Minority participation	Ownership affirmative action (including tax certificates, distress sales, preference in comparative hearings)	Repeal existing regulations;[c] weight lottery in favor of minorities[b]
	EEO rules promulgated by FCC	EEO jurisdiction transferred to EEOC after 10 years[a]
Fairness Doctrine	Continuous enforcement	Repeal after 10 years[c]
Children's television	Advertising limits Vague content requirements	Repeal after 10 years[c]

Notes: a. Regulatory relaxation.
b. Stronger regulation or reregulation.
c. Deregulation.

state and local level) and that states and localities would be prohibited from regulating cable rates. Further, the bill provided that the federal government would opt not to regulate the sector. Nevertheless, H.R. 3333 would require cable companies, through a "retransmission consent" requirement, to compete with broadcasters for programming. Cable system operators would have to pay either broadcasters or program producers for the rights to carry their programming. H.R. 3333 would make broadcast television license terms indefinite after ten years and would eventually give existing broadcasters property rights in their frequencies, a radical proposal as it undermined public ownership of the airwaves.

Essentially, H.R. 3333 proposed to privatize the airwaves. A lottery would be used to allocate any newly available frequencies, and the bill would require broadcasters to pay a spectrum fee. Under H.R. 3333 ownership regulations would be retained at seven stations, but they would be written into law. To the extent that future changes to these limits would require approval by a majority of the 535 members of Congress, plus approval of the president, rather than simply three votes from the FCC, this would actually strengthen the ownership regulations. The bill would repeal all program regulations after ten years, at which time the FCC also would lose jurisdiction over equal employment opportunity in the television industry, which would be moved to the Equal Employment Opportunity Commission (EEOC). H.R. 3333 would repeal the FCC's minority ownership programs. However, minorities would receive weight (two chances to one) in lotteries in addition to low-interest loans from a minority ownership trust fund.

The Death of the Rewrite

At hearings held on the proposed legislation, broadcaster after broadcaster appeared before the subcommittee to praise the bill and its provisions, which largely met all of their policy desires.[8] The one provision to which television broadcasters were opposed, of course, was that of the spectrum fee, which threatened to hit them in their wallets.

Cable companies also generally favored the bill but opposed its retransmission consent provision, which like the proposed spectrum fee for broadcasters would affect their bottom lines. The provision would have required cable system operators to pay broadcasters

before they could retransmit broadcast programming. Cable operators feared that broadcasters would withhold retransmission permission in order to starve cable companies of programming. As Stephen
Effros, executive director of the Community Antenna Television
Association (the trade association representing small cable companies), put it:

> There are local stations which are not terribly prompted to aid their
> local cable system. The one thing they would like to see is . . . the
> cable system go out of business. . . . So if I were a local broadcast-
> er . . . it would be a very simple prospect for me to say to the local
> cable operator: "Sorry, Charlie, I am not going to give you local
> program consent for my local programs that I produce, so you
> don't have any place else to go to."[9]

From the perspective of cable television operators, Van Deerlin's bill
would not ameliorate the "virtual stranglehold" problem. Their fates
and, by definition, the viewing habits of Americans would continue
to be controlled by television broadcasters.

Thus television broadcasters opposed the proposed spectrum fee
and cable companies opposed the retransmission consent provisions.
Van Deerlin intended that these two provisions would serve simultaneously to level the competitive playing field between broadcasters
and cable companies by rescinding both of their subsidies. Though
broadcasters and cable companies opposed these specific measures,
they nevertheless signaled their willingness to bargain. It does not
take a tremendous leap of imagination to suppose that this opposition, which was relatively minor given that cable companies and
broadcasters generally favored the legislation, could have been
blunted merely by restoring their respective subsidies. Conceptually,
the competitive playing field would still be level, but no money
would change hands.

But Van Deerlin never got to that point because of opposition
from other interests, specifically from public interest groups, academics, members of the Communications Subcommittee, and various
agency heads. At heart, these interests argued that the bill relaxed
regulation too much and that the solution to the "toothless tiger"
problem—the idea that the FCC was too lenient with its regulated
industries—was not to deregulate but rather to make regulations
more stringent and to step up regulatory enforcement. To be sure,
public interest groups did support the bill's proposed deregulation of

cable signal carriage—for they had long argued that the FCC's protection of broadcasters had stymied cable's growth and thereby the viewing options presented to the public. However, outside of that provision, they vehemently opposed the bill. They argued that the federal government should not refuse to regulate cable but rather that a federal role was necessary to ensure minimum cable standards and to preserve public access to cable through, for example, mandating public access channels.[10]

It was the broadcast portion of the bill that most stirred up the ire of public interest groups. They believed that, despite the ability of the marketplace to furnish entertainment programming, regulation still was necessary in order to harness television to broader social and political concerns. They did not believe that the marketplace, even in light of further cable development and expansion, would provide diverse programming, news and public affairs programming, and wholesome programming for kids. Indeed, they did not believe that a marketplace of ideas would stem from the new, more competitive television marketplace that the bill proposed to create. As Peggy Charren, head of Action for Children's Television, reasoned by analogy, "Increasing the number of highways does not guarantee the solution of all traffic problems."[11]

The most significant obstacle to the bill came from other Democrats on Van Deerlin's Communications Subcommittee, who echoed the sentiments expressed by public interest groups and without whose support no legislation could pass. Though Erwin Krasnow, Lawrence Longley, and Herbert Terry characterize the "depth of commitment" to Van Deerlin's bill as "unclear," a careful reading of the hearings surrounding the bill shows that the depth of congressional commitment was quite clearly against the bill.[12] Representative Marty Russo (D–Ill.) perhaps best summed up the views of his colleagues when, after listening to the testimony of a public interest group representative, responded: "There are some of us on the committee who . . . will see that your point of view is well voiced. Those of us who are concerned about this bill's basis in economics only will argue these points."[13]

On July 13, 1979, Representative Van Deerlin ended his effort to rewrite the 1934 Communications Act.[14] In an era of economic *deregulation*, Van Deerlin had proposed to strengthen television ownership rules by writing them into law. And in an era of social *regulation*, Van Deerlin proposed to deregulate the content restrictions on television. At precisely the same time that Congress was passing legislation deregulating other infrastructure industries, major legislation deregulating television failed. Van Deerlin subsequently lost his House seat in the 1980 Republican sweep, suggesting that he was probably a marginal player in the Democratic Party by this time. Among his parting words, he predicted that his attempt to rewrite the 1934 Communications Act had succeeded in calling attention to communications issues and challenging the prevailing orthodoxy. Future policymakers, he hoped, would build upon what he had begun. He noted, "Things will never be the same again."[15] Of course, policy developments in subsequent decades would support the old adage that the more things change, the more they stay the same.

Episode 2: The 1980s and Early 1990s—A "Toaster with Pictures"

The Reagan administration took office committed to an agenda of deregulation across the board.[16] As part of his administration's strategy, President Ronald Reagan appointed a staunch free-marketer, Mark Fowler, to chair the FCC. Fowler, who served from 1981 until 1987, offered his own metaphor for television. As he put it, a television was nothing more than "a toaster with pictures."[17] If those who offered the "toothless tiger" metaphor of the FCC advocated stronger regulatory enforcement and those who offered the "virtual stranglehold" metaphor of the FCC advocated the freeing of cable from regulatory constraints, Chairman Fowler was advocating a much more radical agenda. If a television was just a toaster with pictures, then there was no need to regulate it at all. The government does not, after all, regulate toasters, the bread we put in them, or the toast that they produce. The government does not involve itself in who gets to own toaster factories nor in who gets to work for them. In just a few words, Fowler sought to redefine the television problem, radicalize the agenda, and advocate the nearly complete and immediate deregulation of television.

In September 1981, Chairman Fowler issued to Congress a package of policy proposals to that effect. Fowler's proposal failed. While Republicans controlled the Senate (until 1987), Democrats continued to control the House and the leadership of its Telecommunications

Subcommittee, and the subcommittee's parent, the Commerce Committee. Key Democrats remained allied with public interest groups. Conflict was guaranteed. Indeed, in the 1981 budget reconciliation law, Congress repealed the FCC's permanent authorization and substituted a two-year authorization period. Clearly Congress intended more rigorous oversight of the agency.[18]

Faced with such opposition, Fowler attempted to deregulate television administratively via the FCC rule-making process. He had this option available to him because of the wide discretion to make (and unmake) policy granted to the agency by the 1934 Communications Act, for the 1934 act instructed the FCC simply to make policy in the public interest, the definition of which now was in the hands of an FCC chair who saw it as synonymous with competition. In an important 1982 article in the *Texas Law Review,* Fowler threw down the gauntlet and articulated his vision of a new paradigm for television policy characterized by complete reliance on market forces:

> The perception of broadcasters as community trustees should be replaced by a view of broadcasters as marketplace participants. . . . Instead of defining public demand . . . the commission should rely on the broadcasters' ability to determine the wants of their audiences through the normal mechanisms of the marketplace. The public's interest, then, defines the public interest.[19]

To Fowler, it didn't matter whether television was a "vast wasteland," as long as it reflected what the public wanted.

Justifying his views and approach, Fowler noted that technology (cable, satellite, VCRs) was providing substitutes for broadcast television. Further, he implied that scarcity no longer existed, if it ever did, arguing that the television medium should be viewed as part of a larger information market consisting of cable, billboards, books, radio, and motion pictures. He also foreshadowed his intention to deregulate via the FCC rule-making process. Fowler's successor, Dennis Patrick, appointed FCC chairman in 1987, was no less a believer in the market and would seek to advance Fowler's agenda.

This clash of views between congressional Democrats and FCC chairman Fowler (and later Patrick) meant that during this period very few television policy changes occurred consensually. One of these was an extension of broadcast license terms from three years to five and a streamlining of license renewal procedures.[20] The other consensual change culminated in cable signal deregulation (though a later consensus would develop around reregulating cable). While a prior FCC had taken the initiative and deregulated cable signal carriage, Congress would take the initiative in 1984 and deregulate rates. Outside of these two issues, in an era of divided government the opposition engendered by Fowler's initiatives resulted in institutional warfare as proregulation policy actors sought to stem the tide of deregulation. At the end of this period the result of the Reagan-Fowler-Patrick efforts was not so much the removal of government control, but regulatory reduction and reconfiguration, the imposition of some new regulations, and reregulation.

"Deregulating" Cable Television

In 1980 the FCC—still with its Carter-appointed chairman—concluded that cable television posed minimal harm to broadcasters and that, in freeing cable of signal carriage rules, the public stood to gain more than television broadcasters stood to lose. Thus, looking very much like the Civil Aeronautics Board in the airline deregulation example and the Interstate Commerce Commission in the trucking deregulation case, the FCC rescinded its remaining signal rules, allowing cable companies to carry whichever broadcast signals they wanted whenever they wanted. And cable companies were still paying below-market rates for the privilege.[21] Though this change seemed favorable to cable, it effectively transferred remaining regulatory authority over cable from the federal government to localities. The cable industry feared that local regulation would lead to overregulation, differing regulations across municipalities, exorbitant franchise fees, and stringent rate regulation and service requirements.[22]

In the early 1980s, cable companies sought relief from Congress, and cable firms, municipalities, and public interest groups hammered out legislation.[23] After a last-minute compromise between the Democrat-controlled House and the Republican-controlled Senate, Congress passed and President Reagan signed cable deregulation legislation. One issue with which the legislation dealt was franchise fees paid by cable systems to localities in exchange for the right to string their wires along city streets. Cable companies wanted to end franchise fees, but localities and their lobbying arm, the National League of Cities, supported by public interest groups, viewed franchise fees as a revenue-raising device and were reluctant to give them up.

A second issue concerned rates paid by cable customers. Cable companies wanted to set their own rates. The National League of Cities and public interest groups, however, wanted cities to be able to regulate rates. Fowler's arguments about a broader communications marketplace notwithstanding, they viewed cable systems as local monopolies and believed that, absent regulation, prices would rise dramatically, making cable unaffordable for some.[24]

The National League of Cities, the National Cable Television Association, and public interest groups reached a compromise. They agreed to allow local governments to impose franchise fees, to be capped at no more than 5 percent of the annual gross revenues of a cable system. They also agreed to permit localities to regulate subscriber rates whenever a cable system was not subject to effective competition—which would later be defined by the FCC.[25] These issues were embodied in bills in both the Democratic House and the Republican Senate.[26]

The House bill and its Senate counterpart differed in terms of scope, and these differences were evident in the bills' stated purposes. The more politically conservative Senate bill defined its purposes in competitive terms: "To encourage a competitive environment for the growth and development of cable." While the more politically liberal House bill acknowledged the desire to promote competition, it also stated as its purpose to "assure that cable telecommunications provide the widest possible diversity of information sources to the public." The House bill thus included a number of significant public trustee provisions such as cross-ownership rules (prohibiting the ownership of local cable systems by broadcasters, newspapers, and phone companies if their service areas overlapped), rules allowing cities to make programming demands, and application of the FCC's equal employment opportunity rules to cable companies. These provisions had been worked out in the compromise between the cable firms, the cities, and public interest groups. According to the sponsor of the House bill, Representative Ed Markey (D–Mass.), the bill ultimately was intended to "establish the principle that cable operators . . . do have some form of responsibility to provide more than merely entertainment programming."[27] After modifying the equal employment opportunity provisions, as a response to some conservative Senate Republicans, the legislation passed and President Reagan signed it into law. The final provisions of the 1984 Cable Act as passed are depicted in Table 3.2. In the end, far from being a deci-

Table 3.2 The 1984 Cable Act

Issue	Extant Policy	1984 Cable Act
	Economic Issues	
Rates	Regulated by states and localities	Deregulate[c]—unless cable firm not subject to effective competition[b]
Local franchise procedures	Vary from locality to locality	Uniform national procedure[b]
Franchise fees	Determined by states and localities	Capped at 5 percent of cable company's local gross revenues[a]
Cable/broadcast cross-ownership	Allowed	Prohibited[b]
	Social Issues	
Programming regulation	Uncertain legality	Allowed cities to demand public, educational, and governmental channels and categories of programming[b]
Equal employment opportunity	None	Applied to cable firms[b]

Notes: a. Regulatory relaxation.
b. Stronger regulation or reregulation.
c. Deregulation.

sively deregulatory measure, the 1984 Cable Act thus was much more complex. It did include some regulatory relaxation, but also applied new regulations, such as ownership regulations, obscenity rules and rules allowing franchise authorities to mandate public, educational, and governmental channels.

Reregulating Cable Television

By 1988 the cable sector's fortunes had changed. The number of cable subscribers, subscription revenues, and ad revenues all increased dramatically.[28] More important, the cable sector had become vertically integrated, with cable companies holding major financial stakes in programmers. For example, Time Warner cable owned the HBO movie channel. Whereas when television initially reached the policy agenda in the mid-1970s the cable sector was seen as victimized by the "virtual stranglehold" that broadcasters had over the FCC, which was bent on protecting broadcasters, by the late 1980s the cable sector was seen as a powerful behemoth. Indeed, by the late 1980s it was the cable industry that was viewed as having a virtual stranglehold over television. This was evident in a series of congressional oversight hearings.[29]

Technological change was creating new ways of distributing television programming and thus was creating new competitors and therefore new interest groups. Microwave and direct satellite technologies both could distribute programming through a multichannel format. Because they delivered packages of programs, like cable companies, these technologies were dubbed "wireless cable." These competitors argued that cable firms were using their economic power in an anticompetitive manner. Specifically they argued that cable companies were denying them access to programming owned by the large cable systems. Without programming, these nascent competitors would fail. Ironically, this was the same argument that cable firms previously had used against broadcasters. The result, these competitors argued, would be a communications underclass populated by rural citizens and the urban poor, as sparsely populated rural areas and poor urban communities would not provide a return on investment that cable companies would need in order to serve these areas. As Robert Schmidt, president of the Wireless Cable Association, warned the Senate Subcommittee on Communications:

> There are many areas of the country which will never be wired by coaxial cable. Unless wireless cable and other alternatives to cable television . . . are able to overcome obstacles that have been thrown in their way, people living in these areas of the country will in effect continue to be second-class citizens with respect to their ability to view television programming.[30]

Broadcasters also complained about cable firms. Small independent broadcasters (those not affiliated with a network) charged that cable systems were refusing to carry their signals. They also argued that when cable systems did carry their signals, they received poor channel assignments (i.e., channel assignments different from their over-the-air assignments). Finally, independent broadcasters alleged that cable companies frequently and arbitrarily changed their channel assignments, resulting in the loss of those viewers unable to find the station. As Preston Padden, president of the Association of Independent Television Stations, explained, "It is like the phone company gives you a phone number, you establish a business, get it going, and then the phone company . . . take[s] it back."[31]

Large network-affiliated broadcasters had their own concerns. They attracted a large following of viewers, which in turn provided a compelling incentive to cable operators to carry their signals on their original channels. Yet cable companies still were allowed by law to carry the stations for below-market prices. Edward Fritts, president and chief executive officer of the National Association of Broadcasters, noted that these low fees constituted an unfair subsidy by broadcasters to cable companies. Fritts argued that television broadcasters effectively were subsidizing their own competitors.[32]

Customers also rebelled against cable. Cable rates nationally had jumped an average of 50 percent since passage of the 1984 Cable Act, mobilizing irate consumers and their representatives.[33] In one instance, a group of customers in Long Island, N.Y., picketed their local cable operator, Cablevision, because the company did not renew its contract with the Madison Square Garden Channel (which carried the Knicks and Rangers games). Picketers accused Cablevision of discriminating against the Madison Square Garden channel in favor of another sports channel owned by it.[34] Opinion on Capitol Hill galvanized around the need for cable policy reform. As Senator Daniel Inouye (D–Hawaii), chairman of the Senate Communications Subcommittee, warned, "We can't close our ears to the shouts from our constituents. They're pretty loud."[35]

The growing issue salience and public pressure for restraints on cable rates led members of Congress to pass the 1992 Cable Act. The act reregulated cable rates; prohibited programmers from refusing to deal with cable's competitors; capped the number of subscribers a cable system could reach nationwide (similar to the broadcast owner-ship regulations); set uniform, industrywide customer service stan-dards; included both a "must carry" provision (according to which cable companies were required to carry small unaffiliated stations) and "retransmission consent" language (which required cable compa-nies to obtain permission, usually for payment, from larger broad-casters to carry their programming); allowed localities to ban porno-graphic programming; and contained stronger equal employment opportunity regulations. Bipartisan support for the measure was so strong that Congress overrode a veto by President George H. W. Bush—the only successful veto override of the Bush presidency and a rare instance where consumer anger led to regulation in a generally deregulatory environment.[36]

Relaxing Ownership Regulations

In August 1984 the FCC repealed its multiple-ownership limits, which previously sought a balance between competition and economies of scale. To justify this repeal, the FCC attempted to refute the scarcity premise (using arguments about technological development) as well as the need to guard against economic concentration and foster viewpoint diversity. First, the commission reiterated its by now familiar position that the development of cable and home video technologies had brought about the end of scarcity. Indeed, the FCC accepted CBS's argument that television should be conceptualized as sitting within a broader intellectual marketplace. Quoting CBS, the FCC report noted: "Every press outlet—ranging from sidewalk leafleteers to tiny 'underground' newspapers to iconoclastic journals to mass circulation print and electronic outlets—makes an important contribution to the stimulation of society's collective thought process."[37]

Using data provided by the National Association of Broadcasters, which supported repeal of the ownership limits, the FCC suggested that consumers would actually benefit from increased group ownership on the premise that larger groups had the financial resources to produce "better" programming. Thus the FCC argued that there could be "greater viewpoint diversity than there is ownership diversity" and turned on its head the notion that group ownership was antithetical to the public interest in diversity.[38]

Congressional reaction to the FCC's repeal of the ownership rules was swift. Within one week after the FCC's announcement, a Senate conference committee inserted a provision into a supplemental appropriations bill preventing the repeal from taking effect before April 1, 1985.[39]

With congressional hostility evident, Fowler quickly entered into negotiations with Senator Pete Wilson (R–Calif.) and Representatives Timothy Wirth (D–Colo.) and John Dingell (D–Mich.) over a revised multiple-ownership rule. The compromise plan, later codified in FCC rule-making, provided for increased group ownership, though in a controlled way and in exchange for provisions that, law-makers believed, would facilitate viewpoint diversity.[40] As revised, the new limits allowed groups to own up to twelve stations, as long as the combined stations would reach no more than 25 percent of the national audience. The new regulations also provided direct incen-tives for minority ownership. Groups would be allowed to extend the twelve-station limit to fourteen, provided the two additional stations were 51 percent minority controlled. Similarly, groups would be allowed to extend the 25 percent audience reach cap to 30 percent, provided the additional 5 percent was attributable to minority-con-trolled stations.

Repealing the Fairness Doctrine

On August 4, 1987, the FCC, under its new chairman, Dennis Patrick, abolished the Fairness Doctrine.[41] In its report, the commis-sion pointed to the amelioration of scarcity by way of cable develop-ment and noted that the doctrine, "on its face, violates the First Amendment and contravenes the public interest."[42] The commission argued that the Fairness Doctrine actually had a chilling effect, by which television broadcasters so feared Fairness Doctrine challenges that they did not air controversial programming but rather sought to be as bland as possible. The FCC report reasoned that "the net effect of the Fairness Doctrine is to reduce rather than enhance . . . view-point diversity."[43] Though Congress repeatedly attempted to preempt the FCC's action by passing legislation codifying the doctrine, it was unable to overcome a June 1987 veto by President Reagan as many congressional Republicans succumbed to White House pressure to go along with the president's agenda.[44] The FCC repeal of the Fairness Doctrine marked the only decisive deregulation of the period.

Protecting Minority Ownership Policies

Though the FCC during the 1980s made no moves to abolish equal employment opportunity rules, in 1986 it did try to repeal affirmative action ownership policies that, for example, gave preferences to minorities and women in awarding licenses.[45] Senator Ernest Hollings (D–S.C.) reacted by inserting a provision into the fiscal 1988 omnibus spending bill barring the agency from changing poli-cies. The prohibition was extended for fiscal years 1989 and 1990.

Since in 1987 Democrats were once again in control of the Senate, Hollings was particularly well poised to strike as he chaired both the Commerce Committee and the related Appropriations Subcommittee. He was helped in his efforts to stymie the FCC by the Supreme Court, which in 1990 ruled that federal minority preference policies were constitutional particularly as they "serve the important objective of broadcast diversity."[46] From the Court's perspective, diversity of viewpoints over the airwaves was a legitimate government objective.

Revitalizing Children's Television Policies

In 1986 the FCC repealed its rules governing children's television. Television broadcasters, as well as the American Association of Advertising Agencies (which feared *any* limitations on advertising) advocated deregulation, while public interest groups and child advocates urged even stronger rules. The television industry argued that, in light of the expansion of the marketplace (engendered by cable television and also by growth in videocassette recordings), policies mandating children's programming impinged on their First Amendment rights. Public interest groups and child advocates, on the other hand, argued that the government had a compelling interest in protecting children and that regulation was necessary. The FCC sided with broadcasters.[47]

The dust had no sooner settled on the FCC's repeal of children's television policies when Congress began an attempt to reregulate through legislation. In the mid-1980s an explosion of toy-based programs were organized around the products they were intended to sell. The *Strawberry Shortcake, Care Bear,* and *Gummi Bears* programs were designed to sell the children's products of the same names. As Peggy Charren, head of Action for Children's Television, put it, "If you want to make a biography of Helen Keller in today's marketplace, you would have to first talk Mattel into producing a Helen Keller Doll."[48] Coming on a wave of academic studies noting the dearth of good children's programs, the time was ripe for legislation. And though television broadcasters opposed legislation, in 1990 Congress passed the Children's Television Act, which placed limits on advertising during children's programming and required broadcasters to air programming specifically designed to meet the educational needs of the child audience. An ambivalent President Bush—

who had promised to be the "education president" but also disapproved of regulation—allowed the bill to become law without his signature.[49]

Table 3.3 shows the net effect of the policy struggles of the period 1981–1992 versus policy under the 1934 Communications Act (as interpreted and applied by the FCC). Only cable signal carriage rules and the Fairness Doctrine were successfully repealed. Regulations regarding broadcast license terms and renewal as well as broadcast ownership rules were relaxed. The bulk of the cable television issues as well as children's television issues were the subject of stronger regulation and/or reregulation. While deregulation of the airline, trucking, and telephone industries was being consolidated and implemented, policymakers still battled over television policy.

Episode 3: The Information Superhighway and the 1996 Telecommunications Act

On February 8, 1996, President Clinton signed a new Telecommunications Act into law.[50] A great deal of symbolism surrounded the act. Clinton signed it into law at the Library of Congress—the only bill signing ever to occur there—to signify his hope that the new law would accelerate development of an "information superhighway." Symbolizing the emergence of a new commercial and social infrastructure for the twenty-first century, Clinton signed the bill with the same pen that President Dwight Eisenhower used in 1957 to sign the law creating the vast interstate highway system. Moments later the law was posted on a brand new technology, the Internet.

Politicians from both political parties engaged in hyperbole. Clinton noted, "This law is truly revolutionary legislation that will bring the future to our doorstep."[51] Similarly, Representative Thomas Bliley (R–Va.), a bill sponsor, hailed the new law as "the first major overhaul of telecommunications law since Marconi [the inventor of radio] was alive and the crystal set was state of the art."[52]

The legislation received momentum from the zeitgeist of the times, or as President Clinton called it, the "gestalt of the gigabit."[53] The outlook of the times included the acceleration of globalization, the interconnectedness and interpenetration of national economies brought on by the end of the Cold War, which also prompted a shift in the orientation of the U.S. economy away from technological

Table 3.3 Net Policy Change of the 1980s and Early 1990s

Issue	1934 Communications Act	Net Policy Change, 1981–1992
Regulatory standard	Public interest, convenience, and necessity	No change
Cable	State/local rate regulation	Federal rate regulation[b]
	Federal signal carriage rules	None[c]
	Copyright compulsory license	Must carry; retransmission consent[b]
		Competitor access to programming[b]
		Customer service standards[b]
		Localities can make programming demands[b]
		Equal employment opportunity rules[b]
Broadcast television licensing	3-year term	5-year term[a]
	Allocation via comparative hearings	No change
	Free licenses	No change
		Streamlined renewal procedures[a]
Ownership limits	7 stations	12 stations (with 25 percent audience cap)[a]
Minority participation	Ownership affirmative action (includes tax certificates, distress sales, comparative hearings)	Upheld by Supreme Court
	Equal employment opportunity rules by FCC	No change
Fairness Doctrine	Continuous enforcement	Repealed[c]
Children's television	Advertising limits	Ad limits strengthened; written into law[b]
	Vague content regulations	Stronger content regulations[b]

Notes: a. Regulatory relaxation.
b. Regulatory strengthening or reregulation.
c. Deregulation.

research and development for military purposes and toward research and development for civilian purposes. This was to be advanced by the emergence of a "peace dividend," or monies freed up by not having to engage in Cold War–style military buildups.

Concurrent technological advancements had dramatic effects on the very nature of the U.S. economy. The United States continued its trend toward capital- and technology-intensive manufacturing, epitomized by computer-aided design and manufacturing and the rise of service industries, and away from labor-intensive manufacturing processes. Simultaneously, technological developments facilitated "convergence"—or the blurring of the boundaries between telephony, broadcasting, cable television, and satellite.[54] These technological developments, in turn, created additional potential competitors for the television marketplace and therefore additional interest groups active in the television policy arena.

Indeed, with advancements in digital technologies it became technically possible for communications firms to offer packages of services to customers. For example, telephone companies could potentially deliver video programming, cable companies could potentially deliver voice services, and broadcasters could potentially deliver a whole host of services ranging from traditional programming to interactive programming, from home alarm systems to home shopping services. This convergence held the promise that companies in the different sectors of the larger communications industry could actually compete against each other, so that consumers could choose to purchase their telephone service from among a host of telephone and cable companies. Or they could choose to receive television programming from among a variety of telephone companies, cable companies, satellite services, and broadcasters.

The new technological convergence also promised U.S. consumers movies on demand, remote control shopping, and the like. Popular chief executive officers from high-profile firms promoted fantastic visions of future services. Consider the vision promoted by Bill Gates, CEO of Microsoft Corporation. In his 1995 book *The Road Ahead,* Gates imagined:

> On the information superhighway, you won't have to buy special hardware or software to interact with a television show. Imagine the future *Password* or *Jeopardy!* show that will let viewers at home participate and win either cash or credits of some sort.

> Shows will even be able to keep track of and reward their regular audience members by giving them special prizes or mentioning them by name if they choose to join the game.[55]

Further, policymakers and consumers alike hailed the day when convergence, competition, and technological advancement would be an engine of job creation, economic growth, and private investment.[56] As Vice President Albert Gore stated, "The existence of a premiere information marketplace in the United States will give our companies and our citizens an advantage in worldwide competition."[57]

Communications companies and policymakers alike believed that a major deregulatory overhaul of the 1934 Communications Act was necessary to make these visions a reality. The 1934 act's partitioning of the various communications sectors, through sector-specific regulation, hindered convergence. Drawing distinct policy boundaries around each sector (cable, broadcast television, telephony) and regulating each sector differently ensured that there would not be cross-sector competition. In addition, firms in the various communications sectors continued to feel burdened by specific regulations. Similarly, since the 1980s members of Congress continued to be institutionally at odds with an FCC that they perceived as overstepping its bounds. In this context, then, came the call for a major reshaping of the 1934 Communications Act. The effort was couched in terms of bringing the "information superhighway" to U.S. consumers. The rhetoric associated with this vast network captured the collective imagination.[58]

Though various attempts at passing comprehensive legislation occurred during the 103rd Congress, reform gained momentum in the 104th.[59] Several factors contributed to this. First, several mergers and important alliances occurred among key players in the industry. For example, cable television giant Telecommunications Incorporated formed a partnership with the long-distance telephone company Sprint. The two hoped to team up to offer consumers consolidated packages of cable television, long-distance service, and local telephone service. Not only did this alliance demonstrate the potential power of convergence, but it also heightened legislators' perceptions of the necessity for reform of the 1934 Communications Act. Perhaps most important, Republicans won the 1994 midterm elections and took control of the Congress for the first time in forty years. Generally more supportive of deregulation than Democrats, the Republicans, led by Representative Newt Gingrich (D–Ga.), promised to achieve telecommunications reform during the 104th Congress as part of the general GOP efforts to reduce the size and role of government. As Representative Jack Fields (R–Tex.), the new chair of the House Telecommunications and Finance Subcommittee, put it, "You now have a very strong deregulatory and pro-competitive sentiment . . . almost a supermajority of people who believe that less government is best."[60]

Beyond the Rhetoric

The "information superhighway" was a compelling metaphor that attracted bipartisan attention. Consensus thus developed that communications policy was ripe for change. The broad appeal of the notion of the "information superhighway," and the fanfare surrounding the new law, however, masked years of fitful false starts in forging new policy. The hyperbole also masked the opposing approaches evident in the policymaking process.

On one side of the debate surrounding the formulation of the new law stood a new breed of Republican that dominated the congressional majority. These new Republicans were palpably suspicious of government and decidedly in favor of the market. Congressional leaders and senior Republicans generally favored quick and substantial deregulation. On the other side stood those— mostly Democrats and their president—who continued to evoke a suspicion of the marketplace and a desire to ensure their definition of the public interest through government intervention. President Clinton personified these latter ideas. A "New Democrat," Clinton also praised the virtues of the marketplace, but did not endorse a clear path to the free market and did not believe that simple deregulation would necessarily result in competition. Instead he sought to use government intervention to foster competition, believing that government controls should not be significantly removed until competition actually occurred. Responding to what he viewed as legislation that would result in industry consolidation and concentration rather than competition, because it was too deregulatory too quickly, Clinton issued several veto threats. It is worth quoting one such threat at length:

My administration is committed to enactment of a telecommunications reform bill. . . . Such legislation is needed to stimulate investment, promote competition . . . and provide for flexible regulations
for this important industry. Consumers should receive the benefits
of lower prices, better quality and greater choices . . . and they
should continue to benefit from a diversity of voices and viewpoints in radio, television, and the print media.

　　Unfortunately, H.R. 1555 . . . does not reach any of these
goals. Instead of promoting investment and competition, it pro-
motes mergers and concentration of power. Instead of promoting
. . . diversity of content and viewpoints, it would allow fewer people to control a greater number of television, radio and newspaper
outlets in every community.[61]

These differing policy approaches often manifested themselves
in differing commitments to particular interests. For example,
Clinton's veto statement signaled his commitment to the views of
public interest groups, which wanted to ensure government's role in
preventing industry concentration and in ensuring a diversity of
viewpoints over the airwaves and on the new information superhighway. The veto threat also signaled Clinton's commitment to long-distance telephone companies, which feared mergers between local telephone companies and cable companies.

　　The fanfare surrounding the new law also masked the incrementalism, indeed the bipolar nature, of the television portion of the legislation. Like Van Deerlin's attempted "rewrite" of the 1970s, the
bills leading to the 1996 Telecommunications Act dealt with the
entire communications industry: broadcasting, cable, satellites, and
telephony. As with the Van Deerlin proposal, the television portion of
the bill was the most controversial and conflicts over television
issues were the last to be resolved. But without a last-minute, pre-
Christmas 1995 compromise, the bill would have been very different.
At a minimum, the television portion might have been dropped.
More important, the entire legislation might have died, as had the
Van Deerlin measure nearly twenty years previously. As a result of
numerous compromises along the way, the television portions of the
new law were much more complex than the rhetoric surrounding a
"major deregulatory overhaul" of the 1934 Communications Act
would suggest. Like the policy changes of the 1980s and early 1990s,
the new law signified a hodgepodge of regulation and deregulation
and, far from resolving policy disputes, ensured that they would continue in the future.

The Issues and Players

Because bringing the information superhighway into being would involve regulatory changes (to reflect technological change) across the entire communications field, each industry sector had its own specific pet issues. There also were divisions within sectors. The local telephone companies were the main proponents of new legislation. They wanted to be able to offer long-distance service and, more important for the purposes of this book, video programming using their phone wires to compete with cable companies and, by extension, broadcasters.[62] However, many policymakers and cable companies feared that local telephone companies would use their local monopolies in an anticompetitive manner, to cross-subsidize their video services and thereby gain an unfair competitive advantage over cable firms.

Long-distance telephone companies, on the other hand, wanted to restrain the local phone companies. In particular, long-distance phone companies feared that, in a new deregulatory environment in which cable companies could offer voice service and local telephone companies could offer long-distance telephone service as well as video services, cable companies and phone companies would merge rather than compete. Long-distance phone companies wanted policies prohibiting cross-ownership between cable companies and local telephone companies. They also did not want local telephone companies to be able to offer long-distance telephony until the local companies faced competition in local voice service.[63]

Cable companies were allied with the long-distance phone companies. Nevertheless, cable companies wanted to be allowed to merge with local phone companies. Hence they advocated against cross-ownership rules. On the other hand, small cable companies feared being swallowed up by larger cable companies made still larger by mergers with telephone companies. Also, cable companies generally wanted an end to FCC regulation of their rates, as implemented under the 1992 Cable Act.

Television broadcasters had their own wants. To the extent that wires and digital technologies dominated discussions of the legislation, television broadcasters feared being left behind.[64] They argued that since broadcast television is a free public service and a valuable public resource, they too needed to be included in deregulatory policy change in order to preserve "free television" for the public.

Ironically, television broadcasters historically used this same argument to underscore their desire for regulatory protectionism against both new broadcasters and cable companies. Second, they argued that deregulation of cable and telephony would result in larger video programming conglomerates. In order to be able to compete with more and larger companies offering programming, as this argument went, broadcasters too needed to become bigger. Hence, many broadcasters wanted an end to ownership regulations. Nevertheless, the smaller television broadcasters wanted to retain ownership limits out of fear that they would be swallowed up if such limits were removed. Indeed, this issue was so divisive within the television broadcasting sector that the National Association of Broadcasters, which represents both large and small broadcasters, assumed a neutral position on the station ownership issue.

Television broadcasters also stated their desire to enter the digital era and offer high-definition television, which offers a wider screen and enhanced picture clarity but which would require broadcasters to use more of the available spectrum. Hence broadcasters wanted additional slices of spectrum, but not only for this purpose. They also wanted freedom to use the additional spectrum for such ancillary services as home shopping and interactive television. They argued that all of this would enable broadcasters to compete in the new information marketplace and to offer services to those without access to new technologies.[65] Broadcasters also wanted policymakers to address their perennial concerns with license terms by extending them and making them easier to renew.[66]

Public interest groups sought to guard against potential megamergers and anticompetitive cross-subsidies. With regard to television policy, they wanted to ensure that the ownership laws relating to broadcast television were retained. Finally, they wanted to ensure that all would have access to new technologies.[67]

The perennial issue of sex and violence on television was also at play during this period, especially with the development of the so-called V-chip—a computer chip that can be embedded in television sets to screen out violent and sexually explicit programming. In order to function, the chip requires an instruction-encoded signal, and thus some sort of standardized national ratings system. Broadcasters of course loathed this possibility, but as one Congress-watcher put it, the new device appealed to both "anti-violence Democrats" and "anti-indecency Republicans."[68]

Legislation on the Brink

In the end, conference debate over the legislation came down to the broadcast ownership provisions.[69] And on August 5, 1995, Clinton issued his statement threatening to veto the legislation if broadcast ownership were vastly deregulated. But the issue is interesting because it constitutes a microcosm of the larger policy differences between the White House and its allies on the one hand, and the Republican Congress (especially the House of Representatives) on the other. While everyone agreed that competition within and between communications sectors was a desirable and appropriate goal, the two sides differed on what competition actually means, what (if any) role the government should have in facilitating it, and what to do while waiting for it.

The position of the White House, public interest groups, and their allies in Congress was that deregulation—the removal of government control—does not in itself simply result in competition. In fact, they argued, as in the case of the cable–telephone company cross-ownership issue and the case of the broadcast television ownership issue, the removal of government control just might lead to industry concentration. Hence, according to this line of thought, the government ought to continue to have a role in fostering competition (through ownership regulations, for example).

In this, the coalition supporting ownership regulations was the political descendant of Van Deerlin, who in his attempted television policy reform bill in the 1970s proposed to strengthen rather than weaken ownership regulations. Hence, Larry Irving, of the National Telecommunications and Information Administration (Department of Commerce), argued: "Our belief is that you go from monopoly to competition to deregulation. The House Commerce Committee thinks you go from monopoly to deregulation in the hope of reaching competition. . . . We all want to do the same dance, we're just doing the steps in a different order."[70] Representative Markey, the Clinton administration's point person in the House, put it more succinctly, noting: "The point is to demonopolize, not deregulate."[71] And, they argued, in cases where even competition might not produce the desired results (such as children's television programming), continued regulation would be necessary.

The Republican leadership, especially those Republicans who came to power during the 104th Congress, however, emphasized deregulation, though they used the same rhetoric of competition as their opponents. While the Democrats and their allies sought to draw a distinction between deregulation and competition, Republicans equated the two. As Senator Robert Dole put it, "Not regulation, but competition. Not regulation but deregulation."[72] And so, despite the numerous compromises that bill negotiators made along the way, in the end the central debate came down to the overarching debate over philosophy. The focus of that debate was the provisions of television ownership.

The New Law

After several veto threats from President Clinton, legislators reached agreement on the key issues and Clinton signed the bill into law. The new law effected the following:

• Allowed local telephone companies to offer video service. In doing so, they would be regulated in the same fashion as cable companies, and regulations applying to cable companies would also apply to telephone companies providing video services. For example, phone companies offering video services would have to make available channels for use by public, educational, and government entities.

• Provided that cable and telephone companies offering video services could alternatively choose to be regulated as an "open video system." According to this option, they would not have to comply with many traditional cable regulations, but they would have to comply with rules banning discrimination of programmers.

• Abolished rate regulation for the expanded tier of cable programming services (which include channels such as CNN and MTV) for all cable providers after March 31, 1999. For small cable systems, serving fewer than 50,000 subscribers, the law abolished rate regulation immediately. However, rate regulation of the basic tier would remain until a cable system faced competition.

• Allowed cross-ownership by cable companies and phone companies providing it did not exceed 10 percent of the households in a service area.

• Extended the license terms of television broadcasters from five to eight years.

• Streamlined the broadcast television license renewal system.

Only if renewal is first denied would competing applications be considered. Petitions to deny renewal and revocation petitions would still be allowed.

• Provided for use of additional and free spectrum by broadcasters to develop high-definition television and other services. Use of the new spectrum would have to be in line with the "public interest." Broadcasters using the new spectrum for pay services would have to pay a fee to the FCC.

• Repealed the numerical cap for broadcast television station ownership and relaxed the audience cap. Henceforth television broadcasters would be able to own an unlimited number of stations, provided the combined reach did not exceed 35 percent of the national audience.

• Provided for use of the V-chip along with provisions for a program ratings system. Television broadcasters would have one year to develop and agree to a ratings system, or the FCC would craft and implement one.

• Affirmed the public interest standard and applied it to new digital technologies.

The More Things Change, the More They Stay the Same

Any casual viewer could hardly fail to notice the dramatic technological changes that occurred between the mid-1970s and the mid-1990s. Cable television flourished. Originally merely a means of extending broadcast signals to viewers unable to receive them, cable firms began importing and exporting signals into and out of local and distant markets. There was a veritable explosion of specialty cable channels, made possible by satellite technology. Viewers can now choose to have their programs delivered by consumer satellite services as well. Changes in digital technologies created the Internet, high-definition television, and various other communication devices.

There is no doubt that technological change, and the writings of economists advocating deregulation in light of this change, helped place television deregulation on the agenda in the 1970s, as indeed was the case when Van Deerlin sought to rewrite the 1934 Communications Act. Similarly, Mark Fowler sought the near complete deregulation of television in the 1980s from his perch at the

FCC. A major impetus to the 1996 Telecommunications Act was a desire to respond to technological change, hasten it further, and thereby facilitate technological convergence.

Nevertheless, despite technological development in the late 1970s, Van Deerlin stopped short of proposing complete deregulation in his rewrite effort. Though Mark Fowler at the FCC did propose complete deregulation, a hostile Congress encumbered it at every turn. And despite new technologies and the promise of convergence, the 1996 act only perpetuated incremental change in television policy. The 1996 act did not repeal the 1934 law, but rather amended it. The 1996 act did not promote convergence and intersectoral competition either in theory or in practice, at least not on the scale imagined prior to its passage. Rather, the 1996 act preserved the regulatory boundaries between the different sectors that compose the larger communications industry. On its face, the act itself was structured around the different sectors, with a title of the law pertaining to each. Telephone companies would still be regulated differently than cable firms. Both would be regulated differently than broadcasters. Though the law tried to encourage telephone companies and cable companies to offer each other's services, it also provided that, when they did, they would be regulated accordingly.

Though the act retained much of the regulatory partitioning of the 1934 Communications Act, it did deregulate within sectors, though incrementally so. Central to the purposes of this book was its extension of broadcast license terms and the relaxation of broadcast ownership limits. Though the act deregulated the extended tier of cable programming, it left the basic tier regulated. Though the act removed the numerical limits on broadcast ownership, it only relaxed the audience cap. The basic framework of the 1934 act remained in place. Each sector would be regulated separately. The FCC still would oversee the terms of competition between the sectors. The FCC still would award free licenses to broadcasters to operate in the public interest. This is not to suggest that there was no deregulation. Obviously there was. And it has had important consequences, particularly for industry concentration, which increased dramatically after the new act became law.[73]

But the process and nature of television deregulation was decidedly different from that of the airline, trucking, and telephone industries. While legislation deregulating those three industries passed in the late 1970s and early 1980s, legislation deregulating television failed. In the 1980s and early 1990s, while deregulation of other infrastructure industries was being implemented, policymakers waged a pitched battle across the institutions responsible for television policy. The 1996 Telecommunications Act only perpetuated the schizophrenic tendencies evident in television policy in the preceding decades. Despite significant technological change, the basic paradigm of television regulation remained in place upon passage of the 1996 law. Technological change was certainly an important rationale used by those advocating deregulation, and interest groups and government actors were forced to reassess the purposes of regulation in light of this technological change. Nevertheless, a market forces theory, which holds that policy change reflects economic and technological change, cannot explain the lack of dramatic policy change for television.

Notes

1. To be sure, airline, trucking, and telephony deregulation still would have to be implemented, but policy change for these industries had been agreed to by policymakers. Telephony deregulation, of course, was helped along by the Department of Justice, which initiated an antitrust case against AT&T seeking divestiture.

2. Scherer, *Industrial Market Structure and Economic Performance;* and Eads, "The Reform of Economic Regulation."

3. "Rewrite of Communications Act," p. 19.

4. U.S. House of Representatives, Subcommittee on Communications of the Interstate and Foreign Commerce Committee, *The Communications Act of 1979,* vol. 1, pp. 2–239. Van Deerlin did make a previous attempt at such legislation, with the Communications Act of 1978. Given space constraints, however, and to facilitate clarity of exposition, the discussion here focuses on his second effort. See U.S. House of Representatives, Subcommittee on Communications of the Interstate and Foreign Commerce Committee, *The Communications Act of 1978.* For the congressional studies leading up to these bills, see U.S. House of Representatives, Staff of the Subcommittee on Communications of the Committee on Interstate and Foreign Commerce, *Options Papers.*

5. Brown, "Broadcast Regulation."

6. Quoted in "Mass Media Laws, Changes Proposed," p. D20.

7. Krasnow, Longley, and Terry, *The Politics of Broadcast Regulation,* p. 253.

8. See, for example, House Subcommittee, *The Communications Act of 1979,* remarks by Thomas Bolger, chairman of the Television Board of the National Association of Broadcasters, vol. 3, pp. 192–193; Corydon

Dunham, executive vice president and general counsel of NBC, vol. 2, pt. 2, pp. 1371, 1373; Norman Walt, president of McGraw-Hill Broadcasting, vol. 2, pt. 3, p. 1921; Donald Thurston, National Association of Broadcasters, vol. 3, p. 190; and Everett Erlick, senior vice president and general counsel of ABC, vol. 2, pt. 2, pp. 1404, 1434.

9. Quoted in House Subcommittee, *The Communications Act of 1979*, vol. 2, pt. 1, p. 169. On this issue, see also remarks by Ralph Baruch, chairman and chief executive officer of Viacom and representative of the National Cable Television Association, p. 132.

10. For the views of public interest groups, see House Subcommittee, *The Communications Act of 1979*, remarks of Charles Firestone, American Civil Liberties Union; Nolan Bowie, Citizens Communications Center; Peggy Charren, Action for Children's Television; and Ralph Jennings, Office of Communications of the United Church of Christ. For the views of academics, see remarks by Barry Cole, Annenberg School of Communications of the University of Pennsylvania; and Cherie Lewis, Department of Journalism of the University of Southern California. For the views of executive branch officials, see remarks by Henry Geller, National Telecommunications and Information Administration; Barry Robinson, Office of Minority Business Enterprise; Esther Peterson, Office of Consumer Affairs; J. Clay Smith, Equal Employment Opportunity Commission; and Arthur S. Flemming, Commission on Civil Rights.

11. Quoted in House Subcommittee, *The Communications Act of 1979*, vol. 5, p. 100. See also remarks by Charles Firestone, University of California–Los Angeles, vol. 2, pt. 1, p. 559.

12. Krasnow, Longley, and Terry, *The Politics of Broadcast Regulation*, p. 277.

13. Quoted in House Subcommittee, *The Communications Act of 1979*, vol. 2, pt. 1, p. 535. See also remarks by Representative Timothy Wirth (D–Colo.), vol. 2, pt. 1, p. 87; Representative Al Swift (D–Wash.), vol. 2, pt. 1, p. 552; Representative Albert Gore (D–Tenn.), vol. 2, pt. 2, pp. 1355, 1360; Representative Carlos Moorhead (R–Calif.); and Representative Marc Marks (R–Pa.:), vol. 2, pt. 2, pp. 1355–1357, and vol. 2, pt. 1, p. 565.

14. "Rewrite Written Off."

15. Quoted in "Van Deerlin Refuses to Say Die," p. 27.

16. On the Reagan administration's attempts at deregulation, see, for example, Harris and Milkis, *The Politics of Regulatory Change;* and Hoberg, *Pluralism by Design.*

17. Quoted in Nossiter, "The FCC's Big Giveaway Show," p. 402. For more on Fowler's program, see Cooper, "Fowler's FCC Learns Some Hard Lessons."

18. *The Omnibus Budget Reconciliation Act of 1981.*

19. Fowler and Brenner, "A Marketplace Approach to Broadcast Regulation," pp. 209–210.

20. *Omnibus Budget Reconciliation Act of 1981;* and U.S. Federal Communications Commission, *Radio Broadcast Services.* Black Citizens for a Fair Media challenged this change in court but lost. See *Black Citizens for a Fair Media v. Federal Communications Commission.*

21. U.S. Federal Communications Commission, *Cable Television Syndicated Program Exclusivity Rules and Inquiry.* See also *Federal Communications Commission v. Midwest Video Corporation.*

22. For a useful discussion of cable's regulatory problems, see Besen and Crandall, "The Deregulation of Cable Television."

23. *Cable Communications Policy Act of 1984.*

24. For more on these controversies, see "Cable TV Deregulation," pp. 552–554.

25. For journalistic accounts of the negotiations between the National League of Cities and the National Cable Television Association, see "The Bills Are Back"; "S. 66 Markup Postponed"; "Getting Down to Brass Tacks on Cable Deregulation"; "S. 66 Wins Big in the Senate"; "Parties Go Back to the Table for Cable Dereg. Talks"; "Cable Strikes a Deal with Cities"; Calmes, "Fragile Cable Compromise Threatened by Court Ruling"; "Firms Ask for Changes in Cable Bill"; "Seven-Hour Meeting"; and "Cable Industry Seems Happy with H.R. 4103 Compromise."

26. For the Senate measure, see U.S. Senate, Subcommittee on Communications of the Committee on Commerce, Science, and Transportation, *Cable Telecommunications Act of 1983.* For the House measure, see U.S. House of Representatives, *Options for Cable Legislation.*

27. Quoted in House Subcommittee, *Options for Cable Legislation,* p. 171. Other Democrats concurred. See remarks by Representative James Collins, pp. 293–295, and remarks by Representative John Dingell, p. 296.

28. Pytte, "Cable TV: The New Big Kid," p. 3363.

29. U.S. Senate, Subcommittee on Communications of the Committee on Commerce, Science, and Transportation, *Cable TV: Hearing on the Oversight of the 1984 Cable Telecommunications Act,* See also U.S. House of Representatives, Subcommittee on Telecommunications and Finance of the Committee on Energy and Commerce, *Cable Television Regulation.*

30. Quoted in Senate Subcommittee, *Cable TV,* pp. 431–432. See also statement by Matthew Oristano, chairman of People's Choice TV Partners (a microwave concern), in House Subcommittee, *Cable Television Regulation,* pt. 1, p. 539.

31. Quoted in Senate Subcommittee, *Cable TV,* p. 382.

32. Senate Subcommittee, *Cable TV,* p. 376.

33. Data source: A. C. Neilsen Co., Paul Kagan Associates, Inc., in Pytte, "Cable TV: The New Big Kid," p. 3363.

34. Starobin, "Media Ownership Overhaul May Divide Legislators," p. 1317.

35. Quoted in Pytte, "Cable TV: The New Big Kid," p. 3366.

36. For journalistic background on events leading to the 1992 Cable Act, see Pytte, "Cable TV Reregulation Bill Sweeps by Senate Panel"; Pytte, "Cable Reregulation Measure Moves Forward in House," p. 2053; Mills, "Cable Regulation Is Dead—Again"; Mills, "FCC Leaves Mark"; Mills, "Senate Cable Regulation Bill Headed for Another Season"; Mills, "Markey's Cable Re-Regulation Bill Survives Democrats' Defections"; Mills, "Weakened Reregulation Bill Heads to the House Floor"; and Mills, "Scarred by Media War, Cable Bill Wins Solid Vote." For bills leading to the

1992 Cable Act, see U.S. Senate, Subcommittee on Communications of the Committee on Commerce, Science, and Transportation, *Cable TV Consumer Protection Act of 1991.*

37. Quoted in U.S. Federal Communications Commission, *Multiple Ownership,* para. 26.

38. U.S. Federal Communications Commission, *Multiple Ownership,* paras. 44–45, 52.

39. Pressman, "Congress Clears Supplemental FY '84 Funding," pp. 1950–1951.

40. U.S. Federal Communications Commission, *Multiple Ownership Revisions.*

41. For the complex events leading up to the repeal of the Fairness Doctrine, see U.S. Federal Communications Commission, *Fairness Doctrine Inquiry;* Calmes, "Groundwork Laid," p. 1302; and Calmes, "Senate Panel Axes Broadcast 'Freedom of Expression' Bill," p. 1435.

42. U.S. Federal Communications Commission, *Syracuse Peace Council.* The FCC's repeal of the doctrine was facilitated by a decision by the Court of Appeals for the D.C. Circuit, which ruled that the FCC could unilaterally repeal the doctrine. See *Telecommunications Research and Action Council v. Federal Communications Commission.*

43. U.S. Federal Communications Commission, *Syracuse Peace Council.*

44. See Starobin, "'Fairness Doctrine' Has Had a Tangled Past"; Starobin, "FCC and Congress Clash over Proper Roles"; U.S. House of Representatives, Subcommittee on Telecommunications and Finance of the Committee on Energy and Commerce, *Broadcasters and the Fairness Doctrine;* Ronald Reagan, *Veto—S. 742.*

45. U.S. Federal Communications Commission, *Reexamination of the Commission's Comparative Licensing, Distress Sales, and Tax Certificate Policies.*

46. *Metro Broadcasting, Inc. v. Federal Communications Commission.*

47. U.S. Federal Communications Commission, *Children's Television Programming.* The FCC's decision was upheld in *Action for Children's Television v. Federal Communications Commission,* 756 F. 2d 899. With regard to policies limiting advertising during children's programming, the FCC never executed a formal proceeding. Nevertheless, in 1986 it announced that it (mysteriously) had previously repealed them. See U.S. Federal Communications Commission, *Revision of Television Deregulation.* Upon legal challenge, the FCC was required to reinstate those commercial policies. See *Action for Children's Television v. Federal Communications Commission,* 821 F. 2d 741

48. Quoted in U.S. House of Representatives, Subcommittee on Telecommunications and Finance of the Committee on Energy and Commerce, *Commercialization of Children's Television,* p. 5.

49. The bills leading to the Children's Television Act are included in U.S. House of Representatives, Subcommittee on Telecommunications and Finance of the Committee on Interstate and Foreign Commerce, *Commer-*

cialization of Children's Television. For journalistic accounts, see Starobin, "Bill to Boost Quality of Kids' TV Clears"; Starobin, "Fewer Ads, and More Quality Shows"; Starobin, "House Votes"; Pytte, "Congress Ready Once Again to Curb Children's Television"; and Mills, "Congress Ready to Limit Ads on Children's TV Programs."

50. *Telecommunications Act of 1996.*

51. Quoted in Mills, "Ushering in a New Age in Communications," p. C1.

52. Quoted in Stern, "New Law of the Land," p. 8.

53. "Gore: Confident the U.S. Can Become a 'Premiere Information Marketplace.'"

54. For a good definition of convergence, see Krattenmaker, "The Telecommunications Act of 1996." Also see de Sola Pool, *Technologies of Freedom,* for an early technological history of convergence and its potential effects on policy and society.

55. Gates, *The Road Ahead,* p. 208.

56. U.S. White House, "'95 Technology Administration Budget Highlights"; and U.S. Department of Commerce, Office of the Secretary, "Common Ground."

57. Quoted in Mills, "Clinton's Computer 'Highway,'" p. 827.

58. Ronfeldt, "Cyberocracy Is Coming"; and Cassidy, *Dot.con,* chap. 3.

59. For early legislative proposals, see U.S. House of Representatives, *The Antitrust Reform Act of 1993;* U.S. House of Representatives, *The National Communications Competition and Information Infrastructure Act of 1993;* and U.S. Senate, *The Communications Act of 1994.* For journalistic accounts of these early proposals, see Andrews, "HDTV Use for Profit Is Pushed"; Healey, "Senate Sponsors Reinforce Communications Bills"; Andrews, "U.S. May Let a Baby Bell Widen Reach"; and Healey, "Stumped by Bells' Objections, Hollings Kills Overhaul." For a scholarly account, see Aufderheide, *Communications Policy and the Public Interest;* and Olufs, *The Making of Telecommunications Policy.*

60. Quoted in Healey, "Sides Fielding New Teams in Legislative Battle."

61. U.S. White House, "Statement by the President on H.R. 1555," p. 3406.

62. See, for example, statement by James Cullen, vice chairman of Bell Atlantic Corporation, in U.S. House of Representatives, Subcommittee on Telecommunications and Finance of the Committee on Commerce, *Communications Law Reform,* pp. 84–92.

63. See, for example, statement of Robert Allen, chairman and chief executive officer of AT&T, in ibid., pp. 21–29.

64. Mills, "New Bills Make Waves."

65. See Sohn and Schwartzman, *Pretty Pictures of Pretty Profits;* and Carney, "Spate of Squabbles Leaves Bill's Fate Uncertain."

66. See testimony by the National Association of Broadcasters in House Subcommittee, *Communications Law Reform,* pp. 518–527.

67. Sohn and Schwartzman, *Pretty Pictures of Pretty Profits.*

68. Quoted in Healey, "Rejecting Further Regulation, Senate Easily Passes Bill."

69. Carney, "Telecommunications."

70. Quoted in Healey, "GOP Dealing Wins Votes for Deregulatory Bill," p. 1496.

71. Quoted in Healey, "House Committee Leaders Back Senate Provisions," p. 1237.

72. Quoted in Healey, "With Democrats at a Distance, GOP Details Its Own Plan," p. 153.

73. For statistics on industry concentration as of 2002, see Compaine and Gomery, *Who Owns the Media?*

4

Fragmentation, Negotiation, and the Industry's Failure to Determine Policy

IN THE AIRLINE AND TRUCKING DEREGULATION EXAMPLES, THE REGU-lated firms, benefiting from regulatory protection, initially fought deregulation. Clear divisions within the regulated industries, howev-er, provided a few consistent allies for policymakers seeking deregu-lation. Once a few major firms capitulated and ceased their efforts to derail deregulation, other firms followed. Scholars can, and do, debate whether this constitutes evidence for an industry determinism theory of policy change (suggesting that policymakers would not have achieved deregulation had the industries not capitulated) or whether this constitutes evidence that industry interests were overrid-den by more diffuse interests.[1] By contrast, television is an extremely fragmented sector, and due to this fragmentation, firms in the sector were unable to control the course of regulatory policy change.

The role of television firms (local broadcasters, networks, cable companies) is a particularly compelling topic. Television firms are widely perceived as very powerful political actors in the United States.[2] Some scholars, for example, argue that the influence of tele-vision firms derives from their ability to shape the political environ-ment, set the national agenda, facilitate political and cultural social-ization, and influence elections.[3] Another debate concerns the locus of this power—specifically, whether that power resides in the broad-cast television sector or the cable sector, and further, whether it resides in local or national media outlets.[4] Clearly both broadcast and cable television influence the political environment. The broadcast networks and stations reach a large mass audience, while cable offers a variety of twenty-four-hour news channels as well as coverage of

Congress by C-Span (short for Cable Satellite Public Affairs Network).[5] The twenty-four-hour news channels have been credited with the "CNN effect," by which issues are thrust into public consciousness and public opinion is inflamed by extensive news coverage of breaking events.[6] Finally, some scholars emphasize the power of the national media, while others emphasize the influence of local television outlets.[7] While the national media (such as the broadcast networks) cover *issues* that are important to members of Congress and to the institution as a whole, local television stations provide coverage of the *members* of Congress themselves.

Another source of power for television firms is said to stem from their ability to mobilize politically in order to pursue their own self-interest.[8] J. H. Snider and Benjamin Page, for example, argue that the power of the media as an interest group derives from both its vast lobbying prowess, as well as the idea that elected politicians depend on the media for news coverage.[9] Snider and Page argue that television stations and networks can bias their programming to lobby indirectly for their interests. For example, broadcasters can engage in overt bias, by which they provide favorable coverage to their positions on issues, or alternatively, ignore coverage of issues that are important to them that would be offensive to the larger public. Thus, through their programming, broadcasters can expand or narrow conflict. Further, broadcasters can engage in covert bias by, for example, covering issues that a member of Congress doesn't want covered (such as allegations of sexual impropriety) or by refusing to cover a member and thus denying him or her important publicity.[10]

Given the vast quantity of paper devoted to demonstrating and understanding the influence and power of television, one would expect television interests to have dominated and determined policymaking.[11] But policy change did not necessarily reflect the wishes of television firms. We therefore must ask why the television industry was not better able to embed its preferences in policy.

What the Industry Wanted vs. What It Got

In order to make a compelling prima facie case that the television industry *did* determine policy, we would want to see a consistent correlation between the policy wishes of the industry and actual policy outputs. Given the wide range of issues and the long time period under consideration in this book, it is rather difficult to generate a definitive laundry list of industry policy preferences, especially as some of those preferences have changed over time and interacted with the particular political context and policy proposals of the moment. This said, we can approximate such a list, keeping in mind that it is extremely oversimplified.

Cable companies wanted distant signal deregulation so that they could import and export broadcast signals from one market to another. They also wanted rate deregulation so that they could have the freedom to set their own rates. Cable companies did not want any social or public trustee regulations. For their part, television broadcasters did not want deregulation of cable carriage of their signals. Barring that, however, they wanted cable companies to purchase broadcasters' programming at market rates. Broadcasters also wanted licenses in perpetuity and freedom from the Fairness Doctrine, children's television regulations, and affirmative action and equal employment opportunity regulations. Finally, through the years a division occurred within the broadcasting sector over ownership regulations. Large group and chain broadcasters, as well as the television networks, wanted ownership regulations repealed, while smaller and independent broadcasters wanted the regulations maintained.

Based on this general list, we can identify the net policy "wins" and "losses," from the perspective of industry actors, over the period under consideration (the mid-1970s through passage of the 1996 Telecommunications Act). Cable companies did receive distant signal deregulation (win), but had to abide by regulations mandating that small broadcasters could demand carriage on cable systems and that large broadcasters could charge cable systems for carriage (loss). The 1996 act deregulated rates for the expanded tier of programming for small cable systems upon passage of the act (win), while the same tier of programming of the larger cable systems would be deregulated three years after passage (win or loss, depending on one's perspective). Rates for the basic tier of programming remained regulated (loss). At the end of the period under consideration in this book, cable companies also were still subject to regulations requiring public, educational, and governmental channels, equal employment opportunity rules, and various provisions concerning limitations on obscene and pornographic programming (loss).

Television broadcasters "lost" on cable signal deregulation, though small broadcasters benefited from legislation allowing them to demand carriage by cable companies while larger broadcasters benefited from legislation allowing them to charge cable companies for their signals (win). Broadcasters still must be awarded licenses, which must be renewed, for finite terms (loss). Though the Fairness Doctrine and affirmative action ownership policies were repealed by the Federal Communications Commission (FCC) with approval from the courts (win), television broadcasters still were subject to equal employment opportunity rules, children's television regulations that were even stronger than the initial such regulations issued in 1974, and the V-chip program along with its program ratings system (loss). Ownership limits remained in effect, as of passage of the 1996 Telecommunications Act, though they were relaxed (win or loss, depending on one's point of view).

The discussion above indicates that the television industry on balance achieved some favorable policies. However, there is no *consistent* correlation between the policy wishes of the industry and actual policy outputs. How do we explain this? Beyond suggesting that policy outputs reflect industry wishes, industry determinism theories make certain assumptions. First, they assume that there is an inherent conflict between a larger public interest and private interests. Second, they assume that industry "dominance" can be objectively measured. Third, they assume that an industry's success in embedding its preferences in policy correlates with its levels of mobilization, the existence of an organized opposition, and the industry's internal unity. Thus, the better an industry is mobilized, the more we should expect it to receive favorable policy outputs. To the extent that an industry is unified in its policy preferences, we should also expect to see favorable policies. Finally, when an industry faces no opposition from other producer groups, it is more likely to receive favorable policy.[12]

Obviously, the television industry was well mobilized. But debates over the nature and locus of the political influence of the television industry, coupled with the discussion above about policy wins and losses, clearly implicates industry *structure* as an important factor to consider in attempting to explain the ambiguous nature of television deregulation and the role of the industry in policymaking.

The ability of television interests to determine policy outputs was complicated by the very nature of the industry's structure. Unlike the relatively simple structure of the regulated industries in the airline and trucking cases, the television industry is fragmented, both between sectors (for example, between the broadcast and cable television sectors) and within sectors (for example, between larger broadcast chains and networks on the one hand and smaller and independent television stations on the other).

This fragmentation raises a series of important questions, beginning with how it affected television politics. The fragmented nature of industry structure made it plausible to argue that the government should continue to determine and preserve sector boundaries in order to ensure "fair" competition. Industry fragmentation also made coalition building difficult and provided openings for public interest groups and policymakers to exploit. Given this industry fragmentation, we are compelled to ask whether dominant sectors (either broadcast or cable), or dominant firms, were able to determine policy outputs, or whether policy resulted from bargaining among groups—or both.

Intersectoral Fragmentation

Depending on how one looks at the matter, there may or may not be an actual television industry. Far from being a metaphysical statement, this actually is a practical point that had important implications for television policy and politics. Historically, policy has reflected the view that there is no single industry but, rather, distinct sectors.

What we view on our television screens is brought to us by a host of different kinds of firms, using different distribution systems that are themselves based on different technologies. Traditional television—that is, "free," over-the-air television programming—is delivered to us by firms in the broadcast sector using the electromagnetic spectrum. Cable firms, on the other hand, deliver programming to us by wires strung along and under public streets. Cable systems carry the signals (and hence the programming) of broadcasters, as well as a host of other specialized and niche channels, such as twenty-four-hour news networks, sports channels, movie channels, and children's programming channels. Rather than delivering programming to us over wires, home satellite firms beam their programming to receiving dishes installed on our homes.

Though the 1934 Communications Act gave the FCC jurisdiction over both radio and, by definition, television broadcasting, and though the agency was charged with the task of allocating the scarce public resource of the electromagnetic spectrum to broadcasters, the FCC originally had no jurisdiction over cable television. Nevertheless, the agency assumed jurisdiction over cable firms, rather by fiat, in 1965.

Broadcasters complained that cable importation of distant signals into their local markets was fragmenting the size of their audiences and undermining their revenue base, thereby hindering their ability to serve the "public interest." The FCC thus assumed jurisdiction over cable firms to the extent that it was "reasonably ancillary" to the agency's performance in regulating broadcast television. Because cable competition constituted potential harm to broadcasters, as fiduciaries of the public trust, the FCC assumed jurisdiction over cable and proceeded, by imposing a series of highly restrictive measures on the types of signals that cable could import, to protect broadcasters.[13] By the late 1970s, of course, the FCC had removed the vast bulk of its cable signal regulations, though cable rates remained regulated.[14]

By the late 1970s and early 1980s, as discussed in Chapter 3, certain key policymakers, such as Lionel Van Deerlin (then chair of the House Communications Subcommittee) and Mark Fowler (FCC chair from 1981 to 1987), began to advocate the point of view that broadcasting and cable firms did not so much constitute distinct sectors as they composed a larger industry—the television industry—or at least that they should, and that policy could be an instrument for facilitating that larger industry. Van Deerlin's attempt to legislate deregulation in the 1970s, Fowler's attempt to deregulate administratively in the 1980s, and formulation of the 1996 Telecommunications Act each constituted an effort to view these sectors as a larger industry and then deregulate on that basis.

The various kinds of television firms didn't quite see the industry as deregulators wanted to see it. Instead, industry actors argued that, given the sectoral fragmentation, government had an important role to play in establishing and protecting the boundaries of each sector. They also argued that government had to ensure fair competition and protect against market abuses of one sector by another. This was most notable in the two related areas of copyright issues and cable carriage of broadcaster signals.

Though the FCC, with Congress's implicit assent, removed its signal carriage rules in 1979 and 1980, the question of how to compensate television broadcasters for the carriage of their signals by cable companies remained. That cable firms were carrying broad-caster signals meant that they were carrying programming for which television broadcasters had incurred significant costs—either by pay-ing Hollywood producers for programming or by producing it them-selves. Historically, cable companies had paid fees, which were well below market rates, to a copyright tribunal. The tribunal then distrib-uted the monies to broadcasters.

Television broadcasters, of course, thought this arrangement was highly unfair, as they seemed to be subsidizing their own competi-tors. As one broadcaster put it: "Broadcasters need . . . the right to control the retransmission of our signal, which is our only commodi-ty. We need to have a voice in who carries our signals, and on what terms. Without that, little else will matter in the long run."[15] When Representative Van Deerlin attempted to rewrite the 1934 Communications Act in the 1978–1979 period, he included in the legislation a retransmission consent provision, according to which cable system operators would have to obtain the contractual consent, through payment of marketplace rates, from broadcasters for rights to carry their signals and programming. Cable companies argued forcefully that this provision would spell their death and perpetuate the "virtual stranglehold" of broadcasters, as it would place a dispro-portionate amount of market power into the hands of broadcasters—whom cable operators saw as wanting to put them out of business once and for all. Cable operators charged, first, that broadcasters would not consent to cable transmission of their signals (so as to deny them the all-important programming), or alternatively that broadcasters would charge so much for the signal rights that cable companies would be unable to afford the rates.[16] Of course, Van Deerlin's rewrite effort failed and the status quo ante prevailed.

Broadcasters finally won this decades-long dispute in 1992 when Congress passed legislation reregulating cable rates. In the same leg-islation, Congress mandated that small independent broadcasters could demand carriage of their signals by cable systems (the "must carry" rules), or alternatively that the larger group broadcasters and networks could charge cable systems for the privilege of carrying their programming (the "retransmission consent" rules).

Also in the 1992 cable legislation, policymakers prohibited cable companies from discriminating against their competitors in the home satellite sector. By this time, cable was a highly vertically integrated sector and many cable firms either owned outright, or had ownership stakes in, programmers and specific cable networks. Policymakers, along with cable's nascent competitors of direct-to-home satellite firms, feared that cable firms would use their market power in an anticompetitive manner to deny their competitors valuable programming, which after all is the lifeblood of such firms.

Beyond the copyright and signal carriage issues of the 1970s, 1980s, and early 1990s, we also see the importance of sectoral fragmentation in the 1996 Telecommunications Act. Local telephone companies wanted to be able to offer video programming services. Cable companies, however, feared that the local phone companies would cross-subsidize their provision of programming services with revenues from their local phone monopolies. Thus, given the nature of the legislation, which dealt with the entire communications industry, industry fragmentation was a central focus of policymakers.

The key problem that policymakers were attempting to address in formulating the 1996 act was the mechanics involved in making distinct industry sectors, populated by entrenched monopolies and oligopolies, compete in offering each other's services and thereby in offering comprehensive communications packages to consumers. All sectors and firms claimed to want competition, though, not surprising, what they really wanted was to offer the services associated with other sectors while preserving their own monopoly or near-monopoly status. The dilemma that policymakers faced was how to create intersectoral competition without unduly advantaging any one of them. Thus, according to the law, telephone companies could offer video programming, but if they did so they would be regulated either as common carriers or in the manner in which cable companies are regulated. Similarly, cable companies could provide voice telephone services, but the law provided for regulations intended to facilitate this. The law prohibited cable companies and telephone companies from buying each other out, except under certain circumstances.[17] Thus, while early champions of deregulation believed that an ever-expanding television marketplace would facilitate rapid and substantial deregulation, in many ways the opposite happened. This phenomenon thus constitutes an example of what Steven Vogel calls "freer markets, more rules."[18] The 1996 Telecommunications Act perpetuates the sectoral fragmentation and provides for incremental deregulation.[19]

Of course, leveraging this sectoral fragmentation in order to maintain sector boundaries through regulation did not prevent industry actors from claiming that, after all, they did belong to a larger television industry, or television marketplace, when it suited their purposes in the moment. For example, during formulation of the 1996 Telecommunications Act, a consensus emerged that the so-called information superhighway would be brought to Americans by two wires (the so-called two-wire solution).[20] Those two wires were to be those provided by cable companies and telephone companies. With all the talk about wires, broadcasters feared being road-kill on the information superhighway and sought to ensure their place in the larger industry. As John Abel, executive vice president of the National Association of Broadcasters, stated: "Broadcasting is on the sidelines watching as the telephone, cable, and computer companies develop the hype as well as the business."[21]

Ironically, broadcasters echoed the traditional arguments of public interest groups and claimed that "free television," "localism," and a "diversity of viewpoints" in the media were threatened, obviously trying to expand conflict to include important social issues. They thus argued for additional slots on the electromagnetic spectrum. This new spectrum, they suggested, could be used to offer high-definition television, or alternatively, consumer services such as home shopping, interactive television, and video-on-demand. Broadcasters got that additional spectrum, but with regulations attached. If they used their new spectrum for traditional television, they would continue to be subject to public trustee regulations. If they used those additional channels for ancillary services, for which they would charge fees, broadcasters would be required to pay for the spectrum.[22]

When they sought relief from regulations, broadcasters also claimed that a larger television marketplace existed. For example, during the Fowler FCC's 1984 attempt to repeal ownership limitations, as well as a similar attempt during debate over passage of the 1996 Telecommunications Act, broadcasters argued that such regulations were no longer necessary because television broadcasting belonged to a larger marketplace. In making this argument, broadcasters sounded very much like Fowler, who three years previously had argued that television stations exist alongside brochures, billboards, and books, as part of a larger environment. In the 1984 rulemaking, CBS asserted: "Every press outlet—ranging from sidewalk leafleteers to tiny 'underground' newspapers to iconoclastic journals to mass circulation print and electronic outlets—makes an important contribution to the stimulation of society's collective thought process."[23] Whether there exists a television or communications industry is clearly in the eyes of the beholder.

Dominant Sectors and Television Policy

This fragmentation of the television industry might lead us to speculate that dominant industry sectors (either the broadcast television or cable sector) have determined policy outputs. For this variant of an industry determinism theory to be accurate, we would need to see evidence that dominant sectors consistently determined policy outputs. To the contrary, we have seen several examples in which not only did the dominant sector or firm *not* determine policy, but instead the policy wishes of the dominant sector were *overridden* by policymakers.

The clearest example of this was the deregulation of cable signal carriage in 1979 and 1980. The broadcast television sector largely opposed signal deregulation, preferring instead, like the regulated firms in the airline and trucking industries, to retain the protection that those regulations embodied.[24] The broadcast television sector was clearly the dominant actor in this case. Broadcasters were very well organized and mobilized, with representation in Washington, D.C. In fact, at the time, the headquarters of the National Association of Broadcasters and the offices of the major broadcast networks were located right next to the FCC building. Television broadcasters were unanimously opposed to signal deregulation (with the exception of Ted Turner), and if policy inertia existed at all, it was clearly in their favor. Finally, the political influence attributed to the broadcast sector by the fact that every member of Congress has at least one broadcaster in his or her district on which he or she depends for airtime, made this sector seemingly powerful indeed. By contrast, cable was a fledgling industry, not quite yet off its feet financially or politically (having been hindered in the former by regulation), and not comparably well mobilized.

Nevertheless, policymakers overrode the interest of the dominant broadcast television sector and removed the vast bulk of its cable signal carriage rules, thereby allowing cable systems to import and export broadcast signals. This was carried out primarily by the FCC, much like the deregulation associated with the Civil Aeronautics Board and the Interstate Commerce Commission in airline and trucking deregulation. Congress passed no legislation freeing cable of regulatory constraints. However, much like the telephony case, an important segment of Congress, the House Telecommunications Subcommittee, expressed its clear bipartisan position in favor of signal deregulation in the cable oversight hearings in 1976 as well as in the hearings surrounding the failed Van Deerlin rewrite legislation. And as Erwin Krasnow, Lawrence Longley, and Herbert Terry observe, this strongly influenced the FCC to repeal its signal rules.[25] Broadcasters clearly did not get what they wanted.

The 1992 Cable Act constitutes another notable example of a dominant sector receiving unfavorable policy. By 1990, cable was clearly ascendant. The cable sector was vertically integrated, with many cable firms owning, or holding major financial stakes in, programmers. Cable was accused of discriminatory practices against the fledgling direct broadcast satellite sector, which argued that cable firms were denying them programming. Cable customers complained that subscriber rates were skyrocketing and that they were increasingly losing access to their favorite programming. The charge was that cable systems were delivering channels programmed by their own networks rather than with others. Large broadcasters and networks wanted cable companies to pay them for their signals and small broadcasters charged that cable companies were changing their channel assignments willy-nilly.[26]

Cable obviously was the dominant sector. It was well mobilized and was perceived to be influential among members of Congress. Members of Congress, after all, appear regularly on C-Span, which the cable sector created precisely to demonstrate its influence, and the cable sector as a whole was gaining ratings at the expense of broadcasters. And it too, like the broadcast sector in the cable signal deregulation example, had policy inertia on its side. Nevertheless, Congress passed the 1992 Cable Act, which reregulated rates, provided antidiscrimination measures, and provided for "must carry" and "retransmission consent." In each of these examples, the dominant sector did not get the policies it favored.

Intrasectoral Fragmentation

In addition to the sectoral fragmentation, each distinct sector of the television industry also was fractured internally. This prevented firms in each sector from building coalitions in support of the policies they sought. This phenomenon was particularly acute among television broadcasters.

Divisions within the broadcast sector became evident in the 1970s when the television issue was thrust onto the congressional agenda. From 1934 until 1978, Congress only intervened in television policy once. During those decades most policymaking for television took place at the FCC through its rule-making process, and it is in the nature of regulatory rule-makings that they typically deal with one aspect of one issue. Thus, during the years when the FCC dominated television policy, fissures within each sector were not immediately obvious. With the television problem thrust into the legislature, however, especially in the context of trying to achieve major legislative overhaul of the entire communications industry (first in the 1970s and later in the 1990s), these fissures became obvious.

For example, though television broadcasters opposed the deregulation of cable signal carriage, a division within the broadcast sector undermined their arguments that they would be financially harmed. One broadcaster in particular applauded the proposed signal carriage deregulation and suggested that it could actually help broadcasters, rather than hurt them. Ted Turner, owner of Turner Communications, licensee of Atlanta's WTCG-TV, was the broadcast television industry's loose cannon in this regard.[27]

In the early 1970s, when Turner bought it, WTCG was a fledgling UHF station in last place in its market. By 1979, WTCG (which later changed its call letters to WTBS) was a "superstation." Cable systems all over the country were exporting its signal out of Atlanta and into local markets. Why was Turner so delighted with this situation, despite the gloom and doom prognostications from all of his fellow television broadcasters?

In 1971, a year after Turner purchased WTCG, he was approached by the marketing director for the cable company Telecommunications Incorporated, which wanted to distribute Turner's station on its cable systems. Turner would make no money directly from the cable system, but found the prospect alluring. He would be able to reach a larger audience and thereby increase his advertising base. He could have a regional—even national—audience, rather than a local one. This prospect appealed to Turner and WTCG thus went "national."

In part it was Turner's somewhat unique advertising methods

that allowed him to take advantage of the opportunities presented by cable television. Stations typically receive revenue from both national advertisers (especially if they are affiliated with a national television network) and local advertisers. Cable did offer the prospect of increased viewership, which theoretically would increase revenues. Most broadcast stations, however, did not envision increased advertising. As they saw it, local businesses (for example, used car dealers) would not care that their ads would reach a larger, more geographically dispersed audience, since viewers in other states and regions would not have access to the specific product or service advertised.

Turner's ads, however, were relatively unique for the time. He employed a direct advertising approach at WTCG, a sort of predecessor to the home shopping network. Viewers saw an 800 number that, as Turner's biographers explain, invited them to

> call in to buy their very own "incomparable recordings" of country music's greatest hits. Turner's station was flacking a whole bucketful of dubious products: mood rings and genuine family coats of arms and Popiel's Pocket Fisherman—basically a fancy ball of string. Then there were the Ginzu knives—they sliced, they diced, and they were dirt cheap and so sharp you could cut a can with them, though why anybody would want to cut a soda can with a knife was never explained.[28]

Turner was brand new to the television business and, after only one year on the job, was able to jump on board with cable without any preconceived intersectoral ill will. Turner's approach clearly undermined broadcaster arguments that the sky would fall the minute cable signal carriage took effect.

During the same period, a division began between small television broadcasters and larger broadcasters. Two such small local broadcasters appeared at the hearings on the "rewrite" legislation held by Van Deerlin and argued that broadcast television should absolutely remain regulated. Both broadcasters were deeply committed to the public trustee regulatory ideal and they specifically argued that, in the absence of regulation, the search for profits would undermine localism, a diversity of viewpoints, and news and public affairs programming.

Leo Beranek was president of Boston Broadcasters, Inc., the licensee of Boston's Channel 5 (WCVB), which he founded along with a group of Boston-area citizens. As Beranek tells it, while he and his colleagues agreed that they were not out to lose money, they were willing to run the station informally as a nonprofit firm. While most broadcasters were afraid of editorializing for fear of running into Fairness Doctrine complaints or alienating advertisers, or both, Channel 5 editorialized aggressively and was widely recognized as airing record-high levels of locally produced public affairs programming and original children's programming. Beranek attributed Channel 5's programming success and wide reputation in the 1970s to the fact that the station did not need to seek ever-increasing profits.[29]

William Dilday represented Communications Improvement, the licensee of WLBT-TV in Jackson, Mississippi. This station was formally a nonprofit organization. Communications Improvement acquired this station in 1969 when the FCC revoked the license of the previous owner for failing to serve the public interest. Under the direction of Dilday, the station had put in place a broadly representative staff and focused on children's and public affairs programming.[30]

Dilday and Beranek both undermined the arguments of television broadcasters that less regulation was in order. They argued that, absent public trustee regulations, broadcasters would be motivated only by profits and would not continue to offer public services. Mirroring the views of public interest groups, Dilday argued: "The people who control the power and pervasiveness of television must in some way be accountable to the American people. It is the duty of Congress to pass no laws which would remove this accountability."[31]

A similar fracture developed in the broadcast television sector surrounding the ownership rules. Larger broadcasters wanted the rules repealed, while smaller broadcasters, fearing predation, wanted them maintained.[32] This fracture became quite pronounced as the years progressed, and it was on this issue that the 1996 telecommunications legislation nearly failed.[33] And it was over this issue that President Bill Clinton threatened to veto the bill. The 1996 law relaxed but did not repeal the limitations.

A variation on the theme of intrasectoral fragmentation occurs when policymakers attempt intentionally to fragment a sector when seeking to pass policy. For example, the broadcasting sector includes not only television broadcasters but radio broadcasters as well. Indeed, the National Association of Broadcasters, the main trade organization in the sector, represented both radio interests and television interests. The 1978–1979 Van Deerlin effort to rewrite the 1934 Communications Act promised much more, and much quicker, deregulation to radio than to television broadcasters on the assumption that, since there were more radio stations than television stations, there was less scarcity and hence more competition in radio than in television. Van Deerlin's rewrite legislation thus did not propose the extent of deregulation that television broadcasters hoped for. The legislation also asked television broadcasters to make significant trade-offs. As the National Association of Broadcasters represented both radio and television broadcasters, the organization found it extremely difficult to oppose the legislation. In the end, the National Association of Broadcasters voiced general support for the fateful bill.[34] The same issue reared its head during passage of the 1996 Telecommunications Act. While large broadcasters and networks supported repeal of the ownership limits, smaller broadcasters feared being bought by networks and thus opposed repeal of the limits. Conflict over this issue, as it played out across political party lines, nearly spelled the demise of the legislation. Similarly, in passing the 1996 Telecommunications Act, policymakers were able to get the support of smaller cable system operators by promising them much more deregulation, much more quickly, than they were willing to give to larger cable firms.

Group Bargaining and Television Policy

Another version of a theory of industry determinism would suggest that, in the case of a fragmented industry, policy results from negotiation and bargaining between and among sectors and firms. Obviously, however, the producer-group opposition that organized to challenge the dominant sectors in each of these examples was clearly outmobilized by the dominant sector.

Further, public interest groups weighed in significantly on each of these issues. In the cable signal carriage dispute, public interest groups clearly came down on the side of the weaker cable sector, arguing along with cable companies that signal deregulation would break the "virtual stranglehold" that broadcasters had over what Americans watch on television. Their arguments were reinforced by the testimonial of Ted Turner. Because Turner was a lone broadcaster, and new to the television business, he was not powerful enough to determine policy. But public interest groups exploited this fracture within the broadcast sector in that they were able to point to a broadcaster that had actually benefited from cable signal carriage.

And in the debate over the 1992 cable reregulation law, public interest groups adamantly supported reregulation. On the one hand, they too viewed the various television sectors as distinct, and to the extent that cable constituted a local monopoly, they saw that sector as using its power to exact exorbitant subscriber rates. They also worried that such high rates would necessarily preclude some people from subscribing. Further, public interest groups tended to be in favor of the "must carry" provisions in the law, believing as they did that localism was an important goal of policy. Finally, in the case of the 1992 cable reregulation legislation, constituents jumped into the fray as well. So it is rather difficult, if not impossible, to claim that these issues were driven entirely by business groups. Rather, if anything, this demonstrates the weakness of one of the underlying assumptions of industry determinism theories—that the concerns of the larger public, and of public interest groups, are inherently at odds with those of private interests.[35]

The debates surrounding broadcast ownership regulations (whether to retain, relax, or repeal them) provide another compelling case in which it may be possible that policy reflected bargaining among industry groups. The industry determinism theory nevertheless fails to explain this on several counts. First, such a theory assumes that "dominance" can be measured objectively, yet it is extremely difficult to say who exactly is dominant in this case. Clearly the networks (which wanted the rules repealed) broadcast programming dealing with issues that are important to members of Congress and to the institution as a whole. But small local broadcasters (which wanted the rules retained) are also important to members of Congress to the extent that the latter rely on them for coverage not of the issues, but rather of their personal policy, legislative, and constituent- and district-related achievements. The assumption of industry determinism theories, that "dominance" can be measured by objective criteria, cannot account for *perceptions* about dominance.

Were members of Congress merely splitting the difference between two powerful segments of the larger broadcasting sector when they relaxed the ownership rules? Possibly, but with regard to the ownership example public interest groups also came down very strongly in favor of retention of the rules. In part this was due to their anti–big broadcaster ethic and their concomitant interest in preserving the localism and diversity associated with small broadcasters. But because of the fragmentation of the industry, they also wanted to ensure that their version of the public interest would continue to serve those without access to cable and for whom broadcasting remained a primary source of news and entertainment. So again, it is difficult to support an argument that this was entirely driven by bargaining among firms. That the sector was fragmented prevented coalition building by broadcasters and provided public interest groups and their allies with openings to exploit.

The Influence of Television Interests in Perspective

There also are clear examples in which the policy interests of firms were overridden by policymakers in the absence of any organized business opposition, in the absence of industry fragmentation (and therefore in the absence of bargaining among industry groups), and in which the only opposition to industry was that mobilized by public interest groups. These examples, of course, include the maintenance of various social regulations, such as equal employment opportunity and V-chip rules in the 1996 Telecommunications Act. Broadcasters fought each of these.

To be sure, in the 1970s small broadcasters committed to the public trustee ideal, such as Beranek and Dilday, urged the continuation of such social regulations. But Beranek and Dilday were small-time players in the television industry and do not appear any further in any of the public records of this period. Thus they likely didn't determine policy, but again, provided an opening for opponents of deregulation to exploit.

Two other examples in which Congress overrode the policy preferences of industry actors warrant special attention. In 1984, Congress passed the Cable Communications Policy Act, preempting local government rate regulation and deregulating the rates of many cable systems. Cable companies lobbied hard for this legislation, which reflected their concerns and interests as they had been negotiated with public interest groups and the National League of Cities. Nevertheless, the law also imposed on cable system operators several regulations that they specifically did not want and had previously fought against. These regulations included equal employment provisions, as well as provisions according to which local governments could require cable systems to offer public, educational, and governmental access channels, require programs in certain categories (for example, children's programming), and prohibit programming they deemed obscene. There is some evidence that the cable industry explicitly assented to these provisions in order to gain passage of the rate deregulation provisions. Thus, Peter Athanas, president of the Community Antenna Television Association, noted that his organization accepted those provisions as a necessary trade-off for rate deregulation.[36]

A second example involves passage of the 1990 Children's Television Act, which reregulated children's programming. The National Association of Broadcasters lobbied against this legislation, but Congress passed it anyway. Despite its opposition, the association did not want entirely to stonewall the children's television effort precisely because it was looking for advantages in other policy areas. Specifically, during passage of the Children's Television Act, debate was beginning to heat up over the abuses of the cable industry (a debate that eventually would lead to passage of the 1992 cable reregulation legislation). The National Association of Broadcasters thus did not want to obstruct the children's television effort for fear that doing so would jeopardize its potential for receiving the favorable "must carry" and "retransmission consent" provisions. Congress passed the Children's Television Act, and later, as part of the 1992 cable legislation, broadcasters did receive "must carry" and "retransmission consent" benefits.

On their face, these two examples suggest that industry actors did determine their own policy fates, by accepting public interest requirements in exchange for rate deregulation in the cable example, and in exchange for potentially positive future consideration in the broadcast children's television example. Nevertheless, that the private actors in these examples (cable companies in the first and broadcasters in the second) felt compelled to agree to these trade-offs is equally suggestive. Especially in the broadcast example, the children's television issue received widespread attention from public interest groups, children's advocates, and parent and teacher organizations beginning in 1987, when the FCC repealed its children's rules. The first congressional hearings on reregulation were held that same year. The reregulation law was passed in 1990. By contrast, broadcasters had to wait two years (for passage of the 1992 Cable Act) for "must carry" and "retransmission consent" benefits. If these firms seriously determined policy, these issues never would have been on the agenda in the first place. That these issues, public trustee regulations in the cable example and children's television in the broadcast example, were on the agenda in the first place provided the context for industry trade-offs.

The formulation of the 1996 Telecommunications Act provides some of the most compelling evidence for a theory of industry determinism. Because the act dealt with all sectors of the communications industry, and focused on attempting to create competition between entrenched firms and sectors, it had some of the hallmark characteristics of a classic battle of the titans and was thus conducive to intersectoral bargaining. Indeed, Elizabeth Bailey argues that the politics of the act constituted a classic case of what James Q. Wilson calls "interest group politics," in which bargaining takes place among industry actors behind the scenes.[37]

Moreover, public interest groups found it difficult to mobilize against the different facets of what would become the 1996 Telecommunications Act, in part because, given the fragmented nature of the industry, and given that the legislation dealt with all facets of the industry, they simply could not lobby on every policy issue simultaneously. Finally, as Dick Olufs notes, the issues involved in the 1996 Telecommunications Act were highly technical and therefore tended to be ignored by the larger public.[38] If ever there was an example of industry bargaining, this would appear to have been it.

Nevertheless, an ideological debate ensued over how to achieve "competition." Many of the leading and most active and vocal congressional Republicans equated competition with deregulation. Opponents of deregulation, however, believed that simple deregulation would not result in competition, but rather in industry consolidation. They therefore argued that competition would need to be fostered *through* regulation. Further, and more important in their view, they believed that, because competition would not magically appear upon enactment of the law, certain regulations, such as protections against market and subscriber abuses, had to remain in place. This ideological debate over "competition," in essence, whether it was best achieved through regulation or deregulation, was the overarching question in formulating the law and came to be symbolized in the debates surrounding broadcast ownership regulations, which nearly scuttled the legislation entirely at the very last minute. Though the 1996 act may be the best example of bargaining among producer groups, the concerns of the various television interests were filtered through the larger political and ideological context.

Industry Structure and Television Policy

Television firms did not determine policy. This is not to suggest that they never got what they wanted; clearly there are examples in which private interests received favorable policy outputs. But there was no consistent correlation between their preferences and policy outputs. In part, this is because of the nature of industry structure. The industry is highly fragmented, with divisions both between sectors and within sectors. However, neither did dominant sectors or firms determine policy outputs, as the cable signal deregulation, cable rate reregulation, "must carry" and "retransmission consent" regulation, and ownership regulation demonstrate. Industry structure mattered to the incremental nature of television deregulation because the fragmented nature of industry structure made it possible and plausible (some might even say necessary) to argue that government must continue to protect sector boundaries and protect against market abuses. Further, it mattered because the fragmentation hindered coalition building by television interests and thus provided openings for opponents of deregulation to exploit. In television policy, no faction dominated and no deal was final. Just when one faction appeared to get what it wanted, its gains were reversed in the next round.

Notes

1. MacAvoy, *The Regulated Industries and the Economy,* p. 105; Carron and MacAvoy, *The Decline of Service in the Regulated Industries;* and Eads, "The Reform of Regulation in Telecommunications and Transportation." For a contrary view, see Mucciaroni, *Reversals of Fortune,* esp. chap. 5; and for a discussion of this debate, see Derthick and Quirk, *The Politics of Deregulation,* pp. 21–21, 147–206.

2. See, for example, Wayne, "Broadcast Lobby Excels at the Washington Power Game"; "Off the Dole"; and Mills and Farhi, "Dole Statement Snags Phone, Cable TV Bill."

3. For introductions to this literature, see Graber, *Mass Media and*

American Politics; and McQuail, "The Influence and Effects of Mass Media."

4. Even the industry itself engages in this debate from time to time. See Kurtz, "See No Cable, Hear No Cable."

5. For broadcast television influence, see, for example, Robinson, *Over the Sheehan Wire and On TV.* For cable influence, see, for example, Graber, "Media Power and Government Control"; and Livingston and Eachus, "Humanitarian Crisis and U.S. Foreign Policy."

6. The classic example is CNN coverage of starvation in Somalia, which was credited with increasing the salience of the issue and thus driving President George H. W. Bush to send troops to the country in 1992. See Graber, *Mass Media and American Politics,* p. 16.

7. For local television influence, see Snider and Page, "The Political Power of TV Broadcasters." For national television influence, see Adams et al., "Before and After *The Day After*"; and Hess, *The Ultimate Insiders.*

8. For discussions of this influence, see Krasnow, Longley, and Terry, *The Politics of Broadcast Regulation;* and Snider and Page, "The Political Power of TV Broadcasters."

9. Snider and Page, "The Political Power of TV Broadcasters." Snider and Page note that the National Association of Broadcasters alone spent $2.62 million in lobbying expenses during the first six months of 1996.

10. For studies on bias and objectivity in the news, see Bagdikian, *The Media Monopoly;* Gans, *Deciding What's News;* Hackett, "Decline of a Paradigm?"; Schudson, *Discovering the News;* Tuchman, *Making News;* and Bennett, *News.*

11. Several scholars write from this perspective and argue that the television industry does determine its own policy fortunes. See, for example, Tunstall, *Communications Deregulation.* Other studies in this perspective are primarily single-issue studies, such as Brinkley, *Defining Vision* (on the development of high-definition television), and Snider and Page, "The Political Power of TV Broadcasters" (on the issue of digital spectrum).

12. These variables are derived from Mucciaroni, *Reversals of Fortune.* Mucciaroni in turn derives these from Vogel, *Fluctuating Fortunes.*

13. U.S. Federal Communications Commission, *First Report and Order.*

14. Cable rates remained regulated at the local level. Nevertheless, the 1984 Cable Act gave the FCC formal jurisdiction over cable rates.

15. James Hedlund, Association of Independent Television Stations, quoted in U.S. Senate, Subcommittee on Communications of the Committee on Commerce, Science, and Transportation, *Cable TV Consumer Protection Act of 1991,* p. 199.

16. See testimony by Stephen Effros (Community Antenna Television Association) and Ralph Baruch (Viacom) in U.S. House of Representatives, Subcommittee on Communications of the Committee on Interstate and Foreign Commerce, *The Communications Act of 1979,* vol. 2, pt. 1.

17. According to the law, cable and telephone companies could only buy each other in nonurban areas with less than 35,000 people, for example.

18. Vogel, *Freer Markets, More Rules.*

19. The contradictions inherent in the 1996 act became most pronounced in the fate of AOL Time Warner. The act was intended to promote convergence, or the blurring of sector boundaries so that companies could offer packages of services to consumers in a competitive arena. What "convergence" is to regulators, of course, "synergy" is to businesses. Thus, AOL purchased Time Warner in 2000 hoping to achieve synergy between content production and distribution. The new corporate giant's holdings included (among other concerns) America Online, Time Warner Cable, Home Box Office, Turner Broadcasting, and the WB broadcast network. In the summer of 2002, the new AOL Time Warner came under investigation by the Securities and Exchange Commission for alleged accounting fraud. Through the course of media exposure and investigative reporting, commentators began to argue that "convergence" (or "synergy") had become, in the words of one journalist, "an albatross rather than the magical creature it was supposed to be." See, for example, Walker, "Creating Synergy Out of Thin Air." As if to demonstrate the contradictions inherent in the 1996 act, regulators took a year to approve the merger, during which time company executives argued that the various divisions of the conglomerate would be "different in character."

20. Drake, "National Information Infrastructure Debate."

21. Quoted in Mills, "New Bills Make Waves for Broadcasters," p. 161.

22. This issue was highly contentious. For background, see Healey, "Bill Would Provide Flexibility for 'Advanced TV' Frequencies"; Brinkley, *Defining Vision;* and Brinkley, "The Media Business."

23. U.S. Federal Communications Commission, *Multiple Ownership,* para. 26. Broadcasters also made similar arguments seeking deregulation of children's programming requirements (see U.S. Federal Communications Commission, *Children's Television Programming*) and in attempting to prevent reregulation of children's programming requirements (see testimony by the National Association of Broadcasters in U.S. House of Representatives, Subcommittee on Telecommunications and Finance of the Committee on Energy and Commerce, *Commercialization of Children's Television*).

24. Testimony by Thomas Bolger (National Association of Broadcasters), Everett Erlick (ABC network), and Gene Jankowski (CBS network) in U.S. House of Representatives, Subcommittee on Communications of the Committee on Interstate and Foreign Commerce, *The Communications Act of 1978,* vol. 3.

25. Krasnow, Longley, and Terry, *The Politics of Broadcast Regulation,* pp. 260–261.

26. Testimony by Robert Schmidt (Wireless Cable Association) in Senate Subcommittee, *Cable TV;* Matthew Oristano, People's Choice TV, in U.S. House of Representatives, Subcommittee on Telecommunications and Finance of the Committee on Energy and Commerce, *Cable Television Regulation,* pt. 1; Preston Padden, Association of Independent Television Stations, in Senate Subcommittee, *Cable TV;* and National Association of

Broadcasters, in Senate Subcommittee, *Cable TV.* See also Starobin, "Media Ownership Overhaul May Divide Legislators"; Mills, "FCC Leaves Mark on Battle over Cable TV Control"; and Pytte, "Cable TV: The New Big Kid."

27. Testimony by Ted Turner (WTCG) in House Subcommittee, *The Communications Act of 1979,* vol. 2, pt. 1.

28. Goldberg and Goldberg, *Citizen Turner,* pp. 135–136.

29. Testimony by Leo Beranek in House Subcommittee, *The Communications Act of 1979,* vol. 2, pt. 2.

30. Testimony by William H. Dilday (WLBT-TV) in House Subcommittee, *The Communications Act of 1979,* vol. 2, pt. 2.

31. Ibid., pp. 925–926.

32. Healey, "Rejecting Further Regulation, Senate Easily Passes Bill"; and Mills, "Dole Goes to Bat for Media Giants."

33. In the 1980s, when the FCC attempted to repeal the ownership limits, the National Association of Broadcasters supported elimination of the rules, despite the fact that its more numerous but smaller members wanted to retain them. See U.S. Federal Communications Commission, *Multiple Ownership,* esp. para. 44. Over the years, this fracture became far more pronounced, especially in the context of the formulation of the 1996 Telecommunications Act. By 2000, two of the major broadcast networks (NBC and Fox) had resigned their membership in the association. In 2001, CBS also resigned its membership, stating in its resignation announcement: "For some time we have called for the elimination of the national broadcast ownership cap as well as other outmoded regulatory constraints on broadcasters. It has now become clear that we cannot remain within an organization that is actively working against those objectives." Quoted in Srinivasan, "CBS Leaves Broadcast Association over TV Limits."

34. See testimony by Vincent Wasilewski, Thomas Bolger, and Donald Thurston (all of the National Association of Broadcasters) in House Subcommittee, *The Communications Act of 1979,* vol. 3.

35. Indeed, though the press subsequently manipulated the statement, "Engine" Charlie Wilson, of General Motors Corporation, told Congress in 1953, "What's good for America is good for General Motors."

36. U.S. House of Representatives, Subcommittee on Telecommunications, Consumer Protection, and Finance of the Committee on Energy and Commerce, *Options for Cable Legislation,* pp. 266–267.

37. Bailey, "The Evolving Politics of Telecommunications Regulation." See also Wilson, *The Politics of Regulation.* Bailey looks only at the telephony aspects of the 1996 Telecommunications Act.

38. Olufs, *The Making of Telecommunications Policy,* p. 3.

5

Putting Television Policy into a Broader Context

WHY DOES POLICY CHANGE OCCUR? FOLLOWING UP ON A WAVE OF case studies showing spasms of policy change, Frank Baumgartner and Bryan Jones investigate phenomena that go through what they call "punctuated equilibrium."[1] By this they mean that policy associated with specific issue areas may remain stable for long periods of time only to experience rapid change. As distinct from explanations for policy change based in market forces, technology, and industry influences, Baumgartner and Jones argue that such dramatic policy change results from newly dominant problem definitions and policy images (which may have a basis in technological, economic, or business change) that both provide an impetus for, and work in concert with, institutional changes. Though Baumgartner and Jones do not investigate cases of economic deregulation directly, airline, trucking, and telephony deregulation constitute clear examples of punctuated equilibrium. Thus political scientists who study economic deregulation from this perspective emphasize the role of ideas and institutions in the deregulation of the airline, trucking, and telephone industries.

For example, in their analysis of airline, trucking, and telephone deregulation, Martha Derthick and Paul Quirk argue that, although economists had been advocating deregulation for years, deregulation ultimately passed because it appealed to a broad coalition of liberals and conservatives.[2] On the political left, deregulation appealed to consumer advocates, who were deeply suspicious of big business and its collusion with government and who thought consumers would benefit from added competition, lower prices, and better service. Deregulation also appealed to those on the political right who desired a return to free market policies and principles and who saw deregulation as a tool to combat inflation. The idea of deregulation, thus framed, allowed these strange bedfellows to come together and provided momentum for the deregulation movement.

If ideas are essential to policy change, those ideas go nowhere without the appropriate institutional avenues. As E. E. Schattschneider notes, "organization is the mobilization of bias"— institutions exclude the participation of some actors while including that of others, and the exclusion of actors often means the exclusion of alternative points of view.[3] Thus the success of those advocating deregulation hinged on their ability to expand conflict, break into more favorable institutional venues (or to change institutions to enable them to move forward), and upset long-standing subsystem arrangements and policy monopolies. Deregulation advocates in the airline, trucking, and telephony cases were able to achieve this because their ideas resonated with those politicians outside of the protective regulatory agencies. Thus, both President Gerald Ford and President Jimmy Carter appointed proderegulation reformers to the regulatory commissions. Similarly, several members of Congress, leveraging the added institutional and staffing resources that accrued to them after the decentralizing changes in the congressional institutional structure of the 1970s, provided institutional openings for this coalition.[4] Senator Edward Kennedy (D–Mass.), for example, placed transportation deregulation on the political agenda by holding well-publicized hearings in 1975. In the case of telephony, reform and resistance to AT&T was led by Lionel Van Deerlin (D–Calif.), chair of the House Subcommittee on Communications, and Lou Frey (R–Fla.), the ranking minority member of the subcommittee.[5] Deregulation thus resulted from the entrance of new actors, new ideas, and institutional changes.

The policy process surrounding television deregulation from the mid-1970s through passage of the 1996 Telecommunications Act did not fit this now established pattern. As we have seen, some policymakers did seek significant and rapid television deregulation. They sought to upset the existing policy equilibrium. Van Deerlin attempted to repeal and rewrite the 1934 Communications Act in the mid-1970s. And Federal Communications Commission (FCC) chairmen Mark Fowler and Dennis Patrick sought to deregulate administratively. Many claimed to have achieved significant deregulation with the passage of the 1996 Telecommunications Act. Though policy change did occur, much of it can be described as tinkering with the tools of television regulation. The broad contours of television regulation remained in place. The coalition of liberals and conservatives who drove other cases of deregulation never materialized in the television case. To be sure, a broad coalition of liberals and conservatives vaguely supported cable television deregulation beginning in the mid-1970s, and as Robert Britt Horwitz notes, this gave to cable television deregulation "the same veneer of reform that had cloaked the Civil Aeronautics Board and the Interstate Commerce Commission deregulatory actions."[6] But as with all veneers, this consensus was only skin deep. It extended only to cable carriage of signals that compete with broadcasters. Thus liberals saw cable signal deregulation as a way to break the "virtual stranglehold" that the three dominant television networks had over programming, and free market conservatives approved it as a way to foster competition within the television industry. But the consensus did not extend to deregulation of cable rates, services, and programming. Further, the consensus only extended to certain types of signals. Thus while liberals and conservative agreed that cable should be allowed to carry broadcast signals and special programming into local broadcast markets, they did not agree that cable should be free to choose *not* to carry broadcast signals. And the coalition in no way extended to *broadcast* television deregulation. In short, the liberal-conservative coalition, present as a driving force in other cases of deregulation, was notably absent in the television case.

The nature of television policy was an important factor that resulted in competing policy images and conflict within the larger issue context, as the policy and institutional residue of the public lobby regime of social regulation collided with a new deregulatory regime based in considerations of economic efficiency. Television policy historically evolved so that social policies, goals, and objectives were embedded and intertwined in the New Deal paradigm of economic regulation. Liberal public interest groups and their allies, therefore, viewed the issue not as an economic one but as a social one, not as a matter of economic deregulation but as an attack on social regulation. They thus mobilized to fight it. By contrast, in airline, trucking, and telephony deregulation, public interest groups wanted the economic objectives of lower prices and better services. In the television example, "better service" was a broader concept, one laden with normative dimensions. As Nicholas Johnson, then head of the National Citizens Committee for Broadcasting and former chairman of the FCC, once put it, "Economic interests are virtually the only issues involved when considering deregulation of airlines, trucking companies . . . and so forth. They are the least of our concern in broadcasting."[7] In the television example, therefore, public interest groups and their allies expanded the issues around which conflict took place, and they did so in institutional venues that favored them.

Opponents of television deregulation faced a challenge in seeking to define the issue as a social one. Those advocating deregulation saw television as an economic issue and sought to deregulate on the basis of the erosion of scarcity. Thus, public interest groups had to go beyond simply asserting vague ideas and problem definitions. It wasn't enough to simply argue that the FCC was a "toothless tiger" and that it should strengthen regulation. It wasn't enough to assert the important social aspects present in television policy. Instead, public interest groups had to create new arguments and new legal rationales on which continued regulation could be based.

Simultaneously, public interest groups needed institutional allies if they were going to be able to overcome the seeming momentum of deregulation evidenced with airlines, trucking, and telephony. They found such allies in members of Congress, particularly among Democrats, but congressional Republicans joined them at times as well. This is compelling because the television industry by and large wanted deregulation, and anecdotal evidence suggests that the television industry is a most powerful lobby on which members of Congress are particularly dependent.[8] Why, we must ask, were congressional Democrats so willing to work against the interests of an industry on which they so depended? Similarly, why were congressional Republicans so willing to buck Republican presidents, Ronald Reagan and George H. W. Bush, who consistently sided with advocates of deregulation?

The Advocates: Public Interest Groups

The strength of media-focused liberal public interest groups reached critical mass in the 1970s. The movement comprised an array of groups. Some were born of the civil rights movement and sought to increase minority ownership of, and employment in, television outlets. Others, such as the National Citizens Committee for Broadcasting, headed by former FCC chair Nicholas Johnson, came from a more consumer-oriented perspective, as did the Consumer Federation of America and the various organizations affiliated with Ralph Nader. Still others focused on particular issues. Thus Action for Children's Television focused on children's issues and the National Organization of Women focused on women's issues.

Academics from fields other than economics were an informal part of this movement. Academic economists generally took a strict promarket, proderegulation stance toward television policy issues, but academics from journalism, communications, psychology, and sociology often sided with public interest groups and argued that government should continue to take an active role in television policy. By contrast, in airline, trucking, and telephony deregulation, there were no professors of, say, aviation or trucking urging deregulators to slow down and proceed with caution. In those instances, academic economists were able to provide the sole analytical critique of the woes of regulation and offer a prescription for deregulation without facing any intellectual competition.

If the liberal groups active in media policy reached their pinnacle in the 1970s, by the early 1980s they began to undergo a transformation. This transformation was due to changes in funding and sits within the larger context of attempts by the Reagan administration to "defund the left."[9] Conservatives wanted both to remove the alleged tax benefits afforded to public interest groups and to pressure foundations to cut their funding of liberal groups, in order to dilute their influence and thereby adjust the political agenda to a more conservative bent.

As Michael Greve notes, such attempts to defund the left were, on balance, unsuccessful. In part this was because public interest groups generally had a diverse funding base, so removal of funding from any one source did not have a huge effect. Also, the budgetary assaults on public interest groups often prompted a backlash among their supporters, and public interest groups were able to increase support from them as well as find new sources of funding. Finally, foundations maintained their overall level of support for liberal groups.[10]

Though "defunding the left" did not cripple public interest groups generally, it did affect those groups focused on media issues. Perceptions that media-focused liberal public interest groups were unsuccessful at policy advocacy, the increased competition among all kinds of public interest groups for a limited pool of funding during the 1980s, and finally, changing fashions in public interest advocacy (as evidenced by the rise of environmental advocacy, for instance) caused an adjustment and consolidation among media groups.

Hence, for example, in 1980 the Clinical Law Program at Georgetown University absorbed the Citizens Communications Center (which lost its funding) and the Nader organization later absorbed the National Citizens Committee for Broadcasting.

If by the 1980s liberal media-focused public interest groups had "fallen on hard times," as one contemporaneous account put it,[11] an assortment of conservative groups had begun to emerge. The group Accuracy In Media formed around the notion that a chronic liberal bias pervaded the media, and organized to publicize the liberal inaccuracies of journalism.[12] Conservative groups also had a religious and moral component. The Coalition for Better Television, for example, which formed around Reverend Donald Wildmon's National Federation for Decency, sought to decrease the amount of sex and violence on television. Conservative groups tended to use tactics such as publicity against "liberal inaccuracies" and boycotts against the companies that advertised their products during shows that the groups deemed "indecent." But they were perfectly happy to have government work on their behalf whenever possible as well.

Though their specific policy objectives were often diametrically opposed to those of liberal organizations, such conservative groups were the unwitting allies of liberal groups. What liberal and conservative groups had in common was their focus on the social rather than the traditional economic issues involved in television policy. With this in common, they managed to keep such social issues on the public agenda.

Public interest groups faced several challenges during the debate over the 1996 Telecommunications Act. The omnibus nature of the telecommunications bill, dealing with all sectors of the larger industry, meant that media groups had to mobilize simultaneously in each of these issue areas. Hence they were organizationally challenged. Nevertheless, they often were able to form informal coalitions with specific industry segments, and the Clinton administration was a powerful ally. Thus, though challenged, they were able to keep their ideas on the agenda.

The Philosophy of Liberal Media Groups

We can better understand the specific goals and objectives of the liberal media groups by looking at their underlying philosophy. With airline, trucking, and telephone deregulation, public interest groups were concerned with the economic goals of lower prices, better service, and more choices. They believed that deregulation would lead to competitive markets that could serve those goals better than regulation. Of course, they continued to be concerned with *specific* market imperfections. For example, in the airline case, public interest groups were concerned that competition would result in the diminution of service to small and rural communities. Thus they feared that, while a competitive environment would serve most consumers, firms would not find it profitable to serve sparsely populated geographic areas. In the telephony case, they were concerned that prices would rise to the point where the elderly and poor could not afford service. But these concerns with specific market imperfections did not impede their embrace of the marketplace generally and they advocated deregulation while seeking specific corrections to the identified imperfections.[13]

In the television deregulation case, public interest groups also were concerned with market imperfections, such as the concern that the poor would be priced out of cable service or that cable companies would not anticipate a sufficient return on investment to wire rural or inner-city communities.[14] But in the television case, public interest groups expressed open skepticism about the market. They frequently noted that even a perfectly functioning marketplace would not serve important social and political objectives, but would cater solely to the desire of the mass population for entertainment programming. In some sense, the television marketplace, like other marketplaces, is democratic—viewers can vote via their remote controls for the programming they like. Ultimately, the majority "wins." Public interest groups, however, accentuated the antidemocratic aspects of the marketplace. With regard to entertainment programming, one public advocate noted:

> It is an advertiser's market, where audiences are bought and sold at a cost per thousand. The viewer has no marketplace for programs. The critics, and audience, can and do argue over how well this advertiser's market ends up serving the entertainment desires of women between 18 and 49. Many of them feel left out or insulted, too. But it certainly isn't designed to, and doesn't, serve the entertainment desires of retired men over 65—nor young children, the poor, many minority groups, the handicapped and so forth.[15]

In the television marketplace, the argument went, some "votes" are more important than others because advertisers covet some demographic groups over others.

More important, liberal media groups argued, the marketplace does not serve nonentertainment needs: corporate control of information undermines democracy itself. As Jeff Chester, of the Center for Media Education, put it during debate over the 1996 Telecommunications Act, if after deregulation a few large corporations were to dominate the television industry, programming would sink to new lows. "The tabloid programming is cheapest to produce and the violent programming is what sells globally."[16] In effect, Chester was arguing that deregulation would make the programming identified by Newton Minow in his "vast wasteland" speech look like a veritable golden age of television.

In their suspicion of the marketplace, in their critique of capitalism, and in their suspicion of big business, media reform groups echoed the concerns of their counterparts of the time, seeking increases in environmental, health and safety, and consumer protection regulation. Deriving from the belief that citizens had been locked out of meaningful participation in the political process and that the consumer was at the mercy of big business, environmental, consumer protection, and media activists were all motivated by their concern for participatory democracy and a suspicion of the establishment.[17]

Even with these common ideological roots, however, there existed subtle but important differences between the media groups and their public interest group brethren. First, liberal media groups continued to emphasize industry structure. They argued that large media conglomerates ought to be dissolved, not only for economic reasons but, more important, in order to create many outlets for many different voices and perspectives. Thus, for example, they advocated retention, even strengthening, of ownership limits. Public interest groups associated with environmental, health and safety, and consumer protection regulation also subscribed to an anti–big business ethic. Nevertheless, their policy emphasis was not so much on the dissolution of big business as it was on restraining and controlling its products and processes. They sought the control of manufacturing processes that led to pollution and unsafe products, for example. Liberal media groups, too, wanted to control the products and processes associated with television. But they never ceased in their concern with industry structure; indeed, they emphasized it.[18]

Second, liberal media groups displayed more of an antipathy to the consumer or viewer than did their counterparts in other areas of social policy, though they did share a common missionary zeal. Mainstream public interest groups in the areas of the environment, health and safety, and consumer protection also embodied a critique of consumption, consumption patterns, and consumer preferences. But they sought not to denigrate the consumer, nor to change the consumer. Rather, they sought to help the consumer, through product testing, warning labels, and increased public information and awareness. To the contrary, the liberal public interest groups that focused on the media sought to change the consumer and viewer, albeit indirectly through industry regulation.

For example, during the debate over rewriting the 1934 Communications Act, Esther Peterson, then director of the Office of Consumer Affairs, an important ally of liberal public interest groups during Van Deerlin's mid-1970s effort to rewrite the Communications Act, noted that the objective of television regulation should be to develop the political awareness of the viewer:

> The objective here is to increase the knowledge and understanding that members of the public have of current issues and developments so that they may more intelligently function as citizens. The proponents of deregulation seem to assume that this goal would be served so long as listeners and viewers who wanted to absorb some public affairs programming, and were willing to track it down assiduously were able to find it *somewhere* on the dial. Many listeners and viewers would not be so zealous in their search for edification—at least not on a regular basis—and as a consequence the overall civic literacy of the broadcast audience could be expected to decline.[19]

Though liberal public interest groups active in media issues advocated television regulation, they therefore sought indirectly to regulate the viewer. In essence, public interest groups associated with health and safety and consumer protection issues were concerned with consumers as consumers (or with the workers as workers), and they attempted to improve their lot. Media-focused liberal public interest groups were concerned with viewers as *citizens* and wanted to improve them as such. They did so because, for this issue, process and content were almost inseparable.

Media-focused liberal groups thus ultimately were concerned with the quality of U.S. democracy. To be sure, public interest groups associated with the environmental, health and safety, and consumer movements were also concerned with the quality of democracy; indeed, they sought to open up the political system and the regulatory process to individuals and representatives of the public (as did media-focused groups). But media-focused liberal groups surpassed the emphasis on process, as the examples above indicate, and emphasized the content of television and ultimately the content of U.S. politics and public debates.

The underlying ideas of the media-focused liberal groups left them open to charges that they were antidemocratic and anticapitalist. Irving Kristol, a neoconservative critic of the liberal groups, argued that they were "basically suspicious of, and hostile to, the market precisely because the market is so vulgarly democratic—one dollar, one vote" (or in the case of television, ratings and votes).[20] Such groups, however, did not advocate censorship—the intervention of government into programming through prior restraint—directly. They did not seek to prevent television outlets from airing particular programming or viewpoints and they opposed efforts (often by conservative groups) to regulate or prohibit violence, obscenity, and indecency. Rather, liberal groups sought to encourage a variety of types of programming. For example, in a 1996 interview with *Broadcasting & Cable,* a trade magazine, Peggy Charren (of Action for Children's Television) drew the distinction between *censorship* of programming and *encouragement* of programming:

> You have to be very careful when you talk about what you take off [the air]. I'm talking about what you put on. I'm not talking about what you take off. . . . If you start to say what can't appear, then you've got a big problem. Because one person's idea of sex that appears is another person's sex education. And I am violently opposed to saying, "Take it off the air, I don't like it." I am opposed to anybody saying it. Because if anyone can say it, then Jesse Helms can control my television and I'll have a nervous breakdown.[21]

Though liberal groups often were accused of advocating censorship and opposing the market, conservative media-focused groups took an equally antimarket stance, especially in their desire to rid television of sex and violence. However, there are a number of distinctions between the antimarket tendencies of the left and those of the right, stemming ultimately from differences in their ideas about morality. Conservative groups tended to view morality as given (often referencing the Bible) and absolute, while liberal groups tended to view morality as emerging from a process or dialogue. Hence, conservative groups tended to oppose the portrayal of sex and violence more intensely than liberal groups opposed large quantities of entertainment fare. Conservative groups sought to remove sex and violence from the airwaves, while liberal groups sought to balance entertainment (even entertainment riddled with sex and violence) with civic-minded programming. Conservatives seemed most concerned with saving the souls of Americans, liberals with saving democracy.

The Goals of Liberal Media Groups

Based on these values, liberal groups wanted television to serve their goal of creating enlightened citizens: television should provide a "marketplace of ideas." By this they meant that they wanted television to supply news and public affairs programming, air vigorous debates about important public issues, and make sure that all sides in the debates, all voices, would be heard over the nation's airwaves. Behind this rhetoric we can discern three specific objectives that liberal groups held for television. As portrayed in Table 5.1, these broad objectives were manifested and expressed in specific policy goals.

Civic Education

First, liberal groups wanted television to educate its audiences—that is, television should compensate for some of the deficiencies of parents and schools. Far from being a "vast wasteland," public interest groups apparently believed that television *should* be a venue where viewers could find high culture (rather than *Baywatch*), *Sesame Street* (rather than cartoons), and the news (rather than *Entertainment Tonight*). This concern was particularly targeted at children, and thus often manifested itself in their strong and sustained advocacy in favor of government requirements for children's educational television programming.[22]

But their concern extended beyond children to *civic education* for

Table 5.1   Objectives and Policy Goals of Public Interest Groups

Broad Objectives	Specific Policy Goals
Civic education	Public, educational, and government access channels on cable systems
	Mandatory carriage of broadcast stations
	Fairness Doctrine
	Children's television regulation
Diffusion of political power	Cable signal deregulation
	Affirmative action and equal employment opportunity
	Ownership regulations
Social justice and equality	Affirmative action and equal employment opportunity regulation
	Ownership regulations
	Cable rate regulation
	Children's television regulation

all citizens, and this was manifested in both Fairness Doctrine issues and cable issues. In terms of the former, public interest groups wanted to ensure that television stations covered important public issues so as to ensure that viewers could get vigorous debate on the airwaves.[23] In terms of cable television issues, the civic education goal manifested in issues concerning the so-called PEG (public, educational, and governmental) channels that each cable system provides.[24] Public interest groups wanted the law to mandate PEG channels on the premise that they would be a forum not only in which government communicated with citizens but also in which citizens communicated with each other and with government. In this sense, then, they were reflecting a traditional Jeffersonian impulse. Just as Thomas Jefferson envisioned citizen-farmers educating themselves, and their government, through conversations over the fence and in town hall meetings, liberal groups envisioned modern-day citizen-producers, citizen-broadcasters, and citizen–talk show hosts educating themselves, each other, and their government through local programming on cable access channels. For this reason, they also wanted regulations requiring cable systems to carry their local broadcasters.

Diffusion of Political Power

A second specific objective of liberal groups was the diffusion of political power. They equated access to television with access to government and political power. They therefore believed that unequal access to television would only reinforce existing inequalities in the rest of society and government. This concern was manifested in several different issue areas. It manifested in the cable arena as public interest groups advocated deregulation of cable signal carriage. They wanted cable deregulation so that cable companies, and the programming they carried, could break open the "virtual stranglehold" that television broadcasters had over what Americans watched (and by logical extension, what Americans thought about). As Jesse Jackson, then head of Operation PUSH, put it in the 1976 hearings that preceded cable signal deregulation:

> Undoubtedly, one of the most persuasive arguments for cable TV is that blacks and nonwhites in particular are locked out of much of the TV industry and have little input into this programming. One understandable response to this situation is the example of Chicano people in central and south Texas, and black people in Gary, Indiana, moving to cable TV.[25]

According to this view, if citizens could choose not only from among broadcast channels but also between cable and broadcast channels, programmers might be more responsive to the desires of a wider audience, rather than to those audience members with the more "desirable" demographics prized by advertisers. Thus, liberal groups believed that freeing cable from regulation would allow the television marketplace to be more responsive to a wider audience. This desire for television to be responsive to more than the "right" demographics also manifested in debates over affirmative action.

The desire to disperse political power also was evident in debates over ownership regulations. Liberal groups feared that deregulation of ownership limits would lead to consolidation of the television industry and that stations would be owned by massive corporate conglomerates.[26] That, coupled with the removal of regulations such as the Fairness Doctrine, would lead television stations to be responsive only to the profit motive. As Nicholas Johnson put it: "The ideas [of the television marketplace] are ideas about the odors of mouths and armpits—and praises sung to the policies and lifestyles of transnational conglomerate corporations. No, the ideas of the marketplace do not make for a marketplace of ideas."[27]

Social Justice and Equality

Related to the objective of diffusion of political power, a third goal of the public interest groups was social justice and equality. This goal was also related to the fact that many of the more active and influential groups in the movement grew out of the civil rights era. In fact, standing for public interest groups in regulatory proceedings at the FCC (and at other independent regulatory commissions) grew directly out of a case dealing with race issues.

In 1966 the broadcast license of WLBT-TV in Jackson, Mississippi, was up for renewal. Alleging that the station had repeatedly discriminated against black viewers (who constituted 45 percent of the station's potential audience), two residents of Mississippi and the local United Church of Christ and its national Office of Communications sought to intervene in the renewal proceeding. The FCC refused to hold a hearing on the renewal of the license. The Office of Communications of the United Church of Christ appealed the case to the U.S. Court of Appeals. Judge Warren Burger (future chief justice of the Supreme Court) ordered the FCC to hold a hearing and to allow public participation in it.[28] The public was granted standing in FCC proceedings. Subsequently, the Office of Communications continued to inject civil rights issues into media policy.

Clearly, this concern for equality manifested in issues such as affirmative action and equal employment opportunity. It also led liberal groups to want to retain, even strengthen, ownership regulations. They argued that the television industry must be characterized not only by a large number of owners, but by a wide variety of owners and employees as well. Their arguments, in this respect, went beyond the notion of gender and racial equity in the economic system. They argued that if women and racial and ethnic minorities were ever to have effective participation in the political system, then they must share in the ownership of the means of communication. Their central idea was not only that ownership by women and racial minorities would reduce gender, racial, and ethnic stereotyping in the media, but also that these groups must have a powerfully effective way to communicate their ideas to their communities of interest and to the larger U.S. polity, who would benefit from the expansion of voices in the public debate.

The concern for equality included not only gender and race, but socioeconomic status as well. This aspect reared its head in debates over cable rate policies. In the 1970s, when Lionel Van Deerlin made his effort to rewrite the 1934 Communications Act, he proposed to deregulate cable rates. Liberal groups, however, argued that rate regulation was necessary in order to ensure that cable would serve everyone, and not just those wealthy enough to afford it.[29] Similarly, during the movement in 1984 to deregulate cable rates, liberal groups sought to ensure that only cable systems that operated in communities in which there were also broadcast signals would be deregulated.[30] And their concern with cable rates continued to be evidenced in debates surrounding the 1996 Telecommunications Act.[31]

Finally, their concern for socioeconomic equality extended to children's television issues. When Congress was considering reregulating children's television in 1990, for example, University of Michigan psychologist Bruce Watkins argued that socioeconomic status shapes children's television viewing habits, as children aged two to eleven from poor families watched an average of thirty-three hours per week while their middle-income peers watched an average of twenty-two hours and children from upper-income families watched an average of nineteen hours. Socioeconomic status further compounded the divergence in children's viewing habits because, as Watkins commented:

> Poor children, who are less likely to have competing experiences and competing information, rely on television more as a source of news and information, and are more likely to believe television's presentations than are middle and upper income children who have access to more diverse experiences in their own lives to compare with television's portrayal of reality.[32]

Of course, many of these goals, such as citizen education and the diffusion of political power, had always been a part of the discourse surrounding television policy since passage of the 1934 Communications Act and its predecessor, the 1927 Radio Act, though liberals might argue that policymakers historically had merely paid lip service to such goals. Nevertheless, historically, these goals were generally seen by policymakers as laudable potential by-products of television's economic regulatory paradigm under the 1934 act. The actual stated cause for television regulation—the legal rationale on which all such regulation was based—was the technological condition of spectrum scarcity. Thus the challenge that confronted liberal groups beginning in the 1970s was that the scarcity rationale was rapidly eroding, and economists and some policymakers were advocating deregulation based on that erosion. Public interest groups had to create new rationales for regulating television.

New Regulatory Rationales

In light of the erosion of the scarcity rationale, liberal groups and their allies advanced new rationales in support of regulation. In doing so, they argued that television regulation ought to be continued owing to the "pervasiveness" of the medium. They also argued that, to the extent that television constituted a "public domain," policymakers must act to ensure its wise use. Finally, public interest groups attempted to modify, and thereby create a new understanding of, the scarcity rationale.

Pervasiveness

One new regulatory rationale, advanced by these opponents of deregulation, was that television is everywhere and it affects all aspects of life. It affects what we see and think and how we view the world, and that power alone is sufficient to justify regulation. As Peggy Charren, head of Action for Children's Television, once put it, "Television's messages are pervasive."[33] Interestingly, the pervasiveness rationale originated in the Supreme Court when in 1978 it upheld the FCC's authority to regulate indecent speech over the airwaves. The Court emphasized the distinction between the social nature of television and the nature of other media. The majority opinion noted:

> The reasons for these distinctions are complex. . . . First, the broadcast media have established a uniquely pervasive presence in the lives of all Americans. Patently offensive, indecent material presented over the airwaves confronts the citizen, not only in public, but also in the privacy of the home, where the individual's right to be left alone plainly outweighs the First Amendment rights of an intruder.[34]

Two ironies are associated with the use of the pervasiveness rationale by liberal groups. First, the rationale was used by the Court to justify limitations on indecent speech, limitations that liberal groups historically opposed. Nevertheless, after the Supreme Court's 1978 decision, liberal groups went on to use the rationale to justify regulations they did support. A second irony is that the very pervasiveness of the medium, its very abundance, is what undermined the scarcity rationale and placed deregulation on the agenda in the first place. Nevertheless, public interest groups picked up this rationale from the Court and enlarged upon it.

The Public Domain

A second rationale used to justify continued regulation was that television is a "public" resource. This was not so much a new idea as it was a reemphasis of an old idea. In the early days of television, Congress deemed the airwaves a "scarce public resource" and instructed the FCC to regulate the industry in the name of the public interest. In light of the erosion of the scarcity rationale, opponents of deregulation sought to reemphasize not the scarce nature of the electromagnetic spectrum, but rather its *public* nature.[35] The public owns the airwaves, regardless of whether they are scarce or not. In essence, public interest groups were articulating the public domain argument, that the state must act to ensure the safety and wise use of public property. They further were arguing that television constitutes the nation's only public *forum.*

Public interest groups were assisted, rather unwittingly, in this respect by staunch deregulators, such as FCC chairmen Mark Fowler and Dennis Patrick in the 1980s and by proderegulation congressional Republicans in the 1990s. Those who claimed to believe in the market were ready to give away this valuable resource, rather than auction it off. As such, they were not being very faithful to the economic principles they worshipped, and to this extent they undermined their own credibility. They played right into the hands of those public interest groups that wanted television broadcasters and cable system operators to provide public services.

Modified Scarcity

Public interest groups also sought to redefine the old scarcity rationale. The scarcity rationale historically was an absolute construct based on a technological condition. Scarcity either existed or it did not. In the early days of regulation, scarcity was held to exist and was based on the limited nature of the electromagnetic spectrum. Opponents of deregulation sought to very subtly redefine scarcity (hereafter called the "modified scarcity rationale"). They argued, first, that scarcity is not an absolute condition but rather a relative one. Between the two poles of scarcity and abundance lies a large middle ground. Hence opponents of deregulation noted the ability of cable, satellite, and microwave technologies to squeeze more space out of the spectrum. But they argued that technological capacity alone cannot be used to declare an end to scarcity. Rather, they raised an important public policy question—to what extent must these new technologies and new services be *available, accessible,* and *used* to warrant a determination that scarcity was ended?[36]

In keeping with their concern for equity, liberal groups also sought to redefine scarcity not as a technological condition but as a socioeconomic one. They voiced a concern that new technologies, the growth of which was the basis for the deregulation movement, might not be available to, or would be financially out of reach of, the rural and urban poor. They argued that cable companies might not find it profitable to wire poor and rural areas, fearing an insufficient return on the investment in infrastructure. Liberal groups noted also that even if these areas did have new technologies available, the poor would be unable to utilize them if they could not afford them.[37] Liberal groups argued that, regardless of new technologies, broadcast television should remain regulated because, for those of a lower socioeconomic status, the broadcast medium would remain their only source of television. Liberal groups were suggesting that if we cannot determine what scarcity is and how we know when it is gone, then we cannot deregulate on the basis of its erosion.

Liberal groups thus believed that the television environment should pursue three broad objectives: civic education, diffusion of political power, and social equity. These broad objectives were expressed in specific policy goals. Liberal groups agreed that cable signal carriage should be deregulated, and this consensus was similar to the consensus that emerged in the airline, trucking, and telephony cases. But they also believed that other aspects of cable should remain regulated. They wanted public, educational, and governmental access channels. They wanted rules requiring cable system operators to include local broadcast signals on their channel assignments. They wanted cable rate regulation in order to ensure that cable technology remained available and accessible to all. But they also recognized that cable would not be accessible to all, or that some people might not choose to subscribe. Therefore, they wanted broadcast television to remain regulated as well. They wanted the continuation of limited license terms, rather than licenses in perpetuity. They wanted ownership regulations to ensure that the industry did not become overly concentrated, crowding out other voices. And finally, they wanted continuation of the Fairness Doctrine, affirmative action, and equal employment opportunity regulations as well as children's television regulations. They grounded these policy goals in three new regulatory rationales: that television is pervasive, that the television environment constitutes a public domain and public forum, and that while technological scarcity may have ended, socioeconomic scarcity remained.

Institutional Allies

In terms of the institutional allies of public interest groups, the era under consideration here can be divided into two periods. During the 1970s (when Van Deerlin attempted to rewrite the 1934 Communications Act) and the 1980s (when Chairman Fowler, and later Chairman Patrick, attempted to deregulate via the FCC), Democrats either held a majority in Congress or, from 1981 to 1987, shared power when the Republicans had control of the Senate. The second period, during which the 1996 Telecommunications Act was being debated and passed, was characterized by Republican control of Congress. During both of these periods, support came predominantly from congressional Democrats. But during the 1970s and 1980s, there were specific issues on which Republicans joined them. By the 1990s, however, congressional Republicans (especially those allied with Speaker Newt Gingrich) were far more deregulatory.

It is often alleged that politicians pander to the television industry because of its political clout. As J. H. Snider and Benjamin Page note, "The National Association of Broadcasters (NAB), the largest broadcaster trade organization, is widely recognized as one of the most effective lobbies in Washington, D.C."[38] Yet we know that television interests did not get from Congress the extent of deregulation that they wanted. Thus, if television interests are so powerful, why didn't members of Congress simply bow to the interests of the industry? Why didn't members of Congress simply kowtow to dominant sectors or firms or let television interests bargain among themselves? Further, how can we account for the fact that on certain issues Republicans joined Democrats to oppose Republican presidents Ronald Reagan and George H. W. Bush? Finally, why did congressional Republicans in the 1990s turn decisively toward deregulation?

Voices and Echoes in Congress

The most significant opposition to Lionel Van Deerlin's effort to rewrite the 1934 act came from his colleagues on the House Communications Subcommittee who were hostile to the broadcast television deregulation embodied in Van Deerlin's bill. Many, such as Timothy Wirth (D–Colo.), directly challenged Van Deerlin's assumptions that deregulation would lead to competition and the end of scarcity.[39] Others, notably Al Swift (D–Wash.), doubted whether marketplace forces would provide viewers with information and public affairs programming. In an exchange with a head of the CBS network, Swift challenged, "It seems to me that if we go to total deregulation and that the marketplace forces will dictate what you produce, I see no force in the marketplace which is going to encourage this kind of programming."[40] Echoing the sentiments of many members of the subcommittee, Al Gore concluded, "I think the arm's length regulatory framework that has developed . . . in the current [1934] Act is, you know, it may be the best we can come up with."[41]

Van Deerlin's legislation also had little support in the Senate, where Ernest Hollings (D–S.C.), chair of the Senate Subcommittee on Communications, and Barry Goldwater (R–Ariz.), the subcommittee's ranking minority member, each introduced separate bills that were far less deregulatory than Van Deerlin's.[42] Both bills, unlike Van Deerlin's, would have retained the social policies of equal employment opportunity regulations, affirmative action programs, the Fairness Doctrine, and programming regulation.

By the 1980s we see the noticeable ideological polarization of the two parties as the South became more Republican and the views of congressional Democrats came into sharper focus and echoed the views expressed by liberal groups. A report by the majority staff of the House Telecommunications Subcommittee mirrored the regulatory rationales voiced by public interest groups. The report called into question the "end of scarcity" rationale for television deregulation. In its analysis the staff report subtly redefined the concept of scarcity from an absolute construct to a relative one: "Even as cable becomes more available, questions remain as to *what level of passby* and *how many channels* . . . when combined with the availability of outlets from other video technologies, are necessary to warrant determination that the traditional scarcity rationale has been overcome."[43] The majority staff questioned the central premise of deregulators, that the mere existence of new and alternative technologies equaled the end of scarcity. Echoing public interest groups, the report also redefined scarcity from a technological condition to a socioeconomic one, noting:

> The question of the cost of cable service is an issue in cross elasticity that becomes sharply relevant with respect to those who cannot afford the cost of cable service. If rates of basic cable service are not maintained at a low level, prices may put certain cable services beyond the reach of some members of the public, rendering many new outlets inelastic with broadcast television from the standpoint of these viewers.[44]

The report suggested that, despite the ability of innovation to reduce the technological basis of scarcity, scarcity may well become a socioeconomic condition. To deregulate television on the sole basis of technological innovation would disserve those sectors of society that may not have access to new technologies and that would continue to rely on broadcast television. For the poor, scarcity would continue to exist.

Finally, though the report was concerned only with questions of scarcity and competition, it did raise other factors to be considered in television deregulation. For example, alluding to the pervasiveness rationale, the report noted:

> One might argue that the presence of three television stations in a market does not pose a problem of outlet scarcity because, by comparison, if only one daily newspaper is published in the community, video outlets appear more abundant. Nevertheless, one might still make a judgment that continued imposition of television regulation to insure the public interest is necessitated by the power and dominance of the medium.[45]

Similarly, in hearings held by the subcommittee in December 1981, members of the Democratic majority made further arguments in favor of continued regulation. Among these were assertions that broadcasters were using a "public resource" and therefore owed something to the public in exchange for its use.[46] Full committee chairman John Dingell (D–Mich.) argued most forcefully in favor of continued regulation, noting: "The airwaves are a public trust. . . . They do belong to all the people and that licensing which takes place for the broadcasters is for those broadcasters to use the airwaves first of all, as a public trust and to serve the public interest; and second, to make a decent and proper profit."[47] House Democrats in 1981 were siding with public interest groups and throwing down the gauntlet in the face of the new Republican Reagan administration and its appointees at the FCC.

Partisan Agreement and Disagreement in Congress

In the 1970s and 1980s, partisan disagreement in Congress occurred around the issues of affirmative action and equal employment opportunity, with Democrats generally in favor of policies promoting these values and Republicans generally opposed. In fact, Republican opposition to the application of these regulations to cable television firms in the 1984 Cable Act nearly killed the legislation, until Democrats agreed to add antiobscenity measures. The 1992 Cable Act (regulating rates) and the 1990 Children's Television Act (reregulating children's programming) posed problems for Republicans. President Bush was very much in favor of deregulation, but congressional Republicans had incentives to be responsive to constituents, who favored these policies. The ground swell of public opinion surrounding reregulation of children's television in 1990 and cable rate reregulation in 1992 was too loud to ignore. Congressional Republicans thus joined with Democrats to pass the 1990 Children's Television Act into law (without the signature of President Bush) and again in 1992 to pass legislating reregulating cable rates (over President Bush's veto). These same forces had joined the coalition advocating cable signal and rate deregulation in 1984.

Special Concerns of Members of Congress

It is with regard to the FCC's attempt in the 1980s to repeal the ownership regulations and the Fairness Doctrine, however, that the puzzle becomes so interesting. In these two issue areas, Republicans and Democrats joined forces to attempt to overcome both FCC deregulatory actions as well as industry wishes. They did so in the absence of public attention to these issues. And Republicans did so despite the contrary views of their president.

In 1984, when the FCC attempted to repeal its ownership regulations, bipartisan congressional reaction was swift. Within one week after the FCC's announcement a Senate conference committee, working on a supplemental appropriations bill, inserted a provision preventing the FCC's action from taking effect before April 1, 1985,[48] and Representatives Mickey Leland (D–Tex.), John Dingell (D–Mich.), and Timothy Wirth (D–Colo.) introduced H.R. 6134 to codify a modified ownership law. A companion bill, S. 2962, was introduced in the Senate. Because members of Congress entered into negotiations with Chairman Fowler, and they reached an agreement on modified ownership regulations, the House never took up the bills but did stem the tide of the FCC action.

Similarly in the case of the Fairness Doctrine, Republicans and Democrats joined forces to fight the FCC. When the FCC announced its plans to repeal the doctrine, Congress passed legislation codifying it in the spring of 1987.[49] The House bill had forty-two cosponsors from both political parties and support from both liberal and conservative public interest groups. Nevertheless, President Reagan vetoed the legislation on First Amendment grounds and the FCC subsequently repealed the doctrine.[50] The House and Senate again passed legislation in 1989, but the bill stalled in the face of veto threats from President Bush.[51]

Congressional hostility toward FCC action was not based on any economic concerns per se. That is, in the case of ownership regulations, members of Congress were not worried about the economic effects of industry concentration. And in the case of the Fairness Doctrine, they did not base their fight on the technological scarcity issue. Indeed, there is no evidence of such economic concerns in the record. Rather, they believed that repealing the ownership regulations and the Fairness Doctrine would place too much social and political power in the hands of big broadcasters and, especially, the major television networks. Liberals feared a conservative bias among the networks while conservatives feared a liberal bias. For liberals, the fear was that the marketplace of ideas would become more circumscribed absent the diversifying voices of minorities and smaller television groups. For example, Representative Leland said of the FCC action:

> If carried out, the elimination of the multiple ownership rules would seriously undermine the Commission's historic commitment to ensuring diversity of ownership. Such a change would have a devastating impact on the level of ownership of broadcast properties by minorities and small business. The elimination of ownership limits would encourage the large group owners and the networks to expand their ownership interests greatly. The consolidation of station ownership into fewer hands would serve to undermine the diversity of viewpoints.[52]

Conservatives, who perceived a liberal bias in the network news divisions, also feared that expanded network dominance would be to their political disadvantage. Thus, FCC arguments notwithstanding, liberals and conservatives alike rallied around the notion that increased network expansion was antithetical to a marketplace of diverse ideas. One analyst quipped, "Just tell Congress this will increase the power of the networks and they'll throw it out."[53]

The same dynamic occurred in debates over the Fairness Doctrine. Both Democrats and Republicans were concerned that, absent a Fairness Doctrine, television news might work against them. Conservatives had long worried about a liberal bias among the media, particularly among the three networks. Such charges had been led by Reed Irvine, chairman of Accuracy In Media, and columnist Patrick Buchanan.[54] Indeed at hearings on Fairness Doctrine legislation, Phyllis Schlafly, president of the conservative group Eagle Forum, noted the "anti-Reagan bias of the TV network newscasts."[55] Liberals, on the other hand, were concerned about a conservative media bias. Robert M. Gurss, a staff attorney for the liberal group Media Access Project, noted that his organization was concerned about the repeal of the doctrine because of the "little radio station in the middle of nowhere with some guy who runs it as his personal mouthpiece."[56]

Finally, the Fairness Doctrine had long been called an "incumbent's law" by members of the media.[57] This was due to the perception among members of Congress that the doctrine protected them from an inherently adversarial press and journalists who slant their news accounts against the incumbent, regardless of party. The Fairness Doctrine, members of Congress believed, did not protect them from attack journalism, but did allow them the right to respond. As Representative Billy Tauzin (D–La.) noted:

To those of the conservative bent, the Doctrine was sweet because it meant some way to make sure those doggone liberals who control the press were not going to have their way with the airwaves without having somebody respond to them. To those of the liberal bent, it meant that those doggone conservative owners of broadcasting in America were not going to have their doggone conservative way without having someone called forward to respond to their particular views.[58]

Institutional concerns also drove congressional action, especially in the Fairness Doctrine case. After years of attempted administrative policy change, first under Chairman Fowler and then under Chairman Patrick of the FCC, members of Congress wanted to reassert that body's role in communications policymaking. Indeed, Representative Swift challenged: "The FCC is taking full advantage of the fact that Congress is an extremely powerful, but muscle-bound, giant who sometimes has trouble getting up off its inertia to do anything."[59] Even Representative Tauzin, usually no friend of regulation, made a compelling institutional argument:

Let me point out to you there is another imperative for us to act. I'm frankly sick and tired of somebody other than Congress making communications policy in America . . . and I think it's time for Congress, this subcommittee and this committee, to begin declaring what the communications policy of America is again. If the Supreme Court disagrees with us, let us take . . . those acts down as unconstitutional, but whatever the policy is, it ought to be made here as a general rule. It ought to be implemented, more clearly defined, perhaps, in the administrative process, and it ought to be judged in the court system, but it ought to be made here.[60]

Republicans and Democrats echoed regulatory rationales proposed by liberal public interest groups.[61] In particular, Democrats tended to assert the modified scarcity rationale, while Representative Thomas Bliley (R–Va.) alluded to the dominance, or pervasiveness, of the medium, noting: "We know from polls that the American public forms its attitudes 70 percent of the time from what they see on television; not what they read, but what they see. And for me, that's a terrific problem."[62]

Congressional Republicans during the Reagan and Bush years thus joined their Democratic colleagues in seeking to retain the Fairness Doctrine and ownership regulations. By and large, we can account for this by referring to their different political considerations, which are grounded in the separation of powers, and the different constituencies represented by members of Congress and the president. Members of Congress get far less attention in television news than do presidents. Stories about Congress tend to be placed later in newscasts than are stories about presidents. And the networks tend to spend more airtime on stories about presidents. As one analyst put it, "The 435 members of the House and 100 members of the Senate compete for the crumbs of network time left after the president has got his share."[63]

As Doris Graber notes, the presidency is easier to report on because it is embodied in one person, while Congress is far more fragmented. Because the president personifies the nation, it is easier for reporters to dramatize and personalize his or her actions. Further, news stories about the presidency are far easier to tell to the public because reporters can report on what the president has done. Contrast this to the complex process in which members of Congress engage in order to pass legislation.[64] Members of Congress rely more on their local stations for publicity than on the national networks.

Members of Congress, Republicans and Democrats alike, thus feared removal of the Fairness Doctrine and ownership regulation because they believed their removal would give more power to the networks. Republicans feared a liberal bias and Democrats feared a conservative bias. Republicans feared that small owners would be squeezed out, while Democrats feared that women and minorities would be elbowed out of a universe of giant media conglomerates. All members of Congress feared less coverage and, by extension, feared that greater power would flow to the president. Such overtly political considerations were absent from debates over airline, trucking, and telephone deregulation.

Congressional Republicans and the 1996 Telecommunications Act

By the time period leading to formulation, debate, and passage of the 1996 Telecommunications Act, congressional Republicans had become far more uniformly in support of deregulation than they had been in previous years.[65] In part this was due to ideological change. The slew of new, young Republicans who dominated the 104th Congress as a result of the 1994 elections were far more ideologically in favor of the free market and, indeed, opposed to government, having campaigned on promises to deregulate embodied in their "Contract with America." But the political concerns of Republicans also had changed since the 1980s. Although many Republicans in the 1980s fought attempts to deregulate television, some deregulation did take place during that time. In particular, ownership limits were slightly relaxed and the FCC repealed the Fairness Doctrine, and Republicans discovered that they benefited from these changes. With the repeal of the doctrine, television and radio stations no longer had to fear license revocation for failure to air both sides of important public controversies. Hence, after the repeal, ideologically driven talk show hosts such as Rush Limbaugh became popular media figures. With the relaxation of the ownership limitations in the 1980s, these new conservative superstars were splashed across television screens throughout the country. All of this helped Republicans.

Even so, many congressional Republicans continued to express ambivalence over ownership limitations during debate and passage of the 1996 Telecommunications Act. Many had not given up their concern for small broadcasters, many of which are religious broadcasters. This concern manifested in a struggle between Jesse Helms and Robert Dole. Helms offered a successful amendment to retain the ownership limitations of the time. Senator Dole was subsequently able to persuade several Republicans to switch their votes and his amendment, to relax the limits, passed and was signed into law as part of the 1996 act.[66] Given the risk-averse nature of members of Congress, coupled with Republican ambivalence on ownership limitations and staunch Democratic resistance to total deregulation, members of Congress did not entirely unleash the television industry.

Ideas and Interests in Television Policy

Beginning in the mid-1970s, policymakers and activists waged a pitched battle over television regulation and deregulation. A broad consensus did form across the political spectrum around deregulating cable carriage of broadcast signals, but the consensus ended there. Important policymakers (Van Deerlin in the 1970s, Chairmen Fowler and Patrick from their perch at the FCC in the 1980s, and congressional Republicans in the middle to late 1990s) attempted to achieve dramatic deregulation. Though some regulatory relaxation did occur, and while there was a great deal of tinkering with the policy tools of television regulation, they did not get the extent of deregulation that they wanted (nor did important industry actors). The coalition of liberals and conservatives that provided the momentum for airline, trucking, and telephony deregulation never materialized around most aspects of television deregulation.

Rather, in the television case, the philosophical, institutional, and policy aspects of the public lobby regime of social regulation crashed into the drive for deregulation and the concerns for economic efficiency and technological change. Liberal public interest groups and their allies opposed deregulation. They did so by expanding the conflict surrounding television policy to include important social issues that were absent in other cases of economic deregulation. As a result, in the television case, the drive for economic deregulation intersected with a whole host of social policy issues that dramatically complicated policy change. Public interest groups and their allies complicated the terms of the debate. They did so because they emphasized the social aspects of television policy, rather than its economic aspects. They did not focus so much on issues of economic competition (which they didn't believe would result from deregulation anyway), but on their broader objectives, for the television environment, of civic education, the diffusion of political power, and social equity.

In order to do this, beginning in the 1970s they had to push the issue out of the institutional confines of the FCC, which they saw as bound to the interests of the broadcast television industry. To be sure, the FCC historically had developed social policies for television, but public interest groups saw the FCC as a "toothless tiger" and saw the dominant television networks as having a "virtual stranglehold" over what Americans watched on television (and implicit in this latter point, over the FCC's regulatory action or inaction). Implicit in these metaphors was a call for congressional intervention.

The peculiar nature of television policy, however, posed a challenge to public interest groups and their allies. The social policies that they prized were embedded in the broader New Deal paradigm of economic regulation and hinged on the scarcity rationale. With scarcity eroding, public interest groups had to create and advocate new rationales—pervasiveness, public domain, and modified scarcity—for regulation.

Members of Congress were receptive to the calls from public interest groups. In particular, congressional Democrats allied with liberal public interest groups and stymied Van Deerlin's Communications Act rewrite effort in the 1970s. And they consistently fought the efforts of Chairmen Fowler and Patrick in the 1980s and early 1990s to deregulate administratively through the rule-making process at the FCC. In the 1970s and 1980s, however, congressional Republicans often joined the fray on the side of public interest groups and their allies. First, they too were concerned with the social aspects of television, particularly with sexually explicit, violent, and indecent content at least in part as a response to conservative groups. But they also shared with congressional Democrats the special concerns of members of Congress about their relationship with the media and, in particular, with the major television networks. This accounts for the fact that, contrary to the folklore that members of Congress pander to the television industry, they actually sought to keep the industry on a regulatory leash.

By the mid-1990s, congressional Republicans (in the majority) were decidedly more ideologically conservative and hence in favor of the free market and deregulation. Perhaps more to the point, they had benefited from the previous repeal of the Fairness Doctrine and the previous relaxation of ownership limits. The politics of television policy thus became much more partisan and the incremental nature of the 1996 Telecommunications Act resulted in part from partisan compromise.

In short, the politics of television policy since the mid-1970s were characterized by a struggle to define the issue and the problem, a struggle to set the terms of debate. Neither those who stressed the economic aspects nor those who stressed the social aspects were able to dominate this policy arena. Television policy sits at the intersection of the politics of economic regulation and deregulation and the politics of social regulation and deregulation. In this environment, policy change was highly conflict-ridden and policy outputs were highly ambiguous and fluid.

Notes

1. Baumgartner and Jones, *Agendas and Instability in American Politics.*
2. Derthick and Quirk, *The Politics of Deregulation.*
3. Schattschneider, *The Semisovereign People,* p. 71.
4. On these institutional changes, see Dodd, "Rise of the Technocratic Congress"; and Bosso, *Pesticides and Politics,* chap. 7.

5. For additional institutional perspectives on deregulation, see Geller, "Regulation and Public Policy After Divestiture"; Wiley, "The End of Monopoly"; and Behrman, "Civil Aeronautics Board."

6. Horwitz, *The Irony of Regulatory Reform*, p. 259.

7. U.S. House of Representatives, Subcommittee on Communications of the Committee on Interstate and Foreign Commerce, *The Communications Act of 1979*, vol. 2, pt. 1, p. 528.

8. See, for example, Wayne, "Broadcast Lobby Excels at the Washington Power Game"; "Off the Dole"; and Mills and Farhi, "Dole Statement Snags Phone, Cable TV Bill."

9. Stanfield, "'Defunding the Left' May Remain Just Another Fond Dream."

10. Greve, "Why 'Defunding the Left' Failed."

11. Krasnow, Longley, and Terry, *The Politics of Broadcast Regulation*, p. 60.

12. "Crusades Set Out to Clean Up TV," pp. 27–29.

13. They sought subsidies to small communities in the case of airline deregulation and reduced "lifeline rates" for basic telephone service for the elderly and the poor.

14. See testimony by Nicholas Johnson (National Citizens Committee for Broadcasting), Everett Parker (Office of Communications of the United Church of Christ), and Kathleen Nolan (Coalition for Public Rights in Broadcasting) in U.S. House of Representatives, Subcommittee on Communications of the Committee on Interstate and Foreign Commerce, *The Communications Act of 1978*, vol. 3. See also "The Bills Are Back"; "Getting Down to Brass Tacks on Cable Deregulation"; Kerr, "Cable TV Notes"; "Cable Strikes a Deal with Cities"; and Sohn and Schwartzman, *Pretty Pictures of Pretty Profits*. See also testimony by Andrew Schwartzman (Media Access Project) in U.S. House of Representatives, Subcommittee on Telecommunications and Finance of the Committee on Commerce, *Communications Law Reform*.

15. Nicholas Johnson, quoted in House Subcommittee, *The Communications Act of 1979*, vol. 2, pt. 1, p. 529.

16. Quoted in Mills, "Dole Goes to Bat," p. A14.

17. For elaboration of this idea, see Harris and Milkis, *The Politics of Regulatory Change*, esp. chap. 3.

18. See testimony by Nicholas Johnson (National Citizens Committee for Broadcasting) in House Subcommittee, *The Communications Act of 1978*, vol. 1; Nolan Bowie (Citizens Communications Center), vol. 3; Office of Communications of the United Church of Christ, in House Subcommittee, *The Communications Act of 1979*, vol. 2; and the American Civil Liberties Union, vol. 2, pt. 1. See testimony by Gene Kimmelman (Consumer Federation of America) in U.S. House of Representatives, Subcommittee on Telecommunications and Finance of the Committee on Energy and Commerce, *Cable Television Regulation*, pt. 1. Also see Mills, "Dole Goes to Bat."

19. Quoted in House Subcommittee, *The Communications Act of 1979*, vol. 2, pt. 3, p. 1834 (emphasis in original).

20. Kristol, *Two Cheers for Capitalism*, p. 26.

21. Jessell, "Peggy Charren," p. 24.

22. See testimony by Peggy Charren (Action for Children's Television) in House Subcommittee, *The Communications Act of 1978*, vol. 5, pt. 1; and Peggy Charren, Bruce Watkins (Department of Psychology, University of Michigan), Dale Kunkel (Department of Communications, University of California at Santa Barbara), and Ellen Wartella (University of Illinois) in U.S. House of Representatives, Subcommittee on Telecommunications and Finance of the Committee on Energy and Commerce, *Commercialization of Children's Television*.

23. See testimony by Grace Basinger (PTA) and Office of Communications of the United Church of Christ, in House Subcommittee, *The Communications Act of 1979*, vol. 2, pt. 1. See also references to statements made by the Media Access Project and the Telecommunications Research and Action Center in U.S. Federal Communications Commission, *Fairness Doctrine Inquiry*, paras. 88–89.

24. See, for example, testimony by the American Civil Liberties Union in House Subcommittee, *The Communications Act of 1979*, vol. 2, pt. 1.

25. Jesse Jackson, in House Subcommittee, *Hearings on Regulating Cable Television*, p. 730.

26. See testimony by Nicholas Johnson (National Citizens Committee for Broadcasting) in House Subcommittee, *The Communications Act of 1978*, vol. 1; Nolan Bowie (Citizens Communications Center), vol. 3; and Office of Communications of the United Church of Christ and Barry Cole (Annenberg School, University of Pennsylvania) in House Subcommittee, *The Communications Act of 1979*, vol. 2, pt. 2.

27. Quoted in House Subcommittee, *The Communications Act of 1979*, vol. 2, pt. 1, p. 529.

28. *Office of Communications of the United Church of Christ v. Federal Communications Commission*, 359 F. 2d 994. Even after holding the hearing, however, the FCC determined that the complaint did not warrant stripping WLBT of its license. The United Church of Christ appealed again and this time the FCC's decision was overturned. See *Office of Communications of the United Church of Christ v. Federal Communications Commission*, 425 F. 2d 543.

29. See testimony by Charles Firestone (American Civil Liberties Union) in House Subcommittee, *The Communications Act of 1979*, vol. 2, pt. 1.

30. "The Bills Are Back"; "S. 66 Markup Postponed"; "Getting Down to Brass Tacks on Cable Deregulation;" and "S. 66 Wins Big in the Senate."

31. See Healey, "Republicans' Cable Plan Strikes a Nerve."

32. Quoted in House Subcommittee, *Commercialization of Children's Television*, pp. 325–326.

33. Quoted in House Subcommittee, *The Communications Act of 1978*, vol. 5, pt. 1, p. 141; see also the testimony by Nicholas Johnson, vol. 3, p. 676. Finally, see testimony by Bruce Watkins, Ellen Wartella, and Dale Kunkel in House Subcommittee, *Commercialization of Children's Television*.

34. *Federal Communications Commission v. Pacifica Foundation.*

35. See, for example, testimony by Nolan Bowie (Citizens Communications Center) in House Subcommittee, *The Communications Act of 1978,* vol. 3.

36. See, for example, testimony by Nicholas Johnson (National Citizens Committee for Broadcasting), Everett Parker (Office of Communications of the United Church of Christ), and Kathleen Nolan (Coalition for Public Rights in Broadcasting) in House Subcommittee, *The Communications Act of 1978,* vol. 3, pp. 674–680, 496–502, and 263–270 respectively. See also testimony by Barry Cole (Annenberg School, University of Pennsylvania) in House Subcommittee, *The Communications Act of 1978,* vol. 1, p. 460; Nolan Bowie (Citizens Communications Center) in House Subcommittee, *The Communications Act of 1979,* vol. 2, pt. 2, p. 842; and Ralph Jennings (Office of Communications of the United Church of Christ) in House Subcommittee, *Communications Act of 1979,* vol. 2, pt. 2, p. 871. See also submissions by public interest groups in the FCC rulemaking in U.S. Federal Communications Commission, *Revision of Television Deregulation.*

37. See testimony by Charles Firestone (American Civil Liberties Union) in House Subcommittee, *The Communications Act of 1979,* vol. 2, pt. 1, p. 612; and Nolan Bowie (Citizens Communications Center), vol. 2, pt. 2, p. 842; as well as public interest group comments in U.S. Federal Communications Commission, *Revision of Television Deregulation.* See testimony by Bruce Watkins (Department of Psychology, University of Michigan) and Dale Kunkel (Department of Communications, University of California) in House Subcommittee, *Commercialization of Children's Television,* pp. 325–326 and 335 respectively.

38. Snider and Page, "The Political Power of TV Broadcasters," p. 4.

39. House Subcommittee, *The Communications Act of 1979,* vol. 2, pt. 1, p. 87.

40. Quoted in House Subcommittee, *The Communications Act of 1979,* vol. 2, pt. 1, p. 552; see also remarks by Albert Gore (D–Tenn.), vol. 2, pt. 2, p. 1355.

41. Quoted in House Subcommittee, *The Communications Act of 1979,* vol. 2, pt. 2, p. 1360; see also remarks by Carlos Moorhead (R–Calif.), vol. 2, pt. 2, pp. 1355–1357; and Marc Marks (R–Ohio), vol. 2, pt. 1, p. 565.

42. See "Senate Bills 611 & 622," reprinted in U.S. Senate Subcommittee on Communications of the Committee on Commerce, Science, and Transportation, *Amendments to the Communications Act of 1934: Hearings in S.611 and S.622.*

43. U.S. House of Representatives, Majority Staff of the Subcommittee on Telecommunications, Consumer Protection, and Finance of the Committee on Energy and Commerce, *Telecommunications in Transition* (emphasis added).

44. Ibid., p. 362.

45. Ibid., p. 347.

46. See, for example, remarks by Representative Wirth in U.S. House

of Representatives, Subcommittee on Telecommunications, Consumer Protection, and Finance of the Committee on Energy and Commerce, *Broadcast Reform Proposals,* pp. 1–2.

47. Quoted in ibid., p. 63; 66–70.

48. Pressman, "Congress Clears Supplemental FY '84 Funding," p. 11.

49. Starobin, "'Fairness Doctrine' Has Had a Tangled Past."

50. Reagan, *Veto—S. 742.*

51. Calmes, "Deficit-Reduction Measure Already Behind Schedule"; Pytte, "Fairness Doctrine, Dial-a-Porn Coupled on House Measure"; and Calmes, "Bush, Congress Reach Deal on Deficit-Reduction Bill."

52. Quoted in U.S. House of Representatives, Subcommittee on Telecommunications, Consumer Protection, and Finance, *Broadcast Regulation and Station Ownership,* p. 68. See also "Power Envy"; "Striking a Blow for Small Broadcasters"; Cooper, "Fowler's FCC Learns Some Hard Lessons"; and "Knocking the Networks."

53. Quoted in "Power Envy," p. 50.

54. Calmes, "Groundwork Laid," p. 1303.

55. Quoted in U.S. House of Representatives, Subcommittee on Telecommunications and Finance of the Committee on Energy and Commerce, *Broadcasters and the Fairness Doctrine,* p. 247.

56. Quoted in Calmes, "Groundwork Laid," p. 1303.

57. Starobin, "FCC and Congress Clash over Proper Roles," p. 479.

58. Quoted in U.S. House of Representatives, Subcommittee on Telecommunications and Finance of the Committee on Energy and Commerce, *Fairness Doctrine Legislation,* p. 43.

59. Quoted in Starobin, "FCC and Congress Clash over Proper Roles," p. 480.

60. Quoted in House Subcommittee, *Fairness Doctrine Legislation,* p. 43.

61. See House Subcommittee, *Broadcasters and the Fairness Doctrine,* remarks by Matthew Rinaldo (R–N.J.), p. 51; Ed Markey (D–Mass.), p. 277; and Thomas Bliley Jr. (R–Va.), p. 74.

62. House Subcommittee, *Broadcasters and the Fairness Doctrine,* p. 74.

63. Kathleen Hall Jamieson (*Eloquence in an Electronic Age,* p. 14) quoted in Graber, *Mass Media and American Politics,* p. 289.

64. Graber, *Mass Media and American Politics,* pp. 288–291.

65. For an explanation of why the 1996 Telecommunications Act passed, see, for example, Olufs, *The Making of Telecommunications Policy.*

66. Healey, "Rejecting Further Regulation, Senate Easily Passes Bill."

6

The Limits of
Television Deregulation

WE BEGAN WITH THE ASSERTION THAT TELEVISION DEREGULATION WAS incremental, incomplete, and highly ambiguous. We also identified the task of explaining the nature of television deregulation by way of testing three different understandings of regulation and regulatory policy change: market forces theory, industry determinism theory, and a contingency framework. This chapter summarizes the findings and provides a comprehensive understanding of the history and nature of television deregulation. It also uses the television example to shed light on debates over regulation and regulatory theory.

Continuity and Change in Television Policy

This volume has investigated television regulatory policy change from roughly the mid-1970s to the passage of the 1996 Telecommunications Act. As of 1996, the net policy change was decidedly incremental. Cable carriage of broadcaster signals was deregulated and telephone companies could offer video programming services. But government, meaning the Federal Communications Commission (FCC) with significant and substantial oversight from Congress, still oversaw competition between these sectors and regulated each sector accordingly. With regard to broadcast television, license terms were extended and the renewal process was streamlined. The FCC still was responsible for allocating spectrum and broadcasters still were required to seek license renewal periodically. Ownership regulations were relaxed but they were not repealed. Children's television programming was more highly regulated than at any time in history and the FCC still oversaw equal employment opportunity. The only example of decisive deregulation was the FCC's repeal of the Fairness Doctrine in 1987. The latter, of course, was not decisive in the sense that there was agreement on it; there was no agreement on it at all. Rather, it was decisive in the sense that it was repealed entirely (versus incrementally relaxed) and it was never reinstated. What is more, the period under consideration also encompassed several significant policy fluctuations. Thus, for example, children's television programming was deregulated and then reregulated. Cable television rates were deregulated, reregulated, and partially deregulated again.

Since passage of the 1996 Telecommunications Act, there has been no return to policy equilibrium. To the contrary, events in television policy since passage of the act vividly demonstrate the continuation of the patterns described above. Policy change seemed always to be on the agenda and policy always seemed to be in flux. Yet actual change has been incomplete, incremental, divisive, and ambiguous.

Following passage of the 1996 act, President Bill Clinton served out another full term. In January 2001, President George W. Bush was sworn into office. Each of these presidents attempted to shape television policy via appointments to the FCC. Clinton's appointed chairman, Reed Hundt, was an antitrust lawyer with a keen interest in spurring and maintaining competition. But he, like Clinton, believed that government has an important role to play in promoting competition and preserving through regulation the obligations of television firms to behave in socially responsible ways. Indeed, Hundt specifically drew a distinction between himself and Mark Fowler, his Reagan-era predecessor at the FCC:

> There are two distinct paths to follow. One path, brilliantly articulated by my predecessor and friend Mark Fowler . . . replaces the concept of the broadcaster as a public trustee with broadcasters as market participants, responding only to market forces. . . . I prefer a different path—one that reaffirms the idea of broadcasters as public trustees but that brings that concept into the digital age.[1]

In a 1996 speech titled "The Hard Road Ahead"—perhaps a sober response to the dramatic vision of the new telecommunications universe articulated in Bill Gates's book *The Road Ahead*—Hundt laid out a two-pronged approach to what he believed to be the FCC's role. That approach included use of "(a) competition and, where that doesn't work completely or equitably, (b) proactive social policies."[2] Specifically, Hundt wanted not only to reaffirm broadcasters' obligation to serve the public interest, but also to *quantify* their public interest obligations. Thus, in addition to monitoring ownership patterns and media concentration, Hundt pledged to quantify such broadcaster obligations as providing children's television programming.

In 1997 Bill Kennard replaced Hundt as FCC chairman. Kennard was a broadcast attorney who in the early part of his career represented the National Association of Broadcasters (NAB). Seemingly, he would be friendly to television stations. However, he too believed in a positive role for the FCC and promised to actively and aggressively ensure that the industry would remain diverse. At his first speech to the NAB, he noted, "I believe that no single competitor should have the power to unilaterally dictate the choices that you or I or any consumer makes."[3]

In the years following passage of the 1996 Telecommunications Act, the FCC and the Clinton administration often worked collaboratively with public interest groups to strengthen rules over which they had discretion and attempted to circumvent Republican majorities, who were increasingly skeptical of government intervention, in Congress. One such attempt, to strengthen children's television regulation, involved an unusual institutional arrangement. In 1995 the FCC (under Chairman Hundt) issued a proposal to add teeth to the 1990 Children's Television Act by proposing to adopt a quantitative requirement (a quota) for children's programming. Television stations opposed the proposal on First Amendment grounds and out of fear that they would lose ad revenues. Public interest groups strongly supported the proposal. The FCC was hamstrung. With only four members on the commission at the time (one had resigned and had not been replaced), the FCC was divided two to two.

In June 1996, four months after passage of the new telecommunications law, President Clinton announced plans to hold a summit on children's television at the White House, noting, "I've been trying to get the FCC for a year to just say that three hours a week ought to be devoted to children's educational programming by every network."[4] The summit was scheduled for July 29 and the chief executive officers of the networks, who attributed the summit to election-year politics, did not plan to attend. They also did not want to irritate congressional Republicans, whose leadership opposed strengthened requirements.[5] In the days leading up to the summit, however, the industry began to show signs of movement. Vice President Al Gore's domestic policy adviser, Greg Simon, began to broker negotiations between network and station representatives, public interest groups, FCC officials, and Representative Ed Markey (D–Mass.), a longtime children's programming advocate. After days of negotiations, parties to the talks reached a final consensus and broadcasters agreed to a quantitative guideline requiring them, as a condition of license renewal, to air three hours per week of children's educational programming. Alternatively, they could provide the equivalent by either sponsoring programs on other stations or by broadcasting a package of programming that included an equivalent of three hours' worth of specials and public service announcements. Public interest groups pledged not to seek stronger requirements in the future and broadcasters agreed not to challenge the agreement in court. Less than two weeks later, the FCC quietly approved the agreement.[6] A similar process occurred that led to the industry's creation of a ratings system to accompany the V-chip.[7]

The FCC also had to confront a significant challenge to its equal employment opportunity rules. The Lutheran Church–Missouri Synod owned two radio stations in Missouri. Upon seeking license renewal, the FCC questioned the church's equal employment opportunity practices, placed the licenses in jeopardy, and fined the church $25,000. The FCC found that the broadcaster violated the agency's equal employment opportunity rules through its use of religious hiring preferences and inadequate recruitment of minorities.

The church challenged the FCC's ruling in court and, in an important 1998 case, the D.C. Circuit Court ruled in favor of the church.[8] The court found that the FCC's equal employment opportunity rules extended beyond simple outreach efforts, though the FCC argued that the rules did not enforce quotas. Nevertheless, the court reasoned that the rules did "oblige stations to grant some degree of preference to minorities in hiring" and that "[t]he entire scheme is built on the notion that stations should aspire to a workforce that attains, or at least approaches, proportional representation."[9] The court thus overturned the FCC's rules. Chairman Kennard promised to review the rules, and revise them to meet the court's concerns.

On January 20, 2000, the FCC adopted new rules that, according to its chairman, met the court's objections. The new rules emphasized outreach, rather than specific hiring guidelines. The rules required broadcasters to widely disseminate information about job openings in order to ensure that all qualified applicants would have an opportunity to apply for a position. Broadcasters could perform this outreach in two different ways. First, broadcasters could choose to notify of openings all organizations that requested to be notified. Broadcasters also would have to conduct outreach that extended beyond that associated with particular job openings, including job fairs, internship programs, and mentoring programs. Alternatively, broadcasters could seek outreach through any measure they chose, as long as they could show that their outreach efforts reached all segments of a community. The new rules also applied to cable firms.[10]

In January 2001, when President George W. Bush assumed office, he appointed Michael Powell (son of Colin Powell) to chair the new, Republican-dominated FCC. The new members of the FCC were forced by the courts to reconsider the equal employment opportunity rules crafted by their most recent predecessors. A court of appeals ruled that the new rules were unconstitutional. Specifically, the court argued that the alternative method of outreach, which obligated broadcasters to document that their efforts reached all segments of a community, required broadcasters to report the race and gender of each job applicant.[11] Though the court found no constitutional problems with the first outreach option, notification, it did find that the alternative outreach option could not be severed from the rest of the rule. The court thus vacated the rule in its entirety. In November 2002, however, the new FCC adopted new equal employment opportunity rules that were substantially similar to the requirements of the first outreach option, thereby meeting the court's concerns.[12]

Beyond revising the equal employment opportunity rules, however, Chairman Powell has embarked on a deregulatory crusade for other television issues. As Powell has stated, "I believe government has the role and duty of proving the merits of intervention rather than the other way around. If I can't demonstrate with rigor the necessity of intervention, then the obligation of the government is to stay out."[13] Powell's presumption is in favor of deregulation and market forces.

Specifically, Powell strongly supported repeal of the television station ownership regulations. To that, Senator Ernest Hollings (D–S.C.), then chair of the Senate Commerce Committee, responded in July 2001 with high-publicity hearings on the need for continued regulation. He not only subjected Powell to a public tongue-lashing but also introduced legislation seeking to strengthen the ownership rules. Despite the confrontation with Hollings, Powell was helped in his endeavor by the federal appeals court in Washington, D.C., which on February 19, 2002, ruled that the ownership limits were not adequately justified.[14]

By the spring of 2003 the ownership issue was heating up. Though Powell favored repeal, a Democratic colleague on the commission, Michael Copps, who opposed repeal of the rules, initiated a series of field hearings at various locations across the country in order to educate the public and solicit feedback. Meanwhile, Representative Cliff Stearns (R–Fla.), chairman of the House Commerce Committee, introduced legislation proposing to relax the ownership limits from the 35 percent (embodied in the 1996 Telecommunications Act) to 45 percent.[15]

On June 2, 2003, after months of acrimony between Chairman Powell (the most visible proponent of relaxing the rules) and Commissioner Copps (the most visible opponent), the FCC voted to relax the national ownership limits to 45 percent (from 35 percent). The vote was three to two along party lines, with the three Republican commissioners voting to relax the rules and the two Democratic commissioners voting in favor of the status quo. This struggle over ownership limits reflected the continuation of a thirty-year debate between those who sought dramatic change—justified in terms of the technology explosion and the creation of new media outlets (the erosion of scarcity argument)—and those who opposed change—referencing a larger sociopolitical conception of the public interest in a diversity of viewpoints. Further, to the extent that the end result of the proceeding consisted of regulatory relaxation, rather than repeal or deregulation, and in light of the fact that, as of August 2003, bills were pending in Congress to roll back the change, the proceedings represent a continuation of the pattern of policy change that has been described thoughout this book.[16]

Of course, none of this is to suggest that deregulation did not or has not taken place. Clearly it has, and there has been significant tinkering with the tools of regulation as well. Further, the deregulation that has taken place is not without consequence. Indeed, in light of the relaxation of the ownership regulations embodied in the 1996 Telecommunications Act, significant concentration in the television industry has occurred. For example, by some estimates, five companies now account for 75 percent of prime-time television viewers.[17] Nevertheless, the process has been incremental and acrimonious, and deregulation has been incomplete.

Television Policy Change in Perspective

Thus, even after passage of the 1996 Telecommunications Act, television policy remained uncertain and subject to incrementalism, policy fluctuations, and intense conflict. Those who argue that the U.S. system is prone to incrementalism, such as Charles Lindblom, will not be surprised by the ambiguous nature of television deregulation.[18] But this incremental nature of television policy change is surprising in a number of respects. First, it is surprising given that, since the mid-1970s, three concerted attempts at significant deregulation occurred. In the 1978–1979 period, Lionel Van Deerlin (D–Calif.), then chair of the House Communications Subcommittee, made the first attempt at substantial deregulation when he sought to scrap the 1934 Communications Act entirely and start over with new deregulatory legislation. Mark Fowler, FCC chair from 1981 to 1987, and his successor, Dennis Patrick, made the second attempt to deregulate television administratively via the FCC rule-making process. The third attempt occurred when Congress passed and President Clinton signed the 1996 Telecommunications Act.

The incremental nature of television policy change also is surprising given the rapid and relatively complete deregulation undergone by other infrastructure industries, particularly by the airline, trucking, and telephone industries. The major policy changes that resulted in deregulation of these infrastructure industries occurred between 1975 and 1980.[19] In an age of economic and technological transformation, the captured regulatory commissions initially protected their industries, which led to higher prices and deprived consumers of new services, but subsequently initiated deregulation.[20] Congress affirmed deregulation when in 1979 it passed the Airline Deregulation Act and in 1980 it passed the Motor Carrier Act. Congress did not pass telephony legislation but assented to deregulation in 1977 when it defeated an AT&T-sponsored bill. Deregulation also received momentum from a broad coalition of liberals and conservatives. For their part, liberals were deeply suspicious of the apparent collusion between business and government and also applauded the potential benefits of deregulation to consumers. Deregulation appealed to conservatives, who saw it as an anti-inflation policy and an affirmation of free market principles.[21] The resulting policy outputs were dramatic and conclusive. The airline, trucking, and telephone industries became marked by free entry and competitive pricing.

In the 1970s the television industry exhibited many of the same characteristics. Television also is an infrastructure industry. It serves an advertising function for all other businesses, making it an important part of the economy and an important factor in commerce. Further, as a public forum of sorts, it facilitates social discourse. Television firms are governed by an independent regulatory commission, the FCC, born of the New Deal and charged with the economic regulation of the industry. The central role of the FCC, distribution of electromagnetic frequencies through the licensing process, was similar to the control over airline and trucking routes embodied in the Civil Aeronautics Board (CAB) and the Interstate Commerce Commission (ICC). By the early 1970s, television policy had evolved to include socially oriented regulations, such as the Fairness Doctrine, children's programming guidelines, and equal opportunity rules. These social components distinguish television from airline, trucking, and telephony deregulation. Nevertheless, these social regulations were appended to, and dependent on, the primary New Deal economic regulatory system and its underlying scarcity rationale, which supported the whole scheme of television deregulation.

The FCC, like the CAB and the ICC, exhibited signs of capture by the broadcast television sector. Consumers, economists, and potential entrants had long argued that the agency favored incumbent broadcasters and restricted the growth of cable television and other new technologies. Nevertheless, the FCC, like the CAB and the ICC, began to disprove the capture thesis by initiating deregulation. Most notably, in 1972, and subsequently in 1974, the FCC very slightly relaxed the regulatory burden faced by cable system operators.

As in the airline, trucking, and telephone cases, legislators began considering television deregulation in the middle to late 1970s. In 1976 the House Communications Subcommittee held a series of cable oversight hearings that exposed the frequently protectionist actions of the FCC, as well as the many other problems, such as First Amendment, fairness, and equal employment opportunity issues, associated with television regulation under the 1934 Communications Act. Representative Van Deerlin's introduction of "rewrite" legislation followed. Early on it appeared that television policy would follow the same pattern as airline, trucking, and telephony deregulation.

Yet television deregulation did not follow a similar trajectory. Van Deerlin's legislative rewrite effort failed. Fowler's attempt at administrative deregulation largely was stymied by Congress and resulted in only slight modifications to existing policy. The 1996 act left the broad parameters of the 1934 Communications Act in place; regulated competition between sectors, which resulted in "freer markets and more rules," to borrow a phrase from Steven Vogel; and provided for incremental deregulation within sectors.[22]

The Role of Technological Change

Prior to the 1970s, most Americans had access to only three broadcast television networks and, if they were lucky, a handful of local independent stations. Cable television was in its infancy. In the few local markets where cable was available, it served simply as a means of retransmitting local stations and thus providing clearer pictures free of interference. By the late 1970s, with advances in satellite technology, cable technology provided a means to import and export signals from one market to another, thus providing additional programming choices. Later, cable companies began to offer specialized programming channels. The development of direct-to-home satellite technology followed cable in the early 1990s. Today, as a result of these changes, most Americans with the financial means to subscribe can receive up to several hundred channels of programming.

More important, for our purposes, than the actual technological developments associated with television are the policy prescriptions that stemmed from these changes. In the 1970s, academic economists began to notice the technological change in the television industry and anticipate further such development. Based on this rapid change, they argued that television regulation ought to be significantly retrenched, at the very least, or done away with altogether. For example, Roger Noll, Merton Peck, and John McGowan, perhaps the preeminent scholars of television economics, argued that the expansion of the television environment through new technologies would alleviate scarcity and allow for a more efficient distribution of spectrum through the marketplace. They argued that with rapid technological change, "a substantial reduction in regulation of television will be a significant benefit."[23]

Economists prescribed policies oriented to the market, arguing that the relationship between cable operators and television broadcasters could be determined by what the marketplace would support. Thus, for example, economists suggested that cable carriage of broadcaster signals could best be handled through contracts, rather than through rules of the game laid down by government regulators. If consumer demand did not support the carriage of a particular broadcast station by a cable system, then the cable operator should not have to carry that station. Conversely, if consumer demand was such that a cable system wanted to carry a broadcast station, then the financial terms could best be worked out through the contract process. Similarly, economists suggested that broadcast television licenses should be awarded in perpetuity and the marketplace should decide which broadcasters should remain on the air. If viewers did not flock to particular stations, then those stations would either change their programming to better match consumer interest or sell themselves to a person or corporation that could or would. Finally, economists argued that the expansion of the television marketplace undermined the need and rationale for socially oriented television regulations. Whether television broadcasters offered children's programming, news and public affairs programming, or other formats, could best be left to the marketplace.

Cries of "technological change" were an important theme, some might say a mantra, among economists and advocates of deregulation. Indeed technological change and the policy prescriptions of academic economists were important to the extent that key policymakers picked up the arguments of economists, enlarged upon them, and attempted to embody their prescriptions in policy. Thus, for example, Van Deerlin sought to rewrite the 1934 Communications Act in light of technological change, arguing that cable television would expand the television marketplace, which in turn would lead to greater choice for consumers, obviating the need for most regulations. Van Deerlin proposed to deregulate the industry entirely except for ownership regulations, which he saw as a mechanism to preserve competition. Similarly, Fowler attempted to deregulate administratively from the FCC in the 1980s based on the technological change argument. Fowler took an even broader view of technology and the market and argued that television sits within a larger market consisting of books and brochures and billboards. Hence, Fowler's attempt to deregulate surpassed Van Deerlin's to the extent that he did not even see a need for ownership regulations. Finally, the rhetoric associated with development of the 1996 Telecommunications Act included a powerful technological component, as policymakers wanted to deregulate so as to both respond to technological development and produce further technological advancement, particularly in the form of the so-called information superhighway. Despite the rapid and vast technological change, despite the policy prescriptions of economists based on that change, and despite attempts by policymakers to deregulate in light of that change, television deregulation was incremental and incomplete. Policy simply did not respond to technological change.

The Role of Industry Influence

Industry influence also was not a decisive factor in television policy change. Explanations for regulation or regulatory change that hinge on the influence of industry suggest that policy reflects the wishes of important private-sector interests by virtue of their ability to mobilize politically.[24] Clearly, the television industry was highly fragmented, both between and within sectors. Thus we cannot say that "the industry" received the policy benefits it wanted.

This fragmentation, of course, begs the question of whether dominant sectors, or dominant firms within sectors, drove policy. There is no consistent evidence for such a conclusion. The broadcast sector was obviously dominant in the 1970s, when cable was seeking entry into the industry, but the FCC, after being urged by members of Congress, clearly overrode the wishes of the dominant broadcast sector and deregulated cable carriage of broadcast signals. In 1992, when the cable sector was ascendant, Congress again clearly overrode that sector's interests and reregulated cable rates and imposed "must carry" and "retransmission consent" regulations on cable. Further, in each of these examples, public interest groups advocated on the side of the weaker sector and thus were on the "winning" side of policy outputs, undermining a central assumption of industry dominance theories—that there is an inherent conflict and dichotomy between public interests and private interests.

Finally, we have seen some clear examples in which policymakers overrode the policy preferences of industry actors in the absence of *any* intra-industry conflict. Such examples include the maintenance of the various public trustee regulations and, perhaps most well known, imposition of the V-chip requirement and its companion ratings system.

This is not at all to suggest that industry factions do not play a role in shaping policy; indeed they do. But they must, by necessity, operate in a larger issue context and through institutional venues. Thus it is not so much that technological change or industry influence are unimportant. Rather, technological change, as one idea, and industry actors, as one set of interests, interact with other ideas, institutions, and interests.

Ideas, Institutions, and Television Policy

A contingency framework stresses factors that are exogenous to the industry, rather than industry influence or the status of technology development. Such frameworks do not rule out the notion that technology may be important or that industry may be influential. Rather, they suggest that the influence of technological change or industry mobilization is filtered through a larger context circumscribed by ideas and institutions.

A contingency framework typically is used to understand and explain the larger, nonincremental policy changes that occasionally punctuate the normal workings of the U.S. political system. For example, Frank Baumgartner and Bryan Jones use such a framework to understand rapid changes in policies surrounding such issues as smoking, auto safety, and nuclear power in the latter part of the twentieth century.[25] Richard Harris and Sidney Milkis use a similar framework to understand longer-term shifts in policy across issue areas over the course of U.S. history.[26] Gary Mucciaroni argues that changes in the issue and institutional context account for the many policy reversals sustained by business interests from the 1970s through the early 1990s.[27]

As useful as a contingency framework is for helping us to understand substantial, significant, and often rapid change, most policy change in the United States is not rapid or swift. Rather, much like the television case, most policy moves along slowly. As this volume demonstrates, a contingency framework helps us to gain a clearer understanding of the history of television deregulation than does the economic theory or an industry influence model. Thus a contingency framework is equally as effective at explaining relative policy continuity as it is at explaining dramatic policy change. A contingency framework is particularly useful because, even in the context of comparative policy stability, it helps us to probe beyond superficial policy outputs. Indeed, we see that the issue and institutional context was not conducive to dramatic or rapid policy change for television.

The Issue Context

Deborah Stone writes, "Policy is centrally about classification and differentiation, about how we do and should categorize in a world where categories are not given."[28] In the television case, key participants in the policy process essentially categorized the television issue differently. This is vividly demonstrated in their varying use of metaphors.

Those advocating deregulation essentially saw the television issue as an economic problem. As Van Deerlin in the 1970s, Fowler in the 1980s, and the deregulatory Republicans ushered in as part of the 104th Congress saw it, for example, the central problem of television policy was too much regulation. Regulation stifled the natural workings of the "marketplace." Fowler even argued that television was merely a "toaster with pictures" and hence sought the rapid and nearly complete removal of regulation. Those advocating deregulation essentially saw the television problem as analogous to the airline, trucking, and telephone problem. Regulation was hindering the "natural" operation of the free market. They thus thought that the appropriate remedy was deregulation along the lines of that experienced by the airline, trucking, and telephone industries.

Contrast this with the metaphors invoked by public interest groups and their allies. They saw television neither as a "marketplace" nor as a "toaster with pictures" but as a "vast wasteland"—a cesspool of drivel and programming of the lowest common denominator. In the 1970s, when the television issue first arrived on the public agenda, public interest groups, along with cable companies, argued that this was in part due to the fact that the broadcasters had a "virtual stranglehold" over the FCC and, by definition, over what Americans watched on television. Public interest groups took their argument even further, noting that the FCC was little more than a "toothless tiger."

These metaphors contained policy prescriptions. On the one hand, public interest groups and cable companies advocated cable signal deregulation so as to break the tight relationship between the FCC and the broadcast sector and so as to provide more viewing options to the U.S. public. On the other hand, public interest groups also advocated strengthened regulation of television. They wanted to maintain the public trustee scheme of regulation. They wanted television to produce not a "vast wasteland" but a "marketplace of ideas."

The primary opposition to television deregulation thus consisted of public interest groups and their allies, both internal and external to Congress. To be sure, public interest groups did support cable signal deregulation, as they thought that this would break up the cozy protectionist relationship between broadcasters and the FCC. Beyond this issue, however, they adamantly opposed further deregulation. They opposed deregulation because they did not buy into the policy prescription arrived at by economists and other advocates of deregulation.

They did not support the deregulatory prescription because they did not agree that economic rationality ought to be the goal of the nation's television policy. They argued instead that competition would not necessarily result from deregulation and that, even if it did, competition could not serve the more important social objectives that they thought ought to be the appropriate goals of policy. It was thus competing policy images and problem definitions that led to the incremental nature of television policy change.

Public interest groups successfully expanded the conflict surrounding television policy to include a whole host of social and political *issues* that simply were not present in the deregulation politics of other infrastructure industries. This issue context also served to expand conflict to political *actors* that were not present in other examples of economic deregulation. In the airline, trucking, and telephone deregulation examples, the only public interest groups involved in the process were the large associations, such as the Consumers Union, that were focused on consumer issues per se, such as prices and services. The television example, however, included a whole host of industry-specific public interest groups, as well as academics from fields other than economics. The politics of television policy were characterized by a combustible conflict between economic, social, and moral issues.

The Institutional Context

In recent years, much of the literature on institutions has come to focus on how organizational arrangements, norms, and procedures structure and order the preferences of policymakers acting within them.[29] Mucciaroni, while welcoming this focus, nonetheless argues that this perspective pays short shrift to the actual policy preferences of the people who inhabit U.S. institutions, an argument that this book confirms:

> Institutional roles, missions, rules, and norms shape political actors' goals, but whether those goals are translated into meaningful policy preferences and priorities depends on actors' assessments of issues and situations. They must decide which problems are most pressing and which are most amenable to correction, rate the ideological and intellectual appeal of proposed alternatives, and consider the lessons learned from previous policy choices.[30]

The concerns of public interest groups resonated with members of Congress, especially among congressional Democrats, who were the closest allies of public interest groups. It was Van Deerlin's Democratic colleagues in the House, especially junior members, who informed him privately that they would not support his "rewrite" legislation and who very loudly opposed the rewrite measures during hearings in 1978 and 1979. And it was primarily congressional Democrats who managed to stymie the attempts at administrative deregulation by the FCC chairmen in the 1980s. They did so because they too were concerned with the social aspects of television policy. Nevertheless, congressional Republicans often fought deregulation alongside their Democratic colleagues, especially in the 1970s and 1980s. They were especially concerned with the moral issues of sex and violence on television.

In addition to their ideological concerns, members of Congress shared a concern for their relationship with the media. For example, both Democrats and Republicans wanted the FCC to retain its ownership regulations. Democrats feared that deregulation would result in ownership by corporate conglomerates. This, they believed, would have two effects. First, industry concentration would squeeze out ownership by women and racial and ethnic minorities, core Democratic constituencies. They also believed that ownership by corporate conglomerates, absent content regulation, would result in news and public affairs information with a corporate and conservative bias. Congressional Republicans, for their part, worried about a presumed liberal bias among journalists, which they feared would be more pronounced if regulators removed the ownership constraints.

By 1996, however, several changes occurred that gave to television politics a strong partisan veneer. First, the 104th Congress brought to Capitol Hill a swarm of new, younger, more antigovernment Republicans, and the 1994 elections gave control of the Congress to Republicans for the first time since 1954. Further, a series of rule changes dramatically increased the power of the new Republican Speaker, Newt Gingrich, and resulted in a strengthened congressional Republican Party with more influence over the votes of its members.[31] Finally, Republicans benefited from the previous regulatory relaxation of the 1980s, such as the demise of the Fairness Doctrine and the relaxation of the ownership rules. These two changes combined to produce a veritable swarm of right-wing talk shows across the country. Nevertheless, while these changes produced a party far more inclined toward television deregulation than in the past, there remained enough Republican concern for their small business and religious broadcaster constituents that they continued to be ambivalent about deregulation. This, coupled with partisan bickering and bargaining, produced the incrementalism of the 1996 Telecommunications Act.

In short, public interest groups and their allies managed to expand the conflict surrounding economic deregulation of the television industry to intersect with important social issues. In the 1970s and 1980s, these issues cut across partisan cleavages. In the 1990s, however, they fell along those cleavages.

Relative Policy Continuity
Masks Larger Underlying Changes

Normally, when we think about continuity and change in public policy, we tend to focus at the obvious level of policy outputs. In the television case, such a focus demonstrates that there was more continuity than change. On the other hand, investigating television policy at the level of ideas instructs us that there was tremendous unresolved flux in the issue context. Indeed, while we usually consider changes in ideas as a necessary condition for policy change, the television case teaches us that changes in ideas can support policy continuity.

The challenge that public interest groups and their allies faced, in seeking to retain regulation and prevent deregulation, was that technological development was eroding "scarcity," the underlying rationale for the full gamut of television regulation. In light of the erosion of this rationale, however, public interest groups asserted and advanced new regulatory rationales.

Public interest groups argued, first, that television was pervasive and powerful. The television industry must remain regulated owing to the inherent power and influence of the medium. Second, public interest groups argued that even though the spectrum may no longer be a scarce resource, it is still a *public* resource and, moreover, the television environment constitutes a public domain and a public forum. Finally, they also gave new meaning to the concept of "scarcity." While scarcity had always been an objective and absolute construct based on technology, public interest groups argued that scarcity was a relative concept. Public interest groups argued that scarcity cannot be measured and therefore that there is no way to objectively determine when scarcity no longer exists. Further, they argued that scarcity is not simply a technological consideration but a socioeconomic one as well. Some people might not be able to access all the wonderful new television technologies, and therefore, while for the wealthier segments of society scarcity may indeed be ended, for the poorer among us scarcity would remain a constraint. This is akin to concerns about the "digital divide" in the Internet age. Public interest group advocates argued that despite the great abundance of television technologies, there would continue to be a television divide.

Public interest groups used these arguments to provide the rationales for continued regulation. They were successful in that they managed to keep social issues on the agenda, independent of the scarcity rationale. They also were successful in that these rationales were picked up by their congressional allies and thereby shaped the larger issue context. Thus the majority staff of the House Telecommunications Subcommittee in 1981 issued a white paper justifying continued regulation based on these rationales. Similarly, members of Congress (of both parties) perpetuated these rationales as they argued for continued regulation. And these rationales were embedded in the 1984 Cable Act, the 1992 Cable Act, and the 1992 Children's Television Act. More important, these rationales contributed to the larger issue context. During formulation and passage of the 1996 Telecommunications Act, the dominant discourse surrounded "competition" and "jobs" and "technological convergence." Yet even in this case, the discourse and debate surrounding competition—what it was, how to reach it, and how to recognize it if it were achieved— masked the underlying, more fundamental debate over the social versus the economic aspects of television policy.

Context Matters

Neither technology nor the influence of the television industry was determinative or decisive precisely because they were filtered through the larger issue and institutional context. It was not that technology and industry influence did or did not matter. Rather, *ideas* about technology and industry are a way of framing issues and those ideas, and the interests that voice them, are debated and structured within institutions.

The market forces theory of regulation suggests that regulatory rationales are somehow "given" by the particular circumstances of an industry or a business process and that when a regulatory rationale deteriorates or changes, so does, or should, regulation. The television example, however, powerfully demonstrates that rationales are malleable and subject to change, that regulatory rationales are, above all else, political constructs. What mattered most was not technological change per se, but rather ideas (and the goals of the interests that those ideas reflect) about technological change.

To be sure, Van Deerlin and Fowler—and those members of Congress in the 1990s who wanted to deregulate entirely—advocated for deregulation on the basis of technological change and the erosion of the scarcity rationale. But public interest groups and their allies in Congress did not see it that way at all. They redefined scarcity and offered new rationales to support continued regulation.

Similarly, it was perceptions about the television industry and its power that were important factors in the story of television deregulation. Those advocating deregulation looked out across the television landscape and saw one large communications marketplace. Thus, for example, deregulators wanted to deregulate cable rates, even in markets where there was only one cable provider, because they did not see this as an example of monopoly. Rather, they argued, consumers could always do without cable and get their television programming from traditional broadcast stations or from direct-to-home satellite services.

Their opponents, however, did not see a larger television marketplace. Rather they saw a collection of specific industry segments, and this fragmentation made it possible and plausible to argue, often along with industry sectors, that government had to continue to play the important role of setting and preserving sector boundaries, determining the terms of competition, and guarding against market abuses of one sector by another and also of consumers by the firms. Further, each sector, they argued, had special circumstances warranting regulation. Thus they wanted to regulate cable rates to ensure that cable television remained available to as many people as possible, and they wanted to keep broadcast television regulated on behalf of those for whom broadcasting would remain their only source of programming.

The extent to which there was a larger television marketplace truly was in the eye of the beholder. Thus, where Van Deerlin, Fowler, and the deregulatory Republicans of the 104th Congress saw a larger marketplace, public interest groups and their allies did not. This created a rather vicious cycle—a Catch-22 situation. Continued perceptions of industry fragmentation perpetuated sector-specific policies—in essence, different policies for the different sectors of the television industry. These in turn fed the perception of industry fragmentation and thereby provided continued credibility for arguments that regulations within sectors must be maintained. Perceptions of the nature of the industry mattered.

The incremental nature of television deregulation thus resulted from contingency framework phenomena. The issue and institutional context was not conducive to swift or substantial policy change for television. Public interest groups and their allies expanded the relevant issues around which political conflict took place. As a result, the economic issues involved in television regulation and deregulation intersected with an array of social issues that dramatically complicated deregulation.

Larger Lessons and Implications

How does the television story help us better understand regulation and regulatory politics? Scholars who seek to understand the general and dominant sources of regulatory policy change typically focus on the airline, trucking, and telephone cases because deregulation of these industries was so decisive and relatively complete. But to the extent that these cases looked similar to each other, in terms of both policy processes and policy outputs and outcomes, they do not help us to isolate particular causes with any precision. Indeed, in investigating these cases, scholars find evidence for all kinds of explanatory theories. Nevertheless, by comparing these cases with the television example, in which deregulation was far more ambiguous, we can better isolate important factors. If we can say that a particular factor was present in the airline, trucking, and telephone cases but absent in the television example, or vice versa, we can gain a clearer understanding of which theory of regulation and regulatory policy change holds more explanatory power generally.

Some scholars emphasize that airline, trucking, and telephone regulation crumbled in light of changed economic circumstances. As this argument goes, the airline and trucking industries were deregulated because the industries had matured and stabilized and regulation no longer was needed in order to protect firms from excessive competition. Telephony was deregulated because what was once a natural monopoly was no longer so. In short, the regulatory rationales eroded and so did regulation. The television example teaches us, however, that rationales are malleable. To whatever extent such economic factors were important in airline, trucking, and telephone deregulation, they were not important independent variables in the television example. Thus it would be erroneous to argue that economic or technological change, or both, are the important independent variables in policymaking generally.

Similarly, other scholars of airline, trucking, and telephone deregulation suggest that deregulation occurred because the industries came to want it and then got it. Alternatively, as the theory goes, though these industries first opposed deregulation, they eventually ceased their lobbying against it and capitulated. Such a view implies that, had the industries not capitulated, deregulation would not have happened, at least not to the extent that it did. In the television case, however, we see that the industry generally, and specific sectors of it, wanted a great deal of deregulation but did not get it to the desired extent. Thus, while some scholars stress industry influence in airline, trucking, and telephone deregulation, it was not a decisive factor in television deregulation. We cannot argue that industry influence is a decisive factor in policymaking generally.

What the airline, trucking, telephony, and television cases all had in common, rather, was the importance of the factors associated with a contingency framework. In the first three cases, a broad coalition of liberals and conservatives came together in support of deregulation—though for different reasons. This coalition was the central factor that was missing in the television case. In the television example, public interest groups, their academic allies, and their allies in Congress fought deregulation. In the airline, trucking, and telephone cases, new ideas about the primacy of efficiency considerations in regulation and how those ideas were enacted through the institutional context challenged existing policy equilibria. In the example of television, which to some extent had always involved more than just economic regulation, a broad deregulatory coalition never emerged. Liberals and conservatives were divided over the social and moral implications of deregulation. The result was incremental change in the context of broader policy continuity. Thus the central factor that was present in other cases and absent in the television case was an issue and institutional context conducive to change. The comparison of like and unlike cases thus helps us to see that contingency frameworks are of far more explanatory value in regulatory politics and regulatory policy change generally.

The television example also calls into question some of the constructs that political scientists and policymakers use when thinking about regulation. Scholars and policymakers think dichotomously about economic regulation on the one hand and social regulation on the other. But the television story teaches us that the distinction between these different types of regulation is not hard and fast. We have seen that the nature of regulation can change longitudinally. In the early years of television regulation, a consensus formed that the central problem confronting television was spectrum scarcity. The 1934 Communications Act thus instructed the FCC to rationalize the industry through the licensing mechanism. The FCC developed a variety of public trustee regulations, such as the Fairness Doctrine, children's television programming guidelines, and equal employment opportunity rules. But they were dependent on the scarcity rationale and were embedded in, and dependent on, the economic regulatory paradigm.

In the 1970s, that paradigm began to erode. Those who saw television regulation as an example of economic regulation sought to deregulate along the lines of airline, trucking, and telephone deregulation. But public interest groups and their allies did not see television as comparable to transportation and telecommunications. Rather, they saw television as a social issue and saw attempts to deregulate as attacks on social regulation. They emphasized social issues and devised new rationales to justify continued regulation. Whether something is an example of economic regulation or social regulation is in the eye of the beholder. As Deborah Stone writes:

> In a world of continua, boundaries are inherently unstable. Whether they are conceptual, physical, or political, boundaries are border wars waiting to happen. At every boundary, there is a dilemma of classification: who or what belongs on each side? In policy politics, these dilemmas evoke intense passions because the classifications confer advantages and disadvantages, rewards and penalties, permissions and restrictions, or power and powerlessness.[32]

Beginning in the mid-1970s, television politics constituted a political battle over boundaries. Some viewed television policy as an economic matter and as an example of economic regulation and wanted to deregulate accordingly. Others saw it as a social matter and as an example of social regulation. While the textbook definitions of economic regulation and social regulation clearly would place television regulation in the economic category, important political actors simply viewed it as a social issue. The categories that scholars use to understand regulation break down in the case of television.

In the final analysis, the television example also provides us with the opportunity think about *how we think about* policy change in the United States. When thinking about the nature of change we again tend to invoke broad categories—we tend to think in terms of policy breakthroughs on the one hand or gridlock on the other.[33] We tend to think in negative terms about the latter and positively about the former. Thus when the system is gridlocked, or when policy moves slowly and incrementally, we tend to assume that it is "broken." Indeed, looking at the changes in the U.S. political system, beginning in the 1960s and 1970s, that facilitated the emergence of the public lobby regime (changes such as the emergence of public interest groups, the fragmentation and political mobilization of industry, congressional decentralization, and the rise of the mass media), some scholars suggest that the U.S. system became unable to reach policy closure.[34] On the opposite side of the debate, other scholars view the same changes as facilitating a policy system capable of rapid and responsive change.[35] Indeed, Martha Derthick and Paul Quirk investigate airline, trucking, and telephony deregulation and optimistically argue that these changes in part endow the political system "with a greater capacity than is usually acknowledged."[36]

Does the incrementalism, some might even say gridlock, in television policy mean, therefore, that the system, or at least the television policy subsystem, is broken? To be sure, opinion is divided over television policy and in many ways the history of television policy change since the mid-1970s can be characterized as a series of repeat performances, as interest groups and policymakers have danced a slightly different version of the same policy minuet over and over again. Further, policy change *was* incremental and ambiguous. But before we label television policy as broken or as gridlocked, we would do well to take a lesson from Murray Edelman, who in writing about divisive, conflictual issues, noted: "The well-established, thoroughly anticipated, and therefore ritualistic reaffirmation of the differences institutionalizes both rhetorics, minimizing the chance of major shifts. . . . The persistence of unresolved problems with conflicting meanings is vital."[37]

Different participants active in television policy defined the television problem differently and offered competing policy images. The issue context was thus divided. There was no agreement on the terms of the debate. This manifested in the incremental nature of television policy. The division over whether television constitutes an economic problem and economic regulation or a social problem and social regulation is institutionalized. There is a great deal at stake in television policy. The television industry is an important component of the national economy. Most Americans spend several hours each day in front of their television set, and television is a significant component of the public forum in the United States. It is therefore all to the good that we construct different understandings of the television problem and debate them vigorously.

Notes

1. Hundt, "A Letter to the Industry," p. 87.
2. Hundt, "The Hard Road Ahead."
3. Kennard, "An Era of Opportunity."
4. Quoted in McConnell, "It's Unanimous," p. 6.
5. McConnell, "Eleventh-Hour Scramble."
6. Brainard, "Presidential Leadership, Interest Groups, and Domestic Policymaking Summitry."
7. Stern, "TV Makes History at the White House."
8. *Lutheran Church–Missouri Synod v. Federal Communications Commission.*
9. Ibid., pp. 351–352.
10. *Broadcast and Cable EEO Rules.*
11. *MD/DC/DE Broadcasters Association et al. v. Federal Communications Commission.*
12. U.S. Federal Communications Commission, "FCC Establishes New EEO Rules and Policies for Broadcasters and MVPDS."
13. Quoted in Ahrens, "The Great Deregulator," p. C1.
14. *Fox Television Stations v. Federal Communications Commission.*
15. See, for example, Labaton, "F.C.C. Prepares to Loosen Rules on Media Ownership."
16. During this proceeding, the FCC took up a range of ownership issues in addition to the national ownership limits. For example, the FCC relaxed its newspaper-television-radio rules, upheld a rule, prohibited a television network from buying another network, and tightened radio ownership regulations. See Ahrens, "FCC Eases Media Ownership Rules"; Kirkpatrick, "Deregulating the Media: News Analysis"; and Labaton, "Deregulating the Media: The Overview."
17. Fisher, "Sounds Familiar for a Reason," p. B5.
18. Lindblom, "The Science of Muddling Through"; Braybrooke and Lindblom, *A Strategy of Decision;* and Lindblom, *The Intelligence of Democracy.*
19. This is not to suggest that the seeds of deregulation had not been sown earlier. Indeed, for example, in an important 1969 Interstate Commerce Commission route case, the agency acknowledged the benefits that competition would potentially produce, and the FCC's first deregulation decision in long-distance telephony took place in 1968. Nevertheless, it was during the mid-1970s that the seeds of deregulation took root. Thus, for example, in 1975 the Civil Aeronautics Board's procompetition chairman called for the elimination of price and entry regulation, and by the late 1970s the Interstate Commerce Commission had begun to place the burden of proof on those calling for regulation. Similarly, in 1975 the FCC instituted a certification program allowing competition in telephone equipment.
20. The Civil Aeronautics Board was the first institution to call for the elimination of airline regulation. The Carterphone case, which laid the groundwork for telephone deregulation, was an agency decision and it was

the Interstate Commerce Commission that first acknowledged the benefits that could result from removal of government control over the trucking industry.

21. Derthick and Quirk, *The Politics of Deregulation.*

22. Vogel, *Freer Markets, More Rules.*

23. Noll, Peck, and McGowan, *The Economic Aspects of Television Regulation,* p. 276. See also Herzel, "The Public Interest and the Market in Colour Television Regulation"; Coase, "Federal Communications Commission"; Kalven, "Broadcasting, Public Policy, and the First Amendment"; Levin, *The Invisible Resource;* DeVany et al., "A Property System for Market Allocation of Electromagnetic Spectrum"; Walters, "Freedom for Communications"; Demsetz, "Toward an Economic Theory of Property Rights"; and Minasian, "Property Rights in Radiation."

24. Kolko, *The Triumph of Conservatism;* Kolko, *Railroads and Regulation;* Stigler, "The Theory of Economic Regulation"; Becker, "A Theory of Competition Among Pressure Groups"; Buchanan, *The Demand and Supply of Public Goods;* Buchanan and Tullock, *The Calculus of Consent;* Peltzman, "Toward a More General Theory of Regulation"; and Posner, "Theories of Economic Regulation."

25. Baumgartner and Jones, *Agendas and Instability in American Politics.*

26. Harris and Milkis, *The Politics of Regulatory Change.*

27. Mucciaroni, *Reversals of Fortune.*

28. Stone, *Policy Paradox,* p. 380.

29. For reviews of this literature, see March and Olsen, *Rediscovering Institutions;* Shepsle, "Studying Institutions"; and Evans, Rueschemeyer, and Skocpol, *Bringing the State Back In.*

30. Mucciaroni, *Reversals of Fortune,* p. 178.

31. Deering and Smith, *Committees in Congress,* chap. 2.

32. Stone, *Policy Paradox,* p. 382.

33. On gridlock, see, for example, Sundquist, *Back to Gridlock?;* Brady and Volden, *Revolving Gridlock;* Jones, *Political Parties and Policy Gridlock in American Government;* and Biser, *The Ignorant Majority.*

34. Crozier, Huntington, and Watanuki, *The Crisis of Democracy;* King, "The American Polity in the Late 1970s"; and Chubb and Peterson, *Can the Government Govern?*

35. Derthick and Quirk, *The Politics of Deregulation;* Mucciaroni, *Reversals of Fortune;* Baumgartner and Jones, *Agendas and Instability in American Politics;* and Harris and Milkis, *The Politics of Regulatory Change.*

36. Derthick and Quirk, *The Politics of Deregulation,* p. 253.

37. Edelman, *Constructing the Political Spectacle,* p. 19.

Bibliography

Action for Children's Television v. Federal Communications Commission. 756 F. 2d 899 (D.C. Cir. 1985).
————. 821 F. 2d 741 (D.C. Cir. 1987).
Adams, Bill, et al. "Before and After *The Day After:* The Unexpected Results of the Television Drama." In *Media Power in Politics,* 3rd ed., edited by Doris A. Graber. Washington, D.C.: CQ Press.
Ahrens, Frank. "FCC Eases Media Ownership Rules: Party-Line Vote Clears Way for More Consolidation." *Washington Post,* June 3, 2003.
————. "The Great Deregulator." *Washington Post,* June 18 2001.
Alexis, Marcus. "The Political Economy of Federal Regulation of Surface Transportation." In *The Political Economy of Deregulation,* edited by Roger Noll and Bruce M. Owen. Washington, D.C.: American Enterprise Institute, 1983.
Andrews, Edmund. "HDTV Use for Profit Is Pushed." *New York Times,* March 2, 1994.
————. "U.S. May Let Baby Bell Widen Reach." *New York Times,* December 9, 1994.
Aufderheide, Patricia. *Communications Policy and the Public Interest: The Telecommunications Act of 1996.* New York: Guilford, 1999.
Bagdikian, Ben. *The Media Monopoly.* 5th ed. Boston: Beacon, 1997.
Bailey, Elizabeth. "The Evolving Politics of Telecommunications Regulation." In *A Communications Cornucopia,* edited by Roger Noll and Monroe Price. Washington, D.C.: Brookings Institution Press, 1998.
Bailey, Elizabeth R., David R. Graham, and Daniel P. Kaplan. *Deregulating the Airlines.* Cambridge: MIT Press, 1985.
Bardach, Eugene, and Charles Kagan. *Going by the Book: The Problem of Regulatory Unreasonableness.* Philadelphia: Temple University Press, 1982.
Baumgartner, Frank R., and Bryan D. Jones. *Agendas and Instability in American Politics.* Chicago: University of Chicago Press, 1993.

Becker, Gary. "A Theory of Competition Among Pressure Groups for Political Influence." *Quarterly Journal of Economics* 98 (August 1983): 371–400.

Behrman, Bradley. "Civil Aeronautics Board." In *The Politics of Regulation,* edited by James Q. Wilson. New York: Basic Books, 1980.

Bennett, W. Lance. *News: The Politics of Illusion.* 3rd ed. White Plains, N.Y.: Longman, 1996.

Bernstein, Marver. *Regulating Business by Independent Commission.* Princeton: Princeton University Press, 1955.

Berry, Jeffrey M. *The Interest Group Society.* 3rd ed. New York: Longman, 1997.

———. "Subgovernments, Issue Networks, and Political Conflict." In *Remaking American Politics,* edited by Richard A. Harris and Sidney M. Milkis. Boulder, Colo.: Westview, 1989.

Besen, Stanley M., and Robert W. Crandall. "The Deregulation of Cable Television." *Law and Contemporary Problems* 44 (Winter 1981): 77–124.

"The Bills Are Back." *Broadcasting,* January 31, 1983.

Biser, Len. *The Ignorant Majority: Our Reason for National Gridlock.* Fort Washington, Md.: Petra Publishing, 1993.

Black Citizens for a Fair Media v. Federal Communications Commission. 719 F. 2d 407 (1983).

Bosso, Christopher J. *Pesticides and Politics: The Life Cycle of a Public Issue.* Pittsburgh: University of Pittsburgh Press, 1987.

Bowie, Nolan A. "The Communications Act of 1978: An Expression of Congressional Will to End Civil Rights and Equal Employment Opportunity in the Broadcast Industry." In *Telecommunications Policy and the Citizen,* edited by Timothy Haight. New York: Praeger, 1979.

Brady, David, and Craig Volden. *Revolving Gridlock: Politics and Policy from Carter to Clinton.* Boulder, Colo.: Westview, 1998.

Brainard, Lori A. "Presidential Leadership, Interest Groups, and Domestic Policymaking Summitry: Balancing the Values of Efficiency and Representation." *Public Integrity* 2, no. 2 (2000): 91–104.

Braybrooke, David, and Charles E. Lindblom. *A Strategy of Decision: Policy Evaluation as a Social Process.* New York: Free Press of Glencoe, 1963.

Breyer, Stephen. *Regulation and Its Reform.* Cambridge: Harvard University Press, 1982.

Brinkley, Joel. *Defining Vision: The Battle for the Future of Television.* New York: Harcourt Brace, 1997.

———. "The Media Business: Panel to Consider New Rules for Digital TV Broadcasters." *New York Times,* October 23, 1997.

Broadcast and Cable EEO Rules. 65 Fed. Reg. 31, 7448 (February 15, 2000).

"Broadcaster Finds Rights Endangered." *New York Times,* July 21, 1976.

Brock, Gerald W. *The Telecommunications Industry: The Dynamics of Market Structure.* Cambridge: Harvard University Press, 1981.

Brown, Les. "Broadcasters Split on Plan to Revise Communications Act." *New York Times,* February 15, 1977.

———. "Broadcast Regulation: Plan Makes Waves." *New York Times,* June 12, 1978.

Buchanan, James M. *The Demand and Supply of Public Goods.* Chicago: Rand-McNally, 1968.

Buchanan, James M., and Gordon Tullock. *The Calculus of Consent: Logical Foundations of Constitutional Democracy.* Ann Arbor: University of Michigan Press, 1962.

Cable Communications Policy Act of 1984. U.S. Code vol. 47, sec. 521.

"Cable Industry Seems Happy with H.R. 4103 Compromise." *Communications Daily,* September 28, 1984.

"Cable Strikes a Deal with Cities." *Broadcasting,* June 4, 1984.

"Cable TV Deregulation." *Congressional Quarterly Almanac,* 1983.

Calmes, Jacqueline. "Bush, Congress Reach Deal on Deficit Reduction." *Congressional Quarterly Weekly Report,* November 25, 1989.

———. "Deficit-Reduction Measure Already Behind Schedule." *Congressional Quarterly Weekly Report,* July 15, 1989.

———. "Fragile Cable Compromise Threatened by Court Ruling." *Congressional Quarterly Weekly Report,* July 14, 1985.

———. "Groundwork Laid for Push Eliminating Broadcast Equal Time and Fairness Rules." *Congressional Quarterly Weekly Report,* June 2, 1984.

———. "Senate Panel Axes 'Freedom of Expression' Bill." *Congressional Quarterly Weekly Report,* June 16, 1984.

Carney, Dan. "Spate of Squabbles Leaves Bill's Fate Uncertain." *Congressional Quarterly Weekly Report,* December 23, 1995.

———. "Telecommunications: Overhaul Comes Down to Issue of Broadcast Ownership." *Congressional Quarterly Weekly Report,* December 16, 1995.

Carroll Broadcasting Company v. Federal Communications Commission. 258 F. 2d 440 (D.C. Cir. 1958).

Carron, Aaron S., and Paul MacAvoy. *The Decline of Service in the Regulated Industries.* Washington, D.C.: American Enterprise Institute, 1981.

Carter, Grace M. *Analysis for Public Decisions.* 3rd ed. New York: North-Holland, 1989.

Cassidy, John. *Dot.con: The Greatest Story Ever Sold.* New York: HarperCollins, 2002.

Cater, Douglas. *Power in Washington.* New York: Random House, 1964.

Childs, William R. *Trucking and the Public Interest.* Knoxville: University of Tennessee Press, 1985.

Chubb, John E., and Paul E. Peterson, eds. *Can the Government Govern?* Washington, D.C.: Brookings Institution Press, 1989.

Coase, Ronald H. "Federal Communications Commission." *Journal of Law and Economics* 2 (October 1959): 1–40.

Cole, Barry, and Mal Oettinger. *Reluctant Regulators: The FCC and the Broadcast Audience.* Reading, Mass.: Addison-Wesley, 1978.

Compaine, Benjamin M., and Douglas Gomery. *Who Owns the Media?* Mahwah, N.J.: Lawrence Erlbaum, 2000.

Cooper, Ann. "Fowler's FCC Learns Some Hard Lessons About What It Means to Be 'Independent.'" *National Journal,* April 6, 1985.

Crozier, Michel, Samuel P. Huntington, and Joji Watanuki. *The Crisis of Democracy: Report on the Governability of Democracies to the Trilateral Commission.* New York: New York University Press, 1975.

"Crusades Set Out to Clean Up TV." *Broadcasting,* February 9, 1981.

de Sola Pool, Ithiel. *Technologies of Freedom.* Cambridge: Belknap Press of Harvard University Press, 1983.

Deering, Christopher J., and Steven S. Smith. *Committees in Congress.* 3rd ed. Washington, D.C.: Congressional Quarterly Press, 1997.

Demsetz, Harold. "Toward an Economic Theory of Property Rights." *American Economic Review Papers and Proceedings* 57, no. 2 (May 1967): 347–359.

Derthick, Martha, and Paul J. Quirk. *The Politics of Deregulation.* Washington, D.C.: Brookings Institution Press, 1985.

Dery, David. *Problem Definition in Policy Analysis.* Lawrence: University of Kansas Press, 1984.

DeVany, Arthur S., et al. "A Property System for Market Allocation of Electromagnetic Spectrum." *Stanford Law Review* 21 (June 1969): 1499–1561.

"Disney Asked to Pony Up Kids' Fare." *Broadcasting & Cable,* April 17, 1995.

Dodd, Lawrence C. "Rise of the Technocratic Congress: Reform in the 1970s." In *Remaking American Politics,* edited by Richard Harris and Sidney Milkis. Boulder, Colo.: Westview, 1989.

Downs, A. *An Economic Theory of Democracy.* Stanford: Hoover Institution Press, 1957.

Drake, William. "National Information and Infrastructure Debate: Issues, Interests, and the Congressional Process." In *The New Information Infrastructure: Strategies for U.S. Policy,* edited by William Drake. Washington, D.C.: Brookings Institution Press, 1995.

Eads, George. "The Reform of Economic Regulation in Telecommunications and Transportation." Paper prepared for conference on the Impact of Regulatory Reform in Canada and the United States, May 20, 1982.

Edelman. Murray. *Constructing the Political Spectacle.* Chicago: University of Chicago Press, 1988.

Eisner, Marc Allen. *Regulatory Politics in Transition.* Baltimore: Johns Hopkins University Press, 1993.

Eisner, Marc Allen, Jeff Worsham, and Evan J. Ringquist. *Contemporary Regulatory Policy.* Boulder, Colo.: Lynne Rienner, 2000.

Evans, Peter B., Dietrich Rueschemeyer, and Theda Skocpol, eds. *Bringing the State Back In.* New York: Cambridge University Press, 1985.

Federal Communications Commission v. Midwest Video. 440 U.S. 689 (1979).

Federal Communications Commission v. Pacifica Foundation. 438 U.S. 726 (1978).

"Firms Ask for Changes in Cable Bill." *Washington Post,* July 18, 1984.

Fisher, Marc. "Sounds Familiar for a Reason." *Washington Post,* May 18, 2003.

Fowler, Mark, and Daniel Brenner. "A Marketplace Approach to Broadcast Regulation." *Texas Law Review* 60, no. 2 (1982): 207–257.

Fox Television Stations v. Federal Communications Commission. 280 F. 3d 1027 (2002).

Freeman, J. Lieper. *The Political Process.* New York: Vintage, 1955.

Friendly, Fred W. *The Good Guys, the Bad Guys, and the First Amendment.* New York: Vintage, 1977.

Gans, Herbert. *Deciding What's News: A Study of CBS Evening News, NBC Nightly News, Newsweek, and Time.* New York: Pantheon, 1979.

Gates, Bill. *The Road Ahead.* New York: Viking, 1995.

Geller, Henry. "Regulation and Public Policy After Divestiture." In *Disconnecting Bell: The Impact of the AT&T Divestiture,* edited by Harry M. Shooshan III. New York: Pergamon, 1984.

"Getting Down to Brass Tacks on Cable Deregulation." *Broadcasting,* June 13, 1983.

Goldberg, Robert, and Gerald Jay Goldberg. *Citizen Turner: The Wild Rise of an American Tycoon.* New York: Harcourt Brace, 1995.

"Gore: Confident the U.S. Can Become a 'Premiere Information Marketplace.'" *Congressional Quarterly Weekly Report,* April 3, 1993.

Graber, Doris A. *Mass Media and American Politics.* 6th ed. Washington, D.C.: Congressional Quarterly Press, 2002.

———. "Media Power and Government Control." In *Mass Media and American Politics,* 6th ed., by Doris Graber. Washington, D.C.: Congressional Quarterly Press, 2002.

Greenberg, Edward. "Wire Television and the FCC's Second Report and Order on CATV Systems." *Journal of Law and Economics* 10 (October 1967): 181–192.

Greer, Douglas F. *Industrial Organization and Public Policy.* New York: Macmillan, 1984.

Greve, Michael. "Why 'Defunding the Left' Failed." *Public Interest* 89 (Fall 1987): 91–106.

Hackett, R. "Decline of a Paradigm? Bias and Objectivity in News Media Studies." *Critical Studies in Mass Communication* 1, no. 3 (1984): 229–259.

Harris, Richard A., and Sidney M. Milkis. *The Politics of Regulatory Change: A Tale of Two Agencies.* New York: Oxford University Press, 1989.

Healey, Jon. "Bill Would Provide Flexibility for 'Advanced TV' Frequencies." *Congressional Quarterly Weekly Report,* February 18, 1995.

———. "GOP Dealing Wins Votes for Deregulatory Bill." *Congressional Quarterly Weekly Report,* May 27, 1995.

————. "House Committee Leaders Back Senate Provisions." *Congressional Quarterly Weekly Report,* May 6, 1995.

————. "Rejecting Further Regulation, Senate Easily Passes Bill." *Congressional Quarterly Weekly Report,* June 17, 1995.

————. "Republicans' Cable Plan Strikes a Nerve." *Congressional Quarterly Weekly Report,* March 11, 1995.

————. "Senate Sponsors Reinforce Communications Bills." *Congressional Quarterly Weekly Report,* August 13, 1994.

————. "Sides Fielding New Teams in Legislative Battle." *Congressional Quarterly Weekly Report,* November 26, 1994.

————. "Stumped by Bells' Objections, Hollings Kills Overhaul." *Congressional Quarterly Weekly Report,* September 24, 1994.

————. "With Democrats at a Distance, GOP Details Its Own Plan." *Congressional Quarterly Weekly Report,* January 14, 1995.

Heclo, Hugh. "Issue Networks and the Executive Establishment." In *The New American Political System,* edited by Anthony King. Washington, D.C.: American Enterprise Institute, 1978.

Herzel, Leo. "The Public Interest and the Market in Colour Television Regulation." *University of Chicago Law Review* 18, no. 4 (Summer 1951): 816.

Hess, Stephen. *The Ultimate Insiders: U.S. Senators in the National Media.* Washington, D.C.: Brookings Institution Press, 1986.

Hoberg, George. *Pluralism by Design.* New York: Praeger, 1992.

Horwitz, Robert Britt. *The Irony of Regulatory Reform: The Deregulation of American Telecommunications.* New York: Oxford University Press, 1989.

Hundt, Reed. "The Hard Road Ahead: An Agenda for the FCC in 1997." Available at www.fcc.gov/speeches/hundt/97agenda.text (accessed July 14, 2003).

————. "A Letter to the Industry." *Broadcasting & Cable,* October 9, 1995.

Jessell, Harry A. "Peggy Charren: Victory at Last." *Broadcasting & Cable,* August 12, 1996.

Jones, David R. *Political Parties and Policy Gridlock in American Government.* Lewiston, N.Y.: Edwin Mellen, 2001.

Kahn, Frank J., ed. *Documents of American Broadcasting.* New York: Appleton-Century-Crofts, 1968.

Kalven, Harry. "Broadcasting, Public Policy, and the First Amendment." *Journal of Law and Economics* 10 (October 1967): 15–49.

Kennard, William. "An Era of Opportunity: Remarks to the NAB." April 7, 1998. Available at www.fcc.gov/speeches/kennard/spwek811.html (accessed August 1, 2001).

Kerr, Peter. "Cable TV Notes: Gauging the Impact of Deregulation." *New York Times,* November 27, 1983.

King, Anthony. "The American Polity in the Late 1970s: Building Coalitions in the Sand." In *The New American Political System,* edited by A. King. Washington, D.C.: American Enterprise Institute, 1978.

Kirkpatrick, David D. "Deregulating the Media: News Analysis." *New York Times,* June 3, 2003.

"Knocking the Networks." *National Journal,* April 6, 1985.

Kolko, Gabriel. *Railroads and Regulation, 1877–1916.* Princeton: Princeton University Press, 1965.

———. *The Triumph of Conservatism: A Re-Interpretation of American History, 1900–1916.* New York: Free Press, 1963.

Krasnow, Erwin G., and Lawrence D. Longley. *The Politics of Broadcast Regulation.* 2nd ed. New York: St. Martin's, 1978.

Krasnow, Erwin G., Lawrence D. Longley, and Herbert A. Terry. *The Politics of Broadcast Regulation.* 3rd ed. New York: St. Martin's, 1982.

Krattenmaker, Thomas G. "The Telecommunications Act of 1996." *Connecticut Law Review* 29 (Fall 1996): 123–127.

Kristol, Irving. *Two Cheers for Capitalism.* New York: Basic Books, 1975.

Kurtz, Howard. "See No Cable, Hear No Cable." *Washington Post,* August 12, 2002.

Labaton, Stephen. "Deregulating the Media: The Overview, Regulators Ease Rules Governing Media Ownership." *New York Times,* June 3, 2003.

———. "F.C.C. Prepares to Loosen Rules on Media Ownership." *New York Times,* May 13, 2003.

LeDuc, Don. *Cable Television and the FCC: A Crisis in Media Control.* Philadelphia: Temple University Press, 1973.

Levin, Harvey J. *The Invisible Resource: Use and Regulation of the Radio Spectrum.* Baltimore: Johns Hopkins University Press, 1971.

Lilly, Walter III, and James C. Miller III. "The New 'Social Regulation.'" *Public Interest* 47 (Spring 1977): 49–61.

Lindblom, Charles E. *The Intelligence of Democracy; Decisionmaking Through Mutual Adjustment.* New York: Free Press, 1965.

———. "The Science of Muddling Through." In *Classics of Public Administration,* 4th ed., edited by Jay M. Shafritz and Albert C. Hyde. Toronto: Wadsworth Thomson Learning, 1997.

Livingston, Steven, and Todd Eachus. "Humanitarian Crisis and U.S. Foreign Policy: Somalia and the CNN Effect Reconsidered." *Political Communication* 12, no. 4 (1995): 413–429.

Lowi, Theodore. *The End of Liberalism: Ideology, Politics, and the Crisis of Public Authority.* New York: Norton, 1969.

Lutheran Church–Missouri Synod v. Federal Communications Commission. 141 F. 3d 344 (1998).

MacAvoy, Paul. *The Regulated Industries and the Economy.* New York: Norton, 1979.

March, James G., and Johan P. Olsen. *Rediscovering Institutions: The Organizational Basis of Politics.* New York: Free Press, 1989.

"Mass Media Laws, Changes Proposed." *Washington Post,* March 30, 1979.

Mayhew, David. "Congress: The Electoral Connection." In *Public Policy: The Essential Readings,* edited by Stella Z. Theodoulou and Matthew A. Cahn. Englewood Cliffs, N.J.: Prentice Hall, 1994.

McConnell, Chris. "Eleventh-Hour Scramble." *Broadcasting & Cable,* July 29, 1996.

———. "It's Unanimous." *Broadcasting & Cable,* June 17, 1996.

McConnell, Grant. *Private Power and American Democracy.* New York: Vintage, 1966.

McCraw, T. K. *Prophets of Regulation.* Cambridge: Belknap Press of Harvard University Press, 1984.

McFarland, Andrew. "Interest Groups and the Policymaking Process: Sources of Countervailing Power in America." In *The Politics of Interests: Interest Groups Transformed,* edited by Marc P. Petracca. Boulder, Colo.: Westview, 1992.

McQuail, Denis. "The Influence and Effects of Mass Media." In *Media Power and Politics,* 3rd ed., edited by Doris Graber. Washington, D.C.: Congressional Quarterly Press, 1994.

MD/DC/DE Broadcasters Association, et al. v. Federal Communications Commission. 253 F. 3d 732 (2001).

Metro Broadcasting, Inc. v. Federal Communications Commission. 497 U.S. 547 (1990).

Meyer, John R., et al. *Airline Deregulation: The Early Experience.* Boston: Auburn, 1981.

Mills, Mike. "Cable Regulation Is Dead—Again." *Congressional Quarterly Weekly Report,* October 20, 1990.

———. "Clinton's Computer 'Highway' to Spur Information Age." *Congressional Quarterly Weekly Report,* April 3, 1993.

———. "Congress Ready to Limit Ads on Children's Television." *Congressional Quarterly Weekly Report,* September 22, 1990.

———. "Dole Goes to Bat for Media Giants in Senate Debate over Telecommunications Bill." *Washington Post,* June 16, 1995.

———. "FCC Leaves Mark on Battle over Cable TV Control." *Congressional Quarterly Weekly Report,* December 22, 1990.

———. "Markey's Cable Re-Regulation Bill Survives Democrats' Defections." *Congressional Quarterly Weekly Report,* April 11, 1992.

———. "New Bills Make Waves for Broadcasters." *Congressional Quarterly Weekly Report,* January 29, 1994.

———. "Scarred by Media War, Cable Bill Wins Solid Vote from House." *Congressional Quarterly Weekly Report,* September 19, 1992.

———. "Senate Cable Reregulation Bill Headed for Another Season." *Congressional Quarterly Weekly Report,* November 16, 1991.

———. "Ushering in a New Age in Communications: Clinton Signs 'Revolutionary' Bill into Law at a Ceremony Packed with Symbolism." *Washington Post,* February 9, 1996.

———. "Weakened Regulation Bill Heads to House Floor." *Congressional Quarterly Weekly Report,* June 20, 1992.

Mills, Mike, and Paul Farhi. "Dole Statement Snags Phone, Cable TV Bill: Senator Fights Free Digital Broadcast Licenses." *Washington Post,* January 11, 1996.

Minasian, Jora. "Property Rights in Radiation: An Alternative Approach to

Radio Frequency Allocation." *Journal of Law and Economics* 18 (April 1975): 221–272.

Minow, Newton. "Address to the National Association of Broadcasters, May 9, 1961." Reprinted in *Abandoned in the Wasteland: Children, Television, and the First Amendment,* by Newton Minow and Craig L. LaMay. New York: Hill and Wang, 1995.

———. *Equal Time: The Private Broadcaster and the Public Interest.* New York: Atheneum, 1964.

Minow, Newton, and Craig L. LaMay. *Abandoned in the Wasteland: Children, Television, and the First Amendment.* New York: Hill and Wang, 1995.

Mitnick, Barry M. *The Political Economy of Regulation: Creating, Designing, and Removing Regulatory Forms.* New York: Columbia University Press, 1980.

Mucciaroni, Gary. *Reversals of Fortune: Public Policy and Private Interests.* Washington, D.C.: Brookings Institution Press, 1995.

Niskanen, William A., Jr. *Bureaucracy and Representative Government.* Chicago: Aldine and Atherton, 1971.

Noll, Roger, Merton J. Peck, and John J. McGowan. *The Economic Aspects of Television Regulation.* Washington, D.C.: Brookings Institution Press, 1973.

Nossiter, Bernard. "The FCC's Big Giveaway Show." *The Nation,* October 26, 1985.

"Off the Dole." *Wall Street Journal,* January 24, 1996.

Office of Communications of the United Church of Christ v. Federal Communications Commission. 359 F. 2d 994 (D.C. Cir. 1966).

———. 425 F. 2d 543 (D.C. Cir. 1969).

Olson, Mancur. *The Rise and Decline of Nations: Economic Growth, Stagflation, and Social Rigidities.* New Haven: Yale University Press, 1982.

Olufs, Dick W., III. *The Making of Telecommunications Policy.* Boulder, Colo.: Lynne Rienner, 1999.

The Omnibus Reconciliation Act of 1981. U.S. Public Law 97-35. 97th Congress, 1st sess., 1981.

"Parties Go Back to the Table for Cable Dereg. Talks." *Broadcasting,* January 30, 1984.

Peltzman, Sam. "Toward a More General Theory of Regulation." *Journal of Law and Economics* 19 (August 1976): 211–240.

Posner, Richard A. "Theories of Economic Regulation." *Bell Journal of Economics and Management Science* 5 (Autumn 1974): 335–358.

"Power Envy." *Forbes,* December 31, 1984.

Pressman, Steven. "Congress Clears Supplemental FY '84 Funding." *Congressional Quarterly Weekly Report,* August 11, 1984.

Pytte, Alyson. "Cable Reregulation Measure Moves Forward in House." *Congressional Quarterly Weekly Report,* June 30, 1990.

———. "Cable TV: The New Big Kid Confronts Re-Regulation." *Congressional Quarterly Weekly Report,* December 9, 1989.

————. "Cable TV Reregulation Bill Sweeps by Senate Panel." *Congressional Quarterly Weekly Report,* June 9, 1990.

————. "Congress Ready Once Again to Curb Children's Television." *Congressional Quarterly Weekly Report,* July 15, 1989.

————. "Fairness Doctrine, Dial-a-Porn Coupled on House Measure." *Congressional Quarterly Weekly Report,* October 7, 1989.

Quade, Edward S. *Analysis for Public Decisions.* Englewood Cliffs, N.J.: Prentice Hall, 1989.

Reagan, Ronald. *Veto—S. 742: Message from the President of the United States of America Returning Without My Approval S. 742, the Fairness in Broadcasting Act.* Washington, D.C.: U.S. Government Printing Office, 1987.

Redford, Emmette S. *Democracy in the Administrative State.* New York: Oxford University Press, 1969.

"Rewrite of Communications Act Serious Subject on Capitol Hill." *Broadcasting,* August 9, 1976.

"Rewrite II More Radical Than Predecessor." *Broadcasting,* April 2, 1979.

"Rewrite Written Off." *Broadcasting,* July 16, 1979.

Riker, William H. *Liberalism Against Populism: A Confrontation Between the Theory of Democracy and the Theory of Social Choice.* San Francisco: Freeman, 1982.

Robinson, Michael J., and Margaret Sheehan. *Over the Wire and On TV: CBS and UPI on Campaign '80.* New York: Russell Sage Foundation, 1983.

Rochefort, David A., and Roger W. Cobb, eds. *The Politics of Problem Definition: Shaping the Policy Agenda.* Lawrence: University of Kansas Press, 1994.

Ronfeldt, David. "Cyberocracy Is Coming." *Information Society Journal* 8, no. 4 (1992): 243–296.

"S. 66 Markup Postponed." *Broadcasting,* March 28, 1983.

"S. 66 Wins Big in the Senate." *Broadcasting,* June 20, 1983.

Schattschneider, E. E. *The Semisovereign People: A Realist's View of Democracy in America.* New York: Holt, Rinehart, and Winston, 1960.

Scherer, F. M. *Industrial Market Structure and Economic Performance.* Chicago: Rand-McNally, 1970.

Schudson, Michael. *Discovering the News: A Social History of American Newspapers.* New York: Basic Books, 1978.

Schwartz, Evan I. *The Last Lone Inventor: Tale of Genius, Deceit, and the Birth of Television.* New York: HarperCollins, 2002.

"Senate Bills 611 and 622." *Television Digest,* March 19, 1979.

"Seven-Hour Meeting." *Communications Daily,* July 19, 1984.

Shepsle, Kenneth A. "Studying Institutions: Some Lessons from the Rational Choice Approach." *Journal of Theoretical Politics* 1, no. 2 (1989): 131–147.

Shepsle, Kenneth A., and Barry R. Weingast. "The Institutional Foundations of Committee Power." *American Political Science Review* 81 (March 1987): 85–104.

Simmons, Steven J. *The Fairness Doctrine and the Media*. Berkeley: University of California Press, 1978.

Simon, Herbert A. *Administrative Behavior: A Study of Decision-Making Processes in Administrative Organizations*. 4th ed. New York: Free Press, 1997.

Snider, J. H., and Benjamin I. Page. "The Political Power of TV Broadcasters: Covert Bias and Anticipated Reactions." Paper presented at the annual meeting of the American Political Science Association, Washington, D.C., August 1997.

Sohn, Gigi, and Andrew J. Schwartzman. *Pretty Pictures of Pretty Profits: Issues and Opinions for the Public Interest and Non-Profit Communities in the Digital Broadcasting Debate*. Washington, D.C.: Benton Foundation.

Srinivasan, Kalpana. "CBS Leaves Broadcast Association over TV Limits." Associated Press, April 4, 2001.

Stanfield, Rochelle L. "'Defunding the Left' May Remain Just Another Fond Dream of Conservatives." *National Journal*, August 1, 1981.

Starobin, Paul. "Bill to Boost Quality of Kid's TV Clears Despite Veto Possibility." *Congressional Quarterly Weekly Report*, October 22, 1988.

———. "'Fairness Doctrine' Has Had a Tangled Past." *Congressional Quarterly Weekly Report*, February 27, 1988.

———. "FCC and Congress Clash over Proper Roles." *Congressional Quarterly Weekly Report*, February 27, 1988.

———. "Fewer Ads, More Quality Shows Demanded for Kid's Television." *Congressional Quarterly Weekly Report*, May 21, 1988.

———. "House Votes." *Congressional Quarterly Weekly Report*, June 11, 1988.

———. "Media Ownership Overhaul May Divide Legislators." *Congressional Quarterly Weekly Report*, June 3, 1989.

Stern, Christopher. "New Law of the Land." *Broadcasting & Cable*, February 5, 1996.

———. "TV Makes History at the White House." *Broadcasting & Cable*, March 4, 1996.

Stigler, George. "The Theory of Economic Regulation." *Bell Journal of Economics and Management Science* 2 (Spring 1971): 3–21.

Stokey, Edith, and Richard Zeckhauser. *A Primer for Policy Analysis*. 1st ed. New York: Norton, 1978.

Stone, Deborah. *Policy Paradox: The Art of Political Decision Making*. New York: Norton, 2002.

"Striking a Blow for Small Broadcasters." *Business Week*, December 31, 1984.

Sundquist, James L., ed. *Back to Gridlock? Governance in the Clinton Years*. Washington, D.C.: Brookings Institution Press, 1995.

The Telecommunications Act of 1996. U.S. Public Law 104. 104th Congress, 2nd sess., 1996.

Telecommunications Research and Action Council v. Federal Communications Commission. 801 F. 2d 501 (D.C. Cir. 1986).

Tuchman, Gary. *Making News: A Study in the Construction of Reality.* New York: Free Press, 1978.

Tunstall, Jeremy. *Communications Deregulation.* Oxford: Basil Blackwell, 1986.

U.S. Comptroller-General. *Selected FCC Regulatory Policies: Their Purposes and Consequences for Commercial Radio and TV.* Washington, D.C.: U.S. General Accounting Office, 1979.

U.S. Department of Commerce. Office of the Secretary. "Common Ground: Fundamental Principles for the NII." *NII Advisory Report,* December 1994.

U.S. Federal Communications Commission. *Broadcast and Cable Equal Employment Opportunity Rules.* 65 Fed. Reg. 31 (2000).

———. *Cable Television.* 36 FCC 2d 143 (1972).

———. *Cable Television Syndicated Program Exclusivity Rules and Inquiry into the Economic Relationship Between Television Broadcasting and Cable Television.* 79 FCC 2d 652 (1980).

———. *Children's Television.* 50 FCC 2d 1 (1974).

———. *Children's Television Programming.* 96 FCC 2d 634 (1984).

———. *Equal Employment Opportunity Outreach Program Requirements.* 16 FCC Rcd. 2872 (2001).

———. *Fairness Doctrine Inquiry.* 102 FCC 2d 145 (1985).

———. "FCC Establishes New EEO Rules and Policies for Broadcasters and MVPDS." FCC news release, November 7, 2002.

———. *First Report and Order.* 38 FCC 683 (1965).

———. *In the Matter of Mayflower Broadcasting Corporation and the Yankee Network, Inc. (WAAB).* 8 FCC 333 (1941).

———. *Multiple Ownership.* 49 Fed. Reg. 31877 (1984).

———. *Multiple Ownership Revisions.* 100 FCC 2d 74 (1985).

———. *Nondiscrimination in Employment Practices.* 18 FCC 2d 240 (1969).

———. *Radio Broadcast Services: Revision of Applications for the Renewal of License of Commercial and Non-Commercial AM, FM, and Television Licensees.* 49 Rad. Reg. 2d 740 (1980).

———. *Reexamination of the Commission's Comparative Licensing, Distress Sales, and Tax Certificate Policies Premised on Racial, Ethnic, and Gender Classifications.* 1 FCC Rcd. 1315 (1986).

———. *Revision of Television Deregulation.* 104 FCC 2d 358 (1986).

———. *Second Report and Order.* 2 FCC 2d 725 (1966).

———. *Syracuse Peace Council.* 2 FCC Rcd. 5043 (1987).

U.S. Federal Radio Commission. *Great Lakes Broadcasting Co.* 3 FRC Annual Report 32-34 (1929).

U.S. House of Representatives. *The Antitrust Reform Act of 1993.* H.R. 3626. 103rd Congress, 1st sess., November 22, 1993.

———. Committee on Interstate and Foreign Commerce. *Regulation of Broadcasting: Half a Century of Government Regulation of Broadcasting and the Need for Further Legislative Action.* 85th Congress, 2nd sess., 1958.

———. *The National Communications Competition and Information*

Infrastructure Act of 1993. H.R. 3636. 103rd Congress, 1st sess., November 22, 1993.

———. Majority Staff of the Subcommittee on Telecommunications, Consumer Protection, and Finance of the Committee on Energy and Commerce. *Telecommunications in Transition: The Status of Competition in the Telecommunications Industry.* 97th Congress, 1st sess., 1981.

———. Staff of the Subcommittee on Communications of the Committee on Interstate and Foreign Commerce. *Options Papers.* 95th Congress, 1st sess., 1977.

———. Subcommittee on Communications of the Committee on Interstate and Foreign Commerce. *The Communications Act of 1978: Hearings on H.R. 13015.* 95th Congress, 2nd sess., 1978.

———. Subcommittee on Communications of the Committee on Interstate and Foreign Commerce. *The Communications Act of 1979: Hearings on H.R. 3333.* 5 vols. 96th Congress, 1st sess., 1979.

———. Subcommittee on Communications of the Committee on Interstate and Foreign Commerce. *Hearings on the Role of Congress in Regulating Cable Television and the Potential for New Technologies in the Communications System.* 94th Congress, 2nd sess., 1976.

———. Subcommittee on Telecommunications and Finance of the Committee on Commerce. *Communications Law Reform: Hearings.* 104th Congress, 1st sess., 1995.

———. Subcommittee on Telecommunications and Finance of the Committee on Energy and Commerce. *Broadcasters and the Fairness Doctrine: Hearings on H.R. 1934.* 100th Congress, 1st sess., 1987.

———. Subcommittee on Telecommunications and Finance of the Committee on Energy and Commerce. *Cable Television Regulation.* 101st Congress, 2nd sess., 1990.

———. Subcommittee on Telecommunications and Finance of the Committee on Energy and Commerce. *Commercialization of Children's Television: Hearings on H.R. 3288, H.R. 3966, and H.R. 4125.* 100th Congress, 1988.

———. Subcommittee on Telecommunications and Finance of the Committee on Energy and Commerce. *Fairness Doctrine Legislation: Hearings on H.R. 315.* 101st Congress, 1st sess., 1989.

———. Subcommittee on Telecommunications, Consumer Protection, and Finance of the Committee on Energy and Commerce. *Broadcast Reform Proposals: Hearings on H.R. 4726, H.R. 4780, and H.R. 4781.* 97th Congress, 1st sess., 1981.

———. Subcommittee on Telecommunications, Consumer Protection, and Finance of the Committee on Energy and Commerce. *Broadcast Regulation and Station Ownership: Hearings on H.R. 6134.* 98th Congress, 2nd sess., 1984.

———. Subcommittee on Telecommunications, Consumer Protection, and Finance of the Committee on Energy and Commerce. *Options for Cable Legislation: Hearings on H.R. 4103, H.R. 4229, and H.R. 4299.* 98th Congress, 1st sess., 1983.

U.S. Senate. *The Communications Act of 1994.* S. 1822. 103rd Congress, 2nd sess., February 3, 1994.

———. Subcommittee on Communications of the Committee on Commerce, Science, and Transportation. *Amendments to the Communications Act of 1934: Hearings on S. 611 and S. 622.* 96th Congress, 1st sess., 1979.

———. Subcommittee on Communications of the Committee on Commerce, Science, and Transportation. *Cable Telecommunications Act of 1983: Hearings on S. 66.* 98th Congress, 1st sess., 1983.

———. Subcommittee on Communications of the Committee on Commerce, Science, and Transportation. *Cable TV: Hearings on the Oversight of the 1984 Cable Telecommunications Act.* 101st Congress, 1st sess., 1989.

———. Subcommittee on Communications of the Committee on Commerce, Science, and Transportation. *Cable TV Consumer Protection Act of 1991: Hearings on S. 12.* 102nd Congress, 1st sess., 1991.

U.S. White House. "'95 Technology Administration Budget Highlights." February 1994.

———. "Statement by the President on H.R. 1555." Press release, July 31, 1995.

"Van Deerlin Refuses to Say Die." *Broadcasting,* September 17, 1979.

Vietor, Richard H. K. *Contrived Competition: Regulation and Deregulation in America.* Cambridge: Belknap Press of Harvard University Press, 1994.

Vogel, David. *Fluctuating Fortunes.* New York: Basic Books, 1989.

———. "The 'New' Social Regulation in Historical and Comparative Perspective." In *Regulation in Perspective: Historical Essays,* edited by T. K. McCraw. Cambridge: Harvard University Press, 1981.

Vogel, Steven K. *Freer Markets, More Rules: Regulatory Reform in Advanced Industrial Countries.* Ithaca, N.Y.: Cornell University Press, 1996.

Walker, Rob. "Creating Synergy Out of Thin Air." *New York Times* (late edition), July 28, 2002.

Walters, Ida. "Freedom for Communications." In *Instead of Regulation,* edited by Robert W. Pool. Lexington, Mass.: D. C. Heath, 1982.

Wayne, Leslie. "Broadcast Lobby Excels at the Washington Power Game." *New York Times,* May 5, 1997.

Weaver, Paul H. "Regulation, Social Policy, and Class Conflict." In *Regulating Business,* edited by Chris Argyris. San Francisco: Institute of Contemporary Studies, 1979.

Weidenbaum, Murray L. "The New Wave of Government Regulation of Business." *Business and Society Review* 15 (Fall 1975): 81.

Wiley, Richard. "The End of Monopoly: Regulatory Change and the Promotion of Competition." In *Disconnecting Bell: The Impact of the AT&T Divestiture,* edited by Harry M. Shooshan III. New York: Pergamon, 1984.

Wilson, James Q. *The Politics of Regulation.* New York: Basic Books, 1980.

Index

About the Book

DESPITE A BROAD POLITICAL ENVIRONMENT CONDUCIVE TO DEREGU-
lation, television is one industry that consistently fails to completely
loosen government's regulatory grip. To explain why, Lori A.
Brainard explores the technological changes, industry structures, and
political dynamics influencing this policy quagmire.

Contradicting current scholarly and popular accounts, Brainard
demonstrates that new technologies do not determine policy outcomes, nor does the television industry always get its own way in the
policy arena—in fact, public interest groups have been successful at
influencing television policy over the past thirty years. She concludes that the multifaceted social and institutional contexts in which
television exists have resulted in incremental and incomplete deregulation punctuated by numerous episodes of reregulation and institutional warfare, thwarting all attempts at dramatic and decisive
reform.

Lori A. Brainard is an assistant professor in the School of Public
Policy and Public Administration at The George Washington
University.